First World War
and Army of Occupation
War Diary
France, Belgium and Germany

58 DIVISION
Divisional Troops
Royal Army Medical Corps
2/2 Home Counties Field Ambulance
24 January 1917 - 28 April 1919

WO95/2997/4

The Naval & Military Press Ltd
www.nmarchive.com
Published in association with The National Archives

Published by

The Naval & Military Press Ltd

Unit 10 Ridgewood Industrial Park,

Uckfield, East Sussex,

TN22 5QE England

Tel: +44 (0) 1825 749494

www.naval-military-press.com

www.nmarchive.com

This diary has been reprinted in facsimile from the original. Any imperfections are inevitably reproduced and the quality may fall short of modern type and cartographic standards.

© **Crown Copyright**
Images reproduced by permission of The National Archives, London, England, 2015.

Contents

Document type	Place/Title	Date From	Date To
Heading	WO95/2997-4		
Heading	58th Division 2-2nd (H.C.) Fld Ambnce 1915 Aug-1916 Feb And 1917 Jan-1919 Apl		
Heading	War Diary By O.C. 2/2h.C. Field Ambulance Vol 1		
War Diary	Sutton Veny Warminster	24/01/1917	24/01/1917
War Diary	Southampton	24/01/1917	24/01/1917
War Diary	Le Havre	25/01/1917	25/01/1917
War Diary	Sanvic	26/01/1917	26/01/1917
War Diary	Le Havre	26/01/1917	26/01/1917
War Diary	Auxi-Le-Chateau	27/01/1917	27/01/1917
War Diary	Villers L'Hopital	30/01/1917	05/02/1917
War Diary	Map 1/40000 B9c 38	07/02/1917	08/02/1917
War Diary	Sheet 57 DB18b35	09/02/1917	24/02/1917
Heading	War Diary Of Major W.E. Alston Comdg 2/2nd Home Countries Field Ambulance From 22.2.17 To 26.3.17		
War Diary	La Cauchie	22/02/1917	25/02/1917
War Diary	H.Q. Grenas	26/02/1917	26/02/1917
War Diary	La Cauchie	27/02/1917	27/02/1917
War Diary	H.Q. Grenas	01/03/1917	02/03/1917
War Diary	La Cauchie	02/03/1917	25/03/1917
War Diary	Halloy	26/03/1917	26/03/1917
Heading	58th Div 2/2nd Home Counties F.A.		
War Diary	Halloy (Ref Sheet 57 D)	26/03/1917	26/03/1917
War Diary	Halloy	28/03/1917	01/04/1917
War Diary	Ligny Sur Canche	02/04/1917	02/04/1917
War Diary	Cherienne	04/04/1917	04/04/1917
War Diary	Authieuole	06/04/1917	06/04/1917
War Diary	Bus Les Artois	07/04/1917	07/04/1917
War Diary	Bertrancourt	09/04/1917	12/04/1917
War Diary	Bertrancourt Lancashire Dump	14/04/1917	14/04/1917
War Diary	Bertrancourt	15/04/1917	18/04/1917
War Diary	Achiet Le Grand	18/04/1917	25/04/1917
Heading	War Diary Of 2/2nd HC. Fld Amb From 26/4/17 To 25/5/17		
Miscellaneous	O C 2/2 H.C.F.A.	26/05/1917	26/05/1917
War Diary	Achiet Le Grand Map 57c G.9.a.10.8	26/04/1917	12/05/1917
War Diary	Mory (L'abbage) Map 57 C B 22a 85	13/05/1917	13/05/1917
War Diary	Mory (L'abbage)	14/05/1917	14/05/1917
War Diary	Mory (L'abbage) Map 57c B22a 85	14/05/1917	14/05/1917
War Diary	Mory (L'abbage) B22a 85	15/05/1917	16/05/1917
War Diary	MDS Mory B 22a 85 Ref Map 57 C		
War Diary	Mory L'Abbaye Map 57c B22a 85	17/05/1917	17/05/1917
War Diary	Mory L'Abbaye B22a 85	18/05/1917	18/05/1917
War Diary	Mory L'Abbaye Map 57 C B22a 85	19/05/1917	19/05/1917
War Diary	Mory L'Abbaye B22a 85	20/05/1917	21/05/1917
War Diary	Mory L'Abbaye Map 57c B22a 85	22/05/1917	22/05/1917
War Diary	Mory L'Abbaye B22a 85	23/05/1917	24/05/1917
War Diary	Mory L'Abbaye B22a 85 Map 57c	25/05/1917	25/05/1917
War Diary	MDS Mory	23/05/1917	23/05/1917
War Diary	Rearrangement Parts	23/05/1917	23/05/1917

War Diary	MDS Mory (L'Abbaye) B22a 85 Ref Map 57c	26/05/1917	26/05/1917
War Diary	MDS Mory	27/05/1917	28/05/1917
War Diary	MDS Mory (L'Abbaye) B22a 85 Ref Map 57c	29/05/1917	29/05/1917
War Diary	MDS Mory	30/05/1917	31/05/1917
Heading	2/2nd Home Counties F.A. June 1917		
War Diary	MDS Mory (L'Abbaye) B22a 85 Map 57c	01/06/1917	01/06/1917
War Diary	MDS Mory	02/06/1917	02/06/1917
War Diary	MDS Mory L'Abbaye B22a 85 Ref Map 57c	03/06/1917	03/06/1917
War Diary	MDS Mory (L'Abbaye)	04/06/1917	04/06/1917
War Diary	Mory M.D.S. B.22.a. 85 Ref Map 57c	05/06/1917	06/06/1917
War Diary	Ervillers B13d 1.6 Ref Map 57c	07/06/1917	16/06/1917
War Diary	Ervillers	17/06/1917	17/06/1917
War Diary	Ervillers B13d 16 Ref Map 57c	17/06/1917	17/06/1917
War Diary	Ervillers	18/06/1917	19/06/1917
War Diary	Ervillers B13d 16 Ref Map 57c	19/06/1917	19/06/1917
War Diary	Ervillers	20/06/1917	20/06/1917
War Diary	Ervillers B13d 16 Ref Map 57c	21/06/1917	21/06/1917
War Diary	Ervillers	22/06/1917	23/06/1917
War Diary	Courcelles Le Comte B21a 58 (ref Map 57c)	23/06/1917	23/06/1917
War Diary	Courcelles	24/06/1917	24/06/1917
War Diary	Courcelles B21a 58 (ref Map 57c)	25/06/1917	25/06/1917
War Diary	Courcelles	26/06/1917	27/06/1917
War Diary	Courcelles B21a 58 Ref Map 57c	28/06/1917	28/06/1917
War Diary	Courcelles	29/06/1917	30/06/1917
Heading	2/2nd Home Counties F.A. July 1917		
War Diary	Courcelles Le Comte A15.c.7.2 (ref Map 57c)	01/07/1917	01/07/1917
War Diary	Courcelles	02/07/1917	07/07/1917
War Diary	Courcelles Le Comte A 15c 72 (ref Map 57c)	08/07/1917	08/07/1917
War Diary	Maricourt A21a. 8.8 (ref Map 620 1/40000)		
War Diary	Maricourt A21a. 8.8 Ref Map 62c 1/40000	09/07/1917	09/07/1917
War Diary	Maricourt	10/07/1917	11/07/1917
War Diary	Maricourt A21a 8.8 Ref Map 62c 1/40000	12/07/1917	12/07/1917
War Diary	Maricourt	13/07/1917	16/07/1917
War Diary	Maricourt A21a 8.8 Ref Map 62c 1/40000	17/07/1917	17/07/1917
War Diary	Maricourt	18/07/1917	20/07/1917
War Diary	Maricourt A21a 8.8 Ref Map 62c 1/40000	21/07/1917	21/07/1917
War Diary	Maricourt	22/07/1917	25/07/1917
War Diary	Maricourt A21a 8.8 Ref Map 62c 1/40000	26/07/1917	26/07/1917
War Diary	Maricourt	27/07/1917	28/07/1917
War Diary	Maricourt A 21a 8.8 Ref Map 62c 1/40000	29/07/1917	29/07/1917
War Diary	Sailly Au Bois J18b Ref Map 57d	30/07/1917	30/07/1917
War Diary	La Cauchie V 18.a. 3.7 Ref Map 51c	31/07/1917	31/07/1917
Heading	War Diary Of 2/2nd H.Q. Field Ambulance For Month Of August 1917 Vol 7		
War Diary	Izel-Les-Hameau (J2a 8.4)	01/08/1917	08/08/1917
War Diary	Izel-Les-Hameau (J2a 8.4) Ref Map 57c	09/08/1917	18/08/1917
War Diary	Izel Les Hameau J.a.8.4 (ref Map 51c)	19/08/1917	24/08/1917
War Diary	Aubigny	25/08/1917	25/08/1917
War Diary	Gwent Farm A28a 55 (ref Sheet 28)	26/08/1917	26/08/1917
War Diary	Gwent Farm A28a 55 (ref Sheet 28) Map Of Belgium Forma	27/08/1917	27/08/1917
War Diary	Gwent Farm A28a 5.5 Ref Sheet 28	28/08/1917	29/08/1917
War Diary	A.D.S. Duhallow E25d31 Sheet Ref 28	30/08/1917	31/08/1917
Miscellaneous	B.E.F. Summary Of Medical War Diaries Of 2/2nd H.C.F.A. 58th Div. 18th Corps 5th Army From 25/8/1917		

War Diary	Moves and Transfer	25/08/1917	25/08/1917
War Diary	Moves Deatachment	26/08/1917	26/08/1917
War Diary	Moves	29/08/1917	29/08/1917
War Diary	Moves and Transfer	25/08/1917	25/08/1917
War Diary	Moves Deatachment	26/08/1917	26/08/1917
War Diary	Moves	29/08/1917	29/08/1917
Heading	2/2nd Home Counties F.A. Sept 1917		
Heading	War Diary Of 2/2 H.C. Fd. Amb. R.A.M.C.G. From 1st Sept 1917 To 30th Sept 1917		
War Diary	A.D.S. Duhallow C25.d.3.0 (Sheet Ref 28)	01/09/1917	28/09/1917
War Diary	Gwent Farm Sheet 28 A28a 9.9	29/09/1917	30/09/1917
War Diary	Summary Of Medical War Diaries Of 2/2nd H.C.F.A. 58th Div. 18th Corps. 5th Army		
War Diary	Operations R.A.M.C.	01/09/1917	19/09/1917
War Diary	Casualties		
War Diary	Operations	20/09/1917	20/09/1917
War Diary	Casualties		
War Diary	Casualties	21/09/1917	27/09/1917
War Diary	Medical Arrangements	28/09/1917	28/09/1917
War Diary	Moves		
War Diary	Moves and Transfer	30/09/1917	30/09/1917
War Diary	Operations R.A.M.C.	01/09/1917	19/09/1917
War Diary	Casualties		
War Diary	Operations	20/09/1917	20/09/1917
War Diary	Casualties		
War Diary	Casualties	21/09/1917	27/09/1917
War Diary	Medical Arrangements	28/09/1917	28/09/1917
War Diary	Moves		
War Diary	Moves and Transfer	30/09/1917	30/09/1917
Heading	War Diary Of 2/2nd H.C. Fd. Amb. R.A.M.C. (T). From October 1st 1917 To October 31st 1917		
War Diary	Licques Pas De Calais France	01/10/1917	20/10/1917
War Diary	Audruicq	21/10/1917	21/10/1917
War Diary	Poperinghe	21/10/1917	21/10/1917
War Diary	Gwent Farm	22/10/1917	23/10/1917
War Diary	Minty Farm	24/10/1917	25/10/1917
War Diary	Essex Farm Minty Farm	25/10/1917	26/10/1917
War Diary	Minty Farm	26/10/1917	31/10/1917
Heading	War Diary Of 2/2nd H. C. Fd Amb. R.A.M.C. (T) From 1-11-17 To 30-11-1917		
War Diary	Essex Farm (Sheet 28-C.19c.3.0) And A.D.S. Minty Farm (Sheet 28-C10.c.3.6)	01/11/1917	01/11/1917
War Diary	Essex Farm And A.D.S. Minty	01/11/1917	04/11/1917
War Diary	Essex Farm And A.D.S. Minty Farm	04/11/1917	16/11/1917
War Diary	Phillippo Farm Herzeele	17/11/1917	24/11/1917
War Diary	Phillippo Farm Herzeele Parliament Camp	25/11/1917	25/11/1917
War Diary	Parliament Camp Wizernes Lart	26/11/1917	26/11/1917
War Diary	Lart Viel Moulier	27/11/1917	27/11/1917
War Diary	Vieil Moulier	28/11/1917	30/11/1917
Heading	War Diary Of 2/2 H C Fd Amb R.A.M.C. (T) From 1-12-17 To 31-12-17		
War Diary	Le Vieil Moutier Nielle Les Blequin	01/12/1917	01/12/1917
War Diary	Le Vieil Moutier	02/12/1917	06/12/1917
War Diary	Le Vieil Moutier Lart	07/12/1917	07/12/1917
War Diary	Lart	08/12/1917	08/12/1917
War Diary	Gwent Farm Essex Farm	09/12/1917	09/12/1917

War Diary	Minty Farm	09/12/1917	09/12/1917
War Diary	Essex Farm Minty Farm	10/12/1917	10/12/1917
War Diary	Minty Farm & Cement House	10/12/1917	10/12/1917
War Diary	Essex Farm Minty Farm	11/12/1917	11/12/1917
War Diary	Cement House	11/12/1917	11/12/1917
War Diary	Minty Farm & Cement House	11/12/1917	11/12/1917
War Diary	Minty Farm	12/12/1917	12/12/1917
War Diary	Minty Farm & Cement House	12/12/1917	12/12/1917
War Diary	Minty Farm	13/12/1917	13/12/1917
War Diary	Cement House	13/12/1917	13/12/1917
War Diary	Essex Farm	14/12/1917	14/12/1917
War Diary	Minty Farm Cement House	14/12/1917	14/12/1917
War Diary	Cement House	15/12/1917	15/12/1917
War Diary	Minty Farm	15/12/1917	16/12/1917
War Diary	Cement House	16/12/1917	16/12/1917
War Diary	Essex Farm	17/12/1917	17/12/1917
War Diary	Minty Farm	17/12/1917	17/12/1917
War Diary	Cement House	17/12/1917	17/12/1917
War Diary	Essex Farm	18/12/1917	18/12/1917
War Diary	Minty Farm	18/12/1917	18/12/1917
War Diary	Cement House	18/12/1917	18/12/1917
War Diary	Minty Farm & Cement House	18/12/1917	19/12/1917
Miscellaneous	Essex Farm	20/12/1917	20/12/1917
War Diary	Minty Farm	20/12/1917	20/12/1917
War Diary	Cement House	20/12/1917	20/12/1917
War Diary	Minty Farm	21/12/1917	21/12/1917
War Diary	Cement House	21/12/1917	21/12/1917
War Diary	Essex Farm	22/12/1917	22/12/1917
War Diary	Minty Farm	22/12/1917	22/12/1917
War Diary	Cement House	22/12/1917	22/12/1917
War Diary	Minty Farm	23/12/1917	23/12/1917
War Diary	Cement House	23/12/1917	23/12/1917
War Diary	Essex Farm	24/12/1917	24/12/1917
War Diary	Minty Farm	24/12/1917	24/12/1917
War Diary	Cement House	24/12/1917	24/12/1917
War Diary	Minty Farm	25/12/1917	25/12/1917
War Diary	Cement House	25/12/1917	25/12/1917
War Diary	Essex Farm	26/12/1917	26/12/1917
War Diary	Minty Farm	26/12/1917	26/12/1917
War Diary	Cement House	26/12/1917	26/12/1917
War Diary	Minty Farm & Cement House	26/12/1917	26/12/1917
War Diary	Minty Farm	27/12/1917	27/12/1917
War Diary	Cement House	27/12/1917	27/12/1917
War Diary	Minty Farm	28/12/1917	28/12/1917
War Diary	Cement House	28/12/1917	28/12/1917
War Diary	Essex Farm	29/12/1917	29/12/1917
War Diary	Minty Farm	29/12/1917	29/12/1917
War Diary	Cement House	29/12/1917	29/12/1917
War Diary	Minty Farm	30/12/1917	30/12/1917
War Diary	Cement House	30/12/1917	30/12/1917
War Diary	Minty Farm	31/12/1917	31/12/1917
War Diary	Cement House	31/12/1917	31/12/1917
Miscellaneous Heading	War Diary Of 2/2nd H. C. Fd Amb. R.A.M.C. (T) From 1/1/1918 To 31/1/1918 Vol 12		
War Diary	Sheet 28 H.Q. Essex Farm (C.19.c.4.0)	01/01/1918	01/01/1918

War Diary	Minty Farm C.10.c.2.6		01/01/1918	01/01/1918
War Diary	Cement House (U.28.c.2.2)		01/01/1918	01/01/1918
War Diary	Essex Farm		02/01/1918	02/01/1918
War Diary	Minty Farm		02/01/1918	02/01/1918
War Diary	Cement House		02/01/1918	02/01/1918
War Diary	Essex Farm		03/01/1918	03/01/1918
War Diary	Minty Farm		03/01/1918	03/01/1918
War Diary	Cement House		03/01/1918	03/01/1918
War Diary	Minty Farm		04/01/1918	04/01/1918
War Diary	Cement House		04/01/1918	04/01/1918
War Diary	Minty Farm		05/01/1918	05/01/1918
War Diary	Cement House		05/01/1918	05/01/1918
War Diary	Essex Farm		06/01/1918	06/01/1918
War Diary	Minty Farm		06/01/1918	06/01/1918
War Diary	Cement House		06/01/1918	06/01/1918
War Diary	Essex Farm		07/01/1918	07/01/1918
War Diary	Minty Farm		07/01/1918	07/01/1918
War Diary	Cement House		07/01/1918	07/01/1918
War Diary	Gwent Farm		08/01/1918	08/01/1918
War Diary	Minty Farm		08/01/1918	08/01/1918
War Diary	Cement House		08/01/1918	08/01/1918
War Diary	Essex Farm		08/01/1918	08/01/1918
War Diary	Proven		08/01/1918	08/01/1918
War Diary	Div Rest Station Proven		09/01/1918	19/01/1918
War Diary	Villers Bretonneux		20/01/1918	20/01/1918
War Diary	Moreuil		20/01/1918	30/01/1918
War Diary	French Hosp. Lespinoy		30/01/1918	31/01/1918
Heading	War Diary Of 2/2 H.C. Fd. Amb. R.A.M.C. (T) 1st February 1918-28th February 1918			
War Diary	Trench Camp Lespinoy		01/02/1918	08/02/1918
War Diary	Villers Bretonneux Sinceny-Sheet 10d G10 E6.8		08/02/1918	08/02/1918
War Diary	Appilly Sheet 40D Chauny (A26.a.26)		08/02/1918	08/02/1918
War Diary	Chauny		09/02/1918	28/02/1918
Heading	War Diary Of 2/2nd Home Counties Field Amb. R.A.M.C. (T). From 1/3/1918 To 31/3/1918			
War Diary	Sheet 70D (H.Q.) Chauny A.26.a.2.6		01/03/1918	03/03/1918
War Diary	(ADS) Sinceny Q.10.c.6.8		03/03/1918	03/03/1918
War Diary	(H.Q.) Chauny A.26.a.2.6		04/03/1918	04/03/1918
War Diary	(ADS) Sinceny G.10.c.6.8		04/03/1918	04/03/1918
War Diary	Sheet 70D H.Q Chauny A.26.a.2.6		05/03/1918	05/03/1918
War Diary	(A.D.S.) Sinceny G.10.c.6.8		05/03/1918	05/03/1918
War Diary	(H.Q.) Chauny A.26.a.2.6		06/03/1918	06/03/1918
War Diary	(A.D.S.) Sinceny G.10.c.6.8		06/03/1918	06/03/1918
War Diary	(H.Q) Chauny A.26.a.2.6		07/03/1918	07/03/1918
War Diary	(ADS) Sinceny G.10.c.6.8		07/03/1918	07/03/1918
War Diary	Sheet 70D (H.Q.) Chauny A.26.a.2.6		08/03/1918	08/03/1918
War Diary	(H.Q) Chauny A.26.a.2.6		09/03/1918	09/03/1918
War Diary	A.D.S. (Sinceny) G.10.c.6.8		09/03/1918	09/03/1918
War Diary	(H.Q.) Chauny A.26.a.2.6.		10/03/1918	10/03/1918
War Diary	Sheet 70D (H.Q.) Chauny A.26.a.2.6		11/03/1918	11/03/1918
War Diary	A.D.S. Sinceny G.10.c.6.8		11/03/1918	11/03/1918
War Diary	(H.Q.) Chauny A.26.a.2.6		12/03/1918	12/03/1918
War Diary	A.D.S. Sinceny G.10.c.6.8		12/03/1918	12/03/1918
War Diary	(H.Q.) Chauny A.26.a.2.6		13/03/1918	14/03/1918
War Diary	Sheet 70D A.D.S. Sinceny G.10c.6.8		14/03/1918	14/03/1918
War Diary	(H.Q.) Chauny A.26.a.2.6		15/03/1918	15/03/1918

War Diary	A.D.S. Sinceny G.10.c.6.8	15/03/1918	15/03/1918
War Diary	(H.Q.) Chauny A.26.a.2.6	16/03/1918	17/03/1918
War Diary	A.D.S. Sinceny G.10.c.6.8	16/03/1918	17/03/1918
War Diary	(H.Q.) Chauny A.26.a.2.6	16/03/1918	17/03/1918
War Diary	Sheet 70D (H.Q.) Chauny A.26.a.2.6	18/03/1918	18/03/1918
War Diary	A D S Sinceny G.10.c.6.8	18/03/1918	18/03/1918
War Diary	(H.Q.) Chauny A.26.a.2.6	19/03/1918	19/03/1918
War Diary	A.D.S. Sinceny	19/03/1918	19/03/1918
War Diary	(H.Q.) Chauny A.26.a.2.6	19/03/1918	19/03/1918
War Diary	(H.Q.) Chauny A.26.a.2.6	20/03/1918	20/03/1918
War Diary	A.D.S. Sinceny	20/03/1918	20/03/1918
War Diary	Sheet 70D (H Q) Chauny A.26.a.2.6	20/03/1918	20/03/1918
War Diary	A.D.S. Sinceny G.10.c.6.8	20/03/1918	20/03/1918
War Diary	(H.Q.) Chauny A.26.a.2.6	21/03/1918	21/03/1918
War Diary	A.D.S. Sinceny G.10.c.6.8	21/03/1918	21/03/1918
War Diary	Sheet 70D A.D.S. Sinceny G.10.c.6.8	21/03/1918	21/03/1918
War Diary	(H.Q.) Chauny A.26.a.2.6	22/03/1918	22/03/1918
War Diary	A.D.S. Sinceny G.10.c.6.8	22/03/1918	22/03/1918
War Diary	(H.Q.) Sinceny G.10.c.6.8	23/03/1918	23/03/1918
War Diary	Sheet 70D (H.Q.) Sinceny G.10.c.6.8	23/03/1918	23/03/1918
War Diary	(H.Q.) Sinceny G.10.c.6.8	24/03/1918	24/03/1918
War Diary	Bichancourt	24/03/1918	24/03/1918
War Diary	Sheet 70.E. Besme R 14.b. 9.4	24/03/1918	24/03/1918
War Diary	Besme R 14.b. 9.4	24/03/1918	24/03/1918
War Diary	(HQ) Besme R.14.b.9.4	25/03/1918	25/03/1918
War Diary	Sheet 70E. (HQ) Besme R14.b.9.4	25/03/1918	28/03/1918
War Diary	Sheet 70D (A.D.S.) Pierremande G28b.5.2	25/03/1918	28/03/1918
War Diary	(HQ) Besme R.14.b.9.4	29/03/1918	31/03/1918
Heading	War Diary Of 2/2nd H.C.F. Amb. R.A.M.C. (T) From April 1st 1918 To April 30th 1918		
War Diary	Sheet 70E (HQ) Besme R.14.b.9.4	01/04/1918	01/04/1918
War Diary	(H.Q.) Besme R.14.b.9.4	02/04/1918	02/04/1918
War Diary	Sheet 70E. (HQ) Besme R.14.b.9.4	02/04/1918	02/04/1918
War Diary	(HQ) Besme R.14.b.9.4	03/04/1918	03/04/1918
War Diary	Sheet 70E. (HQ) Besme R.14.b.9.4	03/04/1918	03/04/1918
War Diary	Hautebraye	03/04/1918	04/04/1918
War Diary	Ambleny	03/04/1918	05/04/1918
War Diary	St. Pierre Aigle	05/04/1918	05/04/1918
War Diary	Villers Cotterets	06/04/1918	06/04/1918
War Diary	Longeau	06/04/1918	06/04/1918
War Diary	Ecole Des Jeune Filles Faubourg Du Hem Amiens	06/04/1918	08/04/1918
War Diary	Ecole Des Filles Montieres	08/04/1918	15/04/1918
War Diary	Longpres	15/04/1918	15/04/1918
War Diary	Argoeuves	16/04/1918	27/04/1918
War Diary	Abbeville Vauchelles Les Quesnoy	28/04/1918	30/04/1918
Heading	War Diary Of 2/2nd H.C.F. Amb R.A.M.C. (T) From 1/5/1918-To 31/5/18		
War Diary	Vauchelles Les Quesnoy (Abbeville)	01/05/1918	06/05/1918
War Diary	(Sheet 57.D. T.28.a.6.9)	06/05/1918	16/05/1918
War Diary	Grande Rue De Baillon Warloy (U.24.c.3.3)	16/05/1918	16/05/1918
War Diary	Sheet 57D U 24.c.3.3	16/05/1918	31/05/1918
Heading	War Diary Of 2/2 H.C.F. Amb R.A.M.C. (T) From 1/6/18 To 30/6/18		
War Diary	Warloy U 24c.3.3	01/06/1918	01/06/1918
War Diary	T 22c Nr Mirvaux	02/06/1918	10/06/1918
War Diary	Dreuil Les Molliens	11/06/1918	17/06/1918

War Diary	62 E O 3.a.2.5	18/06/1918	18/06/1918
War Diary	Mirvaux Wood 57D T22.c.	18/06/1918	23/06/1918
War Diary	T 22 C.	23/06/1918	27/06/1918
War Diary	St Gratien Wood 62 D. B 20d	27/06/1918	30/06/1918
Heading	War Diary Of 2/2 H. C. F. Amb. R.A.M.C. (T) From 1/7/18 To 31/7/18		
War Diary	St. Gratien Wood 62 D B20d	01/07/1918	31/07/1918
Heading	War Diary Of 2/2 H C F A R A M C (T) From 1/8/18 To 31/8/18		
War Diary	St Gratien Wood 62 D B20d	01/08/1918	02/08/1918
War Diary	Havernas 57 E R31 C 61	03/08/1918	03/08/1918
War Diary	57 E R31 C 61	03/08/1918	04/08/1918
War Diary	Key Wood 62 D 14a	05/08/1918	07/08/1918
War Diary	62 D 14a	07/08/1918	10/08/1918
War Diary	Querrieu H 10a8.6	11/08/1918	13/08/1918
War Diary	Key Wood 62 D I 14a	13/08/1918	18/08/1918
War Diary	62 D I 14a	19/08/1918	23/08/1918
War Diary	Key Wood 62 D I 14a	23/08/1918	24/08/1918
War Diary	Cemetery Copse J 24b 6.8	24/08/1918	24/08/1918
War Diary	62 D J 24b 6.8	24/08/1918	25/08/1918
War Diary	K 17b 7.4	26/08/1918	28/08/1918
War Diary	L 10a.5.8	28/08/1918	29/08/1918
War Diary	A 21b 2.9	30/08/1918	31/08/1918
Heading	War Diary Of 2/2 H C F Amb R A M C (T) From 1-9-18 To 30-9-18		
War Diary	A 30b 3.8	01/09/1918	02/09/1918
War Diary	A 14a.9.7	02/09/1918	07/09/1918
War Diary	B 13b. 5.4 (maurepas)	07/09/1918	08/09/1918
War Diary	B 13b.5.4	08/09/1918	08/09/1918
War Diary	C 18c (Moislains)	09/09/1918	13/09/1918
War Diary	C 18c	13/09/1918	24/09/1918
War Diary	Maricourt A15.c.5.1	24/09/1918	25/09/1918
War Diary	Heilly	25/09/1918	26/09/1918
War Diary	Gouy Servins Q35d 3.3 (44 B)	27/09/1918	30/09/1918
Heading	War Diary Of 2/2 Home Counties Fld. Amb R.A.M.C. (T) From 1/10/18 To 31/10/18		
War Diary	Fosse 10 Sheet 44 B R8 Central	01/10/1918	12/10/1918
War Diary	St Pierre 44A. M11 C7.9	13/10/1918	17/10/1918
War Diary	Fouquieres 44A. O.21a.4.5	17/10/1918	18/10/1918
War Diary	Ostricourt 44A. P6b 3.3	19/10/1918	19/10/1918
War Diary	Mons En Pevele 44A. K24a.0.4	20/10/1918	20/10/1918
War Diary	Vert Bois 44 G 14a. 5.7	21/10/1918	31/10/1918
Heading	War Diary Of 2/2 Home Counties Fld. Amb R A M C (T) From Nov 1st 1918 To Nov. 30th 1918		
War Diary	Vert Bois 44.G 14a 5.7	01/11/1918	08/11/1918
War Diary	Rumegies Sheet 44 (Brewery)	09/11/1918	09/11/1918
War Diary	Rumegies (Brewery)	09/11/1918	09/11/1918
War Diary	Bleharies Sheet 44 (Brewery)	10/11/1918	10/11/1918
War Diary	Basecles (Convent) Sheet 45. A20a9.5	11/11/1918	30/11/1918
Heading	War Diary Of 2/2 Home Counties Field Amb R.A.M.C. (T) 1/12/18 31/12/18		
War Diary	Basecles Sheet 45. A20a 9.5	01/12/1918	05/12/1918
War Diary	Basecles A 20a 9.5	05/12/1918	31/12/1918
Heading	War Diary Of The 2/2 Home Counties Field Amb R.A.M.C. (T) From 1/1/19 To 31/1/19		
War Diary	Basecles (Convent) Sheet 45 A20a.95	01/01/1919	11/01/1919

War Diary	Basecles A20a9.5	12/01/1919	31/01/1919
Heading	War Diary Of 2/2 H C F Amb R.A.M.C. (T) From 1-2-19 To 28-2-19		
War Diary	Basecles (convent) Sht 45 H20a9.5	01/02/1919	28/02/1919
Heading	War Diary Of 2/2 H.C.F. Amb R.A.M.C. (T) From 1.3.19 To 31.3.19		
War Diary	Basecles (Convent) Sht 45 A 20a.9.5	01/03/1919	08/03/1919
War Diary	Chapelle A Wattines	13/03/1919	30/03/1919
Heading	War Diary Of 2/2 H C F Amb R A M C From 1-5-19 To 31-5-19		
War Diary	Chapelle A Wattines	04/05/1919	30/05/1919
Heading	War Diary Of 2/2 H C F Amb R A M C (T) From 1-4-19 To 30-4-19		
War Diary	Chapelle-A-Wattines Belgium	04/04/1919	28/04/1919
Miscellaneous	Transport		

WO 95/29974

58TH DIVISION

2-2ND (H.C) FLD AMBNCE

~~JAN 1915 — DEC 1918~~

1915 AUG — 1916 FEB
       AND
1917 JAN — 1919 APL

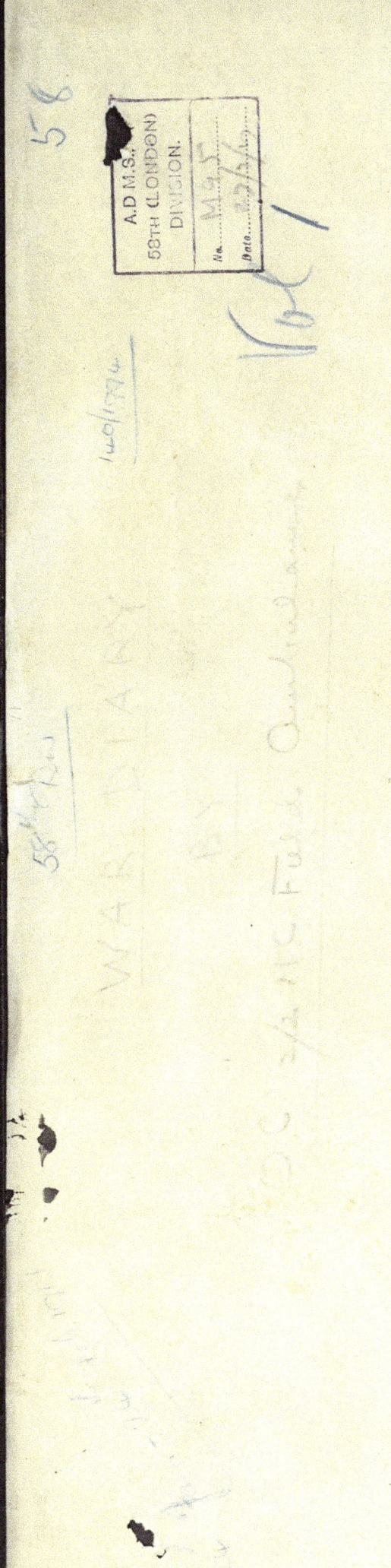

WAR DIARY

BY

O.C. 2/1 A.M.C. Field Ambulance

WAR DIARY
or
INTELLIGENCE SUMMARY.

(Erase heading not required.)

Army Form C. 2118.

Hour, Date, Place	Summary of Events and Information	Remarks and references to Appendices
8.20 am 24-1-17 SUTTONVENY. WARMINSTER.	Left No 6 Camp, SUTTONVENY for entraining for embarkation overseas. Strength of unit, 9 Officers, 217 other ranks including A.S.C. attached, & Battalion Staff & 3 Divisional Bandsmen (the last two named for embarkation only.) WW	
4.0 pm 24-1-17 SOUTHAMPTON	Embarked on S.S. "LYDIA" & S.S. "NORTH WEST MILLER"	
1 am 25-1-17 LE HAVRE	Disembarked from S.S. "LYDIA". S.S. "NORTH WEST MILLER" arrived later with transport. The unit marched to the 2 Camp, SANVIC. WW	
10.0 am 26-1-17 SANVIC	Left No 2 Camp, SANVIC for entraining at LE HAVRE. WW	
3 pm 26-1-17 LE HAVRE.	Unit-entrained. WW	
1 pm 27-1-17 AUXI-LE-CHATEAU	Unit- detrained & marched to VILLERS L'HOPITAL WW	
30-1-17 VILLERS L'HOPITAL 31-1-17 VILLERS L'HOPITAL	4 men M.T.A.S.C. temporarily taken on strength with 2 motor ambulances 3 Divisional Bearers men left for D.H.Q. WW (& 2 motor cycles.	
1-2-17 VILLERS L'HOPITAL	4 men M.T.A.S.C. attached, returned to units. WW	
2-2-17 VILLERS L'HOPITAL	1 Sergeant, 1 Corporal & 11 Drivers M.T.A.S.C. reported for duty with unit with 7 motor ambulances. WW	
3-2-17 VILLERS L'HOPITAL	2 Officers, 30 N.C.O.s & men left for special instruction with 1/3rd North Midland Field Ambulance. GAUDIEMPRE WW	
5-2-17 VILLERS L'HOPITAL	Marched to new position. Map 40000 B9c 38. WW	
7-2-17 Map 40000 B9c 38	Capt T.B. McKEE attached temporarily to 2/6 Batt as R.M.O. Capt W.A. SLATER attached temporarily to 2/7 Batt as R.M.O. WW	

Army Form C. 2118.
Sheet 2

WAR DIARY
or
INTELLIGENCE SUMMARY.
(Erase heading not required.)

Instructions regarding War Diaries and Intelligence Summaries are contained in F.S. Regs., Part II. and the Staff Manual respectively. Title pages will be prepared in manuscript.

Hour, Date, Place	Summary of Events and Information	Remarks and references to Appendices
8.2.17. MAP 1/40000 B9 c 38	Detention staff returned to D.H.Q. WW	
2/m 8.2.17 MAP 1/40000 B9 c 38	Unit moved to Sheet 57D B16 c 35 WW	
9.2.17 Sheet 57D B16 c 35	Opened Reception Hospital at new station. Capt S.Y.WALSH reported for duty with unit WW	
11.2.17 Sheet 57D B16 c 35	2 Officers & 30 other ranks left for special instruction, attached to "H" West Riding field Ambulance. Party detailed for special instruction returned to unit. WW	
12.2.17 Sheet 57D B16 c 35	Capt T.B. McKEE & Capt W.A. SLATER returned to duty with unit WW	
16.2.17 Sheet 57D B16 c 35	Capt S.K. McKEE detailed as Q.M.O to 2/6 L'don Regt (temp.) WW	
17.2.17 Sheet 57D B16 c 35	Capt S.Y. WALSH detailed as R.M.O to 2/4 L'don Regt. (temp.) WW	
19.2.17 Sheet 57D B16 c 35	Second twenty on special instruction returned to unit WW	
21.2.17 Sheet 57D B16 c 35	Capt S.Y. WALSH detached for duty with a D.M.S., 46" Divn and struck off strength. Capt T.B. McKEE detailed to act as R.M.O.F. 2/7" L'don Regt vice Capt S.Y.WALSH. C WW. Capt McGILLIVRAY & Capt SLATER & 40 other ranks & 20 motor ambulances detached for duty with "13th H. Midland Fd Ambr at Sheet 51C V17 b 98 WW	
22.2.17 Sheet 57D B16 c 35	Capt A.C. WATKIN detailed to attend Gas Course at ST. POL. WW	
23.2.17 Sheet 57D B16 c 35	"B" section tent sub-division left for duty at 51C V17 b 98, Capt B.A. BULL in charge. WW	

Army Form C. 2118.
Sheet 3

WAR DIARY
or
INTELLIGENCE SUMMARY.
(Erase heading not required.)

Hour, Date, Place	Summary of Events and Information	Remarks and references to Appendices
23-2-17 Sheets 7D B18 C35	Capt A.J. BLAXLAND detailed for duty as R.M.O. to 2/12 L'dn. Regt. W.A.	
24-2-17 Sheets 7D B18 C35	The remainder of "B" section left for duty at 5/C V17 & 9C7 W.A.	
24-2-17 Sheets 7D B18 C35	Capt CHALMERS with orderly of 2/1st H.C.F.A. attached for duty with unit.	

W. Eaton
Major O.C.
212ND H. C. FLD. AMB.

Manual
Vol #2

140/2002

From 23.2.17 – 26 Mar 1917

Contradicted
War Diary
of
Major W.E. Acton

Comdg 3/1 nd Home Counties Field Ambulance

COMMITTEE FOR THE
MEDICAL HISTORY OF THE WAR 26.3.17.
Date 11 MAY 1917

Army Form C. 2118.

WAR DIARY
or
INTELLIGENCE SUMMARY.
(Erase heading not required.)

Instructions regarding War Diaries and Intelligence Summaries are contained in F.S. Regs., Part II. and the Staff Manual respectively. Title pages will be prepared in manuscript.

Hour, Date, Place	Summary of Events and Information	Remarks and references to Appendices
22/2/17 "LA CAUCHIE"	Party of One Officer and 16 Other Ranks proceeded from Unit detachment at main dressing station at LA CAUCHIE to A.D.S. at GROSVILLE. W.C.A.	
23/2/17 " "	Party of One Officer and 15 Other Ranks proceeded from M.D.S. to A.D.S. W.C.A.	
24/2/17 " "	Party of 15 Other Ranks proceeded from M.D.S. to A.D.S. W.C.A.	
25/2/17 " "	Capt MAXWELL of 2/3 H.C.F.Amb. detailed for duty at M.D.S. W.C.A.	
26/2/17 H.Q. GRENAS.	Party of 6 Other Ranks proceeded from M.S. to A.R. W.C.A.	
27/2/17 "LA CAUCHIE"	One man proceeded to R.F.C. at BELLEVUE to act as medical orderly; struck off strength. W.C.A.	
1/3/17 H.Q. GRENAS.	Capt. T.B. McKEE reported for duty at M.D.S. W.C.A.	
	Capt. A.J. BLAXLAND returned for duty with Unit. W.C.A.	
2/17 2/3/17 H.Q. GRENAS.	Capt. A.C. WATKIN returned from Course for duty with Unit. W.C.A.	
4/3/17 "LA CAUCHIE"	"A" Section marched to "LA CAUCHIE". W.C.A.	
7/3/17 "	Reinforcement of 7 R.A.M.C. personnel arrived. W.C.A.	
8/3/17 "	Capt A.J. BLAXLAND struck off strength and posted to 1/1 LONDON. C.C.S. W.C.A.	
	Capt. H.J.B. FRY reported for duty with Unit at M.D.S. W.C.A.	
10/3/17 "	Party of 10 Other Ranks detailed for duty at A.D.S. W.C.A.	
	Capt. H.J.B. FRY detailed as R.M.O. 2/7 LONDON REGT. W.C.A.	
	Lieut. J.R. CLARK from 2/1 LOND. REGT. reported for duty with Unit. W.C.A.	
11/3/17 "	One reinforcement of R.A.M.C. personnel arrived. W.C.A.	
12/3/17 "	Party of 12 Other Ranks returned from A.D.S. to M.D.S. W.C.A.	
13/3/17 "	One N.C.O. detailed to attend Course of Instruction at Gas School. BAVINCOURT. W.C.A.	
15/3/17 "	Party of 12 Other Ranks left M.D.S. for Course of Instruction at 37 C.C.S. AVESNES-LE-COMTE W.C.A.	

WAR DIARY or INTELLIGENCE SUMMARY

Army Form C. 2118.

(Erase heading not required.)

Hour, Date, Place	Summary of Events and Information	Remarks and references to Appendices
10.30 a.m. 22/3/17 LA CAUCHIE	One Officer (Capt BABULT) one man detailed for duty with 2/6 LOND. REGT. W.A. One Officer and two Other Ranks proceeded on Road making duty at MONCHY. (Returned the same day) W.A.	
" " "	'B' Section returned from A.D.S. to M.D.S. W.A.	
23/3/17 "	Mobile Dental Surgery Staff with Lorry attached for duty. W.A.	
3.30 P.M. 25/3/17 "	Unit changed stations, by Route March to HALLOY. W.A. Hospital at LA CAUCHIE handed over to 65th Fld. Amb. W.A.	
26/3/17 HALLOY.	Opened Hospital at new station. W.A.	

W Watson
Major
O.C.
2/2ND H.C. FLD. AMB.

58th Div.

140/2086.

2/2nd Home Counties F.A.

COMMITTEE FOR THE
MEDICAL HISTORY OF THE WAR
Date −6 JUN.1917

Army Form C. 2118.

WAR DIARY
or
INTELLIGENCE SUMMARY.
(Erase heading not required.)

Instructions regarding War Diaries and Intelligence Summaries are contained in F.S. Regs., Part II. and the Staff Manual respectively. Title pages will be prepared in manuscript.

2/2 H.C. 2/nd Lowland

Hour, Date, Place	Summary of Events and Information	Remarks and references to Appendices
26-3-17. HALLOY. (Ref Sheet 57D).	Capt. S.K. McKEE and servant returned to Unit on termination of R.M.Cb. duties with 2/6th London Regt. W.A. One N.C.O. and 10 men returned from Course with 37-cd C.C.S. AVESNES au COMTE. (Ref Sheet 51D). W.A.	
28-3-17. HALLOY.	Capt. W.A. SLATER and LIEUT. J.R. CLARK detailed for duty at German Prisoners Camp. W.A.	
8:15 a.m. 1-4-17. HALLOY.	Unit changed Station, marching from HALLOY to LIGNY SUR CANCHE. (Ref Sheet 57D). Captain G.M. McGILLIVRAY and 10 Other Ranks proceeded to 43rd C.C.S. WARLINCOURT to attend Course. (Ref Sheet 57D) W.A.	W.A.
9.0 a.m. 2-4-17. LIGNY SUR CANCHE.	Unit marched from LIGNY SUR CANCHE to CHERIENNE (Sheet 51D)	W.A.
7.30 a.m. 4-4-17. CHERIENNE.	Unit marched from CHERIENNE to AUTHIEVOLE. One light Draught Horse and 1 Heavy Draught Horse left with A.V.C. en route. (Sheet 57D.) W.A.	
9.0 a.m. 5-4-17. AUTHIEVOLE.	Unit marched from AUTHIEVOLE to BUS Les ARTOIS (57D). W.A.	
9.0 a.m. 7-4-17. BUS Les ARTOIS.	Unit marched from BUS-les-ARTOIS to BERTRANCOURT. (57D). Hospital at new station taken over from 2/1st 2/1st 2nd R.A.M.C. (T). W.A.	
9-4-17. BERTRANCOURT.	Two Buglearing Sergeants attend Gas Course at BUS les ARTOIS. Capt. O. DE MUTH taken on the strength. W.A.	
4.30 p.m. 11-4-17. BERTRANCOURT.	"B" Section marched to LANCASHIRE DUMP (57D). Two N.C.Os. and 7 O.R. take over "billeting Arts" at COUIN and COIGNEUX. (Both 57D). W.A. One Heavy Draught cart to Base.	

W. Alston
Major
Comd'g 2/2 H.C. F. Amb

Army Form C. 2118.

WAR DIARY
or
INTELLIGENCE SUMMARY.
(Erase heading not required.)

Instructions regarding War Diaries and Intelligence Summaries are contained in F.S. Regs., Part II. and the Staff Manual respectively. Title pages will be prepared in manuscript.

Hour, Date, Place	Summary of Events and Information	Remarks and references to Appendices
12-4-17. BERTRANCOURT.	One man detached for water duty with 2/1st Lond. Regt. W.A.	
14-4-17. BERTRANCOURT, LANCASHIRE DUMP.	Two Dispensing Sergeants returned from Gas Course. "B" Section taken over Hospital from 2/1st West Riding Field Ambulance. W.A.	
15-4-17. BERTRANCOURT.	Notification received of 1 Man sent to ENGLAND, from Hospital. W.A.	
16-4-17. BERTRANCOURT.	One Reinforcement arrived from ROUEN. W.A.	
9.0 a.m. 18-4-17. BERTRANCOURT.	Unit march from BERTRANCOURT to ACHIET-LE-GRAND. W.A.	
18-4-17. ACHIET-LE-GRAND.	Capt. B.A. BULL and H.J.B. FRY struck off strength. Lieut. J.R. CLARK taken on strength. W.A.	
" "	One Heavy Draught Horse evacuated for Remount Reserve. W.A.	
20-4-17. ACHIET-LE-GRAND.	"B" Section joined Unit from LANCASHIRE DUMP. One Light Draught Horse transferred to A.V.C. W.A.	
22-4-17. ACHIET-LE-GRAND.	Notification received of 2 men evacuated to Base. W.A.	
23-4-17. ACHIET-LE-GRAND.	Serious accident to R.A.M.C. Pte. while on duty in the Trenches, portion of left hand being blown away while examining unexploded detonator. W.A.	
	Notification received of 1 man evacuated (sick) to ENGLAND. W.A.	
25-4-17. ACHIET-LE-GRAND.	One Riser transferred to A.V.C. W.A.	

11 March 1917
26th Apr - 25 May
Medical.
68th Div.
140/2161
Vol 4

CONFIDENTIAL
****

W A R   D I A R Y

OF

2/2nd Hghld. Fld Amb.

From 26/4/17
To 25/5/17

COMMITTEE FOR THE
MEDICAL HISTORY OF THE WAR
Date   10 JUL. 1917

From: O.C. 2/2 H.C.F.A.,
R.A.M.C.(T).

To: A.D.M.S.,
58 Division

Herewith War Diary for this Unit for the month of May, please.

H. Fuller
Maj. R.A.M.C.(T)
O.C.
2/2nd H.C. FLD. AMB.

881
26-5-17

Army Form C. 2118.

Medical

WAR DIARY
or
INTELLIGENCE SUMMARY
(Erase heading not required.)

2/2 Home Counties Field Amb.

Instructions regarding War Diaries and Intelligence Summaries are contained in F. S. Regs., Part II. and the Staff Manual respectively. Title Pages will be prepared in manuscript.

Place	Date	Hour	Summary of Events and Information	Remarks and references to Appendices
Achiet le Grand M.D.S. N.A.L.B	26th Apr 1917	Noon	Majors A.W. French R.A.M.C.T. & Captain J.E. Turtle R.A.M.C.T. reported for duty from Base & taken on strength of unit.	acw
	27th Apr	9AM	Capt. J.R. Clark attached for duty as R.M.O. 2/4th London Regiment struck off unit strength from & including 28th April.	
	28th Apr	12AM	Major A.W. French R.A.M.C.T. assumed command of the unit this day. Authority DGMS' B/1496/32, on Relinquishment of the Command by Major W.E. Alston. Present distribution of unit:— Whole unit open, with Cadres, receiving Sec 17/174 Brigade & various details in Corps area. Detachments: ① Lancashire Dump — 1 NCO & 4 Men ② Bertrancourt — 1 NCO & 1 Man ③ Holding Post at Couigneux & Courir — 2 NCO & 7 Men. 1 Farrier Corpl. reported from 511 HT Coy A.S.C. & taken on strength of unit.	acw

Army Form C. 2118.

2/2 Home Counties Field Amb.

WAR DIARY or INTELLIGENCE SUMMARY

Medical

(Erase heading not required.)

Instructions regarding War Diaries and Intelligence Summaries are contained in F. S. Regs., Part II. and the Staff Manual respectively. Title Pages will be prepared in manuscript.

Place	Date	Hour	Summary of Events and Information	Remarks and references to Appendices
Achiet le Grand Map 57C G.9.a.108	Apl 29th 1917	9AM	Captain O. De Nutt. TC detached as MO to 2/6th London Regt & Spruce off unit strength vice Captain B.A. Bulot who reports on this taken on the unit strength.	new
"	Apl 30th	11AM 11.30A	DOMS V.n Copt visited Field Ambulance & inspected hospital 58th Division visited Field Ambulance.	new
"	May 1st/17	4.PM	APMS 58th Division visited Field Ambulance.	
"	May 2nd	Noon	2 NCO. & 7 Men report back from Couin & Coigneux - holding posts.	
"	May 3	2.PM	Captain A.C. Watkin & 1 NCO & 1 nursing section sent to Ervillers MDS for 48 hours instruction. 1 nursing NCO. to Morey for same period & purpose; 1 riding & 5 L.D. Horses from Remounts & taken on strength. Warning to stand by, ready to move, Received	new
"	May 4		1 NCO. & 3 men returned from Lancashire Dump. Captain A.C. Watkin & 1 NCO recalls from Ervillers & 1 NCO from Morey. 1 Motor Cyclist Returned from Duty in ADMS' Office.	new

Army Form C. 2118.

Medical

2/2 Home Counties Field Amb: **WAR DIARY** or **INTELLIGENCE SUMMARY**

(Erase heading not required.)

Instructions regarding War Diaries and Intelligence Summaries are contained in F.S. Regs., Part II. and the Staff Manual respectively. Title Pages will be prepared in manuscript.

Place	Date	Hour	Summary of Events and Information	Remarks and references to Appendices
Achiet Le Grand Map 57.C G.9.a.10β	May 5 1917	8 AM	Captain A.C. Watkin and B section Tent Sub-Division & Transport coupled, together with 108 Bearers under Captain W.A. Slater moves to Anzac MDS - 1000 yards SW of Vaulx - 57 C. Ref. Map. Point I/C; move completed by Noon; Detachment under orders of DDMS. Anzacs.	
		7 PM.	C section of 2/3 H.C. Field Amb. arrived, to replace B section of 2/2. This evening 80 bearers, under Captain Slater, moved forward to Anzac Wagon Post ADS on Vaulx - Lagnicourt Road to Relieve Anzac Bearers & also Relieved Wagon Post, 1000 yards W by S of Lagnicourt. Bearer detachment as Regt Aid Post in Sunken Road to Noreuil.	
"	May 7		3 O.R. joined as reinforcement from Base. Staff Run a Sheugh - A seeling	
		10.30 AM	O.C. visits Detachment at Anzac MDS - accompanied ADMS 58th Divn on tour of Advanced Dressing stations, Wagon Post, & Regt Aid Post on Lagnicourt front.	
	May 9	10 AM	Lt J.R. Clark reported back from tour of duty as R.M.O. 2/4 London Regt.	
		10 AM 1 PM	O.C. apptd to GOC 174 Brigade re Tactical Scheme No 3, & surveys sites for Medical Arrangements.	
"	"	mid night	Gas Alarm - All ranks assumed Box Respirators, but no gas definitely reported either here or from ADS.	

2/2 Home Counties Field Amb:

WAR DIARY or INTELLIGENCE SUMMARY

Army Form C. 2118. **Medical**

Place	Date 1917	Hour	Summary of Events and Information	Remarks and references to Appendices
Achiet le Gd Map 57C G.9.a.10.8	May 10th	3PM	2 NCO + 30 bearers reported back from Anzac ADS.	
		5PM	O.C. + 1 Officer to MDS. at MORY to note medical arrangements of combined 7th + 62nd DIVISIONS	
		11.30 PM	Received orders to close tomorrow + hand over Hospl to O.C. 2/3 HCFA	acw
	11th	7AM	1 Amb Wagon & 3 Bearer Squads, under Capt. Bull, sent to represent Skeleton Medical arrangements of 174 Bgde Tactical Scheme No 3	
		9AM	Report from Officer i/c detachment at Anzac MDS. that one our Amb: Horses slightly wounded yesterday, in action.	
			Hospital taken over by 2/3 HCFA & all cases transferred to their AMD. Unit stood by awaiting orders rest of day	acw
Achiet le Gd Map 57C G.9.a.10.8	12th	8.45am	One tent sub division, all available (from Orderly Room Staff with C Section's transport) paraded for change of station to MORY, and marched to MORY. 3 O.R. left in Hosp: at A.&B. 3 O.R. proceeded to Vamping camp for 14 days.	
		Noon	Rear party left us at A.&S. Capt. Bull, Lieut Knowles, and 4 O.R. RAMC and transport of A Section	
			Capt. Jarob and servant reported at home from details duty with C.R.E. 58th Divn	acw

Army Form C. 2118.

2/2 Home Counties Field Ambulance

WAR DIARY or INTELLIGENCE SUMMARY

(Erase heading not required.)

Medical

Instructions regarding War Diaries and Intelligence Summaries are contained in F. S. Regs., Part II. and the Staff Manual respectively. Title Pages will be prepared in manuscript.

Place	Date 1917	Hour	Summary of Events and Information	Remarks and references to Appendices
MORY (C'Ottage) Map 57c B22.a.85	May 13	10am	Capt S K McKEE posted for duty with 2 NCO's and 20 men at Advanced Dressing Station. ECOUST C2.c 48	
		Noon	Rest of transport and personnel arrived at MORY. Lieut J R CLARK detailed to report to O.C. 2/4 LOND REGT to replace (with casualty)	
		9pm	Capt WATKIN and Capt T B McKEE reported back from ANZAC Main Dressing Station VAULX with B section tent our division and transport and heavy our division of A T B section.	O.C.
MORY (C'Ottage)	14		Personnel of 2/1 R H C A A at MAIN DRESSING STATION at l'abbaye MORY who arrived at O.C. taken over from 2/1st 2/0 Ambulance 7th Division. Only wounded and (with casualties to be dealt with: also received by 21st FA Ambulance from Ecoust) ADVANCED DRESSING STATION at ECOUST C2.c 48 2 Medical Officers and 2 stretcher squads post the WAGGON POST ADS at C9.d 42 2 M.O.s and 3 stretcher squads. One motor ambulance, 1 M.O. and room station beam RELAY POST C4.c 32 ten stretcher squads. RELAY POST C13.c 45	O.C. O.C.

Army Form C. 2118.

2/2 HOME COUNTIES Field Ambulance

WAR DIARY or INTELLIGENCE SUMMARY

MEDICAL

Instructions regarding War Diaries and Intelligence Summaries are contained in F. S. Regs., Part II. and the Staff Manual respectively. Title Pages will be prepared in manuscript.

(Erase heading not required.)

Place	Date	Hour	Summary of Events and Information	Remarks and references to Appendices
MORY (L'attery) Map 57c B22 a 85	1917 May 14		RELAY POST C7 a 9½ two stretcher squads. REGIMENTAL AID POST at U26 c 80 two stretcher squads	acw
MORY (C attery) B22 a 85	15th		MAJOR TRENCH took over command of MDS and affiliate post from O.C. 2/1 E.A. Capt LAWSON and 100 O.R. of 2/2 WEST RIDING FIELD AMBULANCE reported for duty. 3 O.R. discharged from hospital and 52 O.R. and 2/3 WRFA proceeded to duty in the Capt BULL and 40 O.R. of mid v 2/3 WRFA advanced dressing stations and relay posts. Capt S K McKEE brought to MDS slightly gassed.	acw
MORY (attery) B22 a 85	16th		3 RAMC orderlies and 6 MTASC attached to 2/3 H.C.F.A. reported for duty with unit. 1. O.R. 2/3 WRFA wounded. Capt McKENZIE and 1 O.R. 2/1 WRFA reported for duty Capt S K McKEE returned to d.T. at ADS C6 c48	acw

Army Form C. 2118.

2/2 HOME COUNTIES FIELD AMBULANCE

WAR DIARY or **INTELLIGENCE SUMMARY**

MEDICAL

(Erase heading not required.)

Place	Date	Hour	Summary of Events and Information	Remarks and references to Appendices
MDS MORY	1917		Plan showing distribution of personnel and location of posts when the M.D.S. was taken over from O.C. 21st Field Ambulance on MAY 15th 1917	
B32.c.85				
Ref MAP 57C				

Plan (sketch):

- MDS MORY O — TENT DIVISION — BEARERS 2/2 H.C.F.A.
- DURNOS POST C12.c.45 — MOTOR AMB. / 1 MED. OFFICER / RESERVE STRETCHER BEARERS
- TREGLANS POST C7.q.91 — 2 STR. SQUADS / 1 N.C.O
- RAP C6.d.82
- ADS ECOUST C2.c.48 — 2 MED. OFFICERS / 2 STR. SQUADS
- RAP U26.c.80 — 1 MO / 2 SQUADS
- RELAY POST C4.c.32 — 10 STR. SQUADS
- RAP U19.d.68
- RAP U22.d5
- ADS O'REILLYS POST C9.a.42 — 2 MED. OFFICERS / 3 STRETCHER SQUADS

ACW

Army Form C. 2118.

2/2 HOME COUNTIES FIELD AMBULANCE

WAR DIARY or INTELLIGENCE SUMMARY

MEDICAL

(Erase heading not required.)

Place	Date 1917	Hour	Summary of Events and Information	Remarks and references to Appendices
MORY L'Abbaye Ref 57C B22 a 85	May 17th		Capt CHALMERS and LIEUT DUTHIE both of 2/1st HCFA reports for duty with the unit. Capt McGILLIVRAY took charge of post at Fontaine C13 c45. No. 49522b Pte Black killed in action and 3 OR wounded. 2 Bearer Sub division of 2/3 HCFA i/c of Capt CUMMINGS reports at MDS and proceeded for duty in collecting wounded from divisional front	acw
MORY (L'Abbaye) B22 a 85	18		3 OR reinforcement from base. Capt CUMMINGS and 1 OR of 2/3 HCFA killed in action, and 3 wounded also 2 OR 2/3 WRFA wounded, all at ADS, C9 a 42. Capt LAWSON evacuated to CCS with shell concussion at ADS C9a4t.	acw
MORY (L'Abbaye) B22 a 85			MAJOR FRENCH relinquished command and handed over the unit to Lieut Col BARKLEY O.C. 2/3 H.C. F. Amb. under orders of ADMS 58th Division.	acw

Army Form C. 2118.

2/2 Home Counties Field Ambulance

WAR DIARY or INTELLIGENCE SUMMARY

MEDICAL

(Erase heading not required.)

Instructions regarding War Diaries and Intelligence Summaries are contained in F.S. Regs., Part II. and the Staff Manual respectively. Title Pages will be prepared in manuscript.

Place	Date 1917	Hour	Summary of Events and Information	Remarks and references to Appendices
MORY platoon Map 57C B.22 a 85	May 19		MAJOR FULTON 2/3 H.C.F.A. R.A.M.C. took over command of the unit from Lieut Col BARKLEY under orders of A.D.M.S. 58th Division. LIEUT BURRELL of 2/2 W.R.F.A. reported for duty with unit. 20 O.R. of 2/1 H.C.F.A. temporarily attached to unit for fatigue work at M.D.S. and to carry out sanitary attention under direction of Capt SAVAGE of 2/1 H.C.F.A. who will visit the M.D.S. daily with this work in English. Appointment of Major H. FULTON as O.C. 2/1 HCFA to date from 18.5.17	Auth DMS 5th Army P/4/235 ALLm 23.6.1917 DDMS 247/21 dated 5/4/16 new
MORY (platoon) B.22 a 85	20		Capt CHALMERS 2/1 H.C.F.A. evacuated sick to his own unit. Capt McKENZIE returned from ADS eq942, for duty at M.D.S. D.D.M.S. 5th Corps visited the MDS	new
MORY (platoon) Map 57C B.22 a 85	21		2 O.R. of unit slightly wounded. S.O.C. 58th Div. visited the M.D.S. Capt KENWORTHY 2/2 W.R.F.A. reported for duty at MDS, having returned from ADS at eq 42. Lieut BURRELL 2/2 WRFA reported for duty at MDS CAPT GERATY R.A.M.C. 2/3 H.C.F.A. reported for duty at the ADS	new

2449 Wt. W14957/M90 750,000 1/16 J.B.C. & A. Forms/C.2118/12.

Army Form C. 2118.

2/2 Home Counties Field Ambulance

WAR DIARY or **INTELLIGENCE SUMMARY**

MEDICAL

(Erase heading not required.)

Instructions regarding War Diaries and Intelligence Summaries are contained in F. S. Regs., Part II. and the Staff Manual respectively. Title Pages will be prepared in manuscript.

Place	Date 1917	Hour	Summary of Events and Information	Remarks and references to Appendices
MORY (Village) Map 57c B22 a 85	May 22		Lieut BURRELL of 2/2 WRFA wounded and evacuated to C.C.S. Adv Dressing stn at C9 a 42 transferred owing to repeated shelling and personal transferred to front at Croisilles C13 c 45. Capt FERGUSON RAMC 2/3 HCFA reported for duty at M.D.S. Capt HAYES SMITH reported for duty at M.D.S. having been relieved at ADS by Capt GERATY — Officers 3 O.R. 52 wounded passed thro MDS from noon 21st to noon 22 —	
MORY (Village) B22 a 85	23	11am 9.45p	LIEUT CLARK evacuated to 2/3 HCFA suffering from P.U.O. CAPT L. H. GUEST RAMC reported for duty at MDS Wounded passed through MDS from noon 22nd to noon 23rd my Officers 8 OR 95 acc	
MORY (Village) B22 a 85	24th		Capt SLATER proceeded to ADS at C,13 Central and relieve Capt GERATY who returned to the MDS Capt GUEST proceed to the ADS at ECOUST C2 c 48 Wounded all missing from noon 23rd to noon 24th Officers 4 O.R. 66 acc	

Army Form C. 2118.

2/2 HOME COUNTIES FIELD AMBULANCE WAR DIARY
2/2 H.C. Field Ambulance *or* INTELLIGENCE SUMMARY

MEDICAL

(Erase heading not required.)

Place	Date 1917	Hour	Summary of Events and Information	Remarks and references to Appendices
NORY (Fultry) B22 a 85 Map 57c	May 25th	6 pm	Capt SK MCKEE RAMC returned from ECOUST ADS to the Main Dressing Station having been relieved by Capt GUEST	
		11 AM	Capt CORRIE RAMC in charge of Motor Ambulance Convoy at BEHAGNIES Capt GERATY RAMC left to rejoin his unit at the M.D.S. took over the duty of supervising M.A.C. cars at the M.D.S. Wounded admissions from noon 24th to noon 25th. Officers 2. OR 36	

Army Form C. 2118.

2/2 HOME COUNTIES FIELD AMBULANCE **WAR DIARY** or **INTELLIGENCE SUMMARY** — MEDICAL

Instructions regarding War Diaries and Intelligence Summaries are contained in F. S. Regs., Part II. and the Staff Manual respectively. Title Pages will be prepared in manuscript.

(Erase heading not required.)

Place	Date 1917	Hour	Summary of Events and Information	Remarks and references to Appendices
MDS MORY	MAY 23 1917		DIAGRAM SHOWING REARRANGEMENT OF POSTS ON MAY 23rd 1917	

MDS — Main dressing Station
ADS — Advanced dressing station
RP — Relay post
RAP — Regimental Aid Post
W.P. — Waggon Post

A ROUTE 10 SQUADS
B ROUTE 14 SQUADS

REF. MAP 57C

Key symbols: ⊕ MDS ◎ ADS ● RP ✚ RAP ○W W.P.

Diagram labels:

- 2 RAP EMBANKMENT 4 SQUADS [C.5.a.33]
- RAP BULLECOURT [U.27.c.7.2] RP 2 SQUADS
- ADS ECOUST [C.2.c.48] 2 M.O. 4 SQUADS + 2 in RESERVE
- RAP [U.26.c.7.1]
- RP VALLEY [C.4.c.32] 1 NCO 6 SQUADS
- O'REILLY'S POST [C.9.a.4.2] (EVACUATED)
- RP 4 TREES [C.8.c.93] 1 NCO 2 SQUADS
- TREGIANS POST [C.7.a.91] SUB WAGGON POST 1 NCO 2 MEN 2 FORD CARS BY DAY 1 HORSE AMB AT NIGHT
- ADS + WAGGON POST (BYRNES POST) [C.10.c.45] 2 M.O. + STAFF 2 MOTOR AMB. Horse amb. by day & motor amb by night
- YOUNG'S POST [B.24.d.7.8]
- Cars day & night
- MDS MORY [B.22.a.8.5] TENT DIVISION ½ HC FA

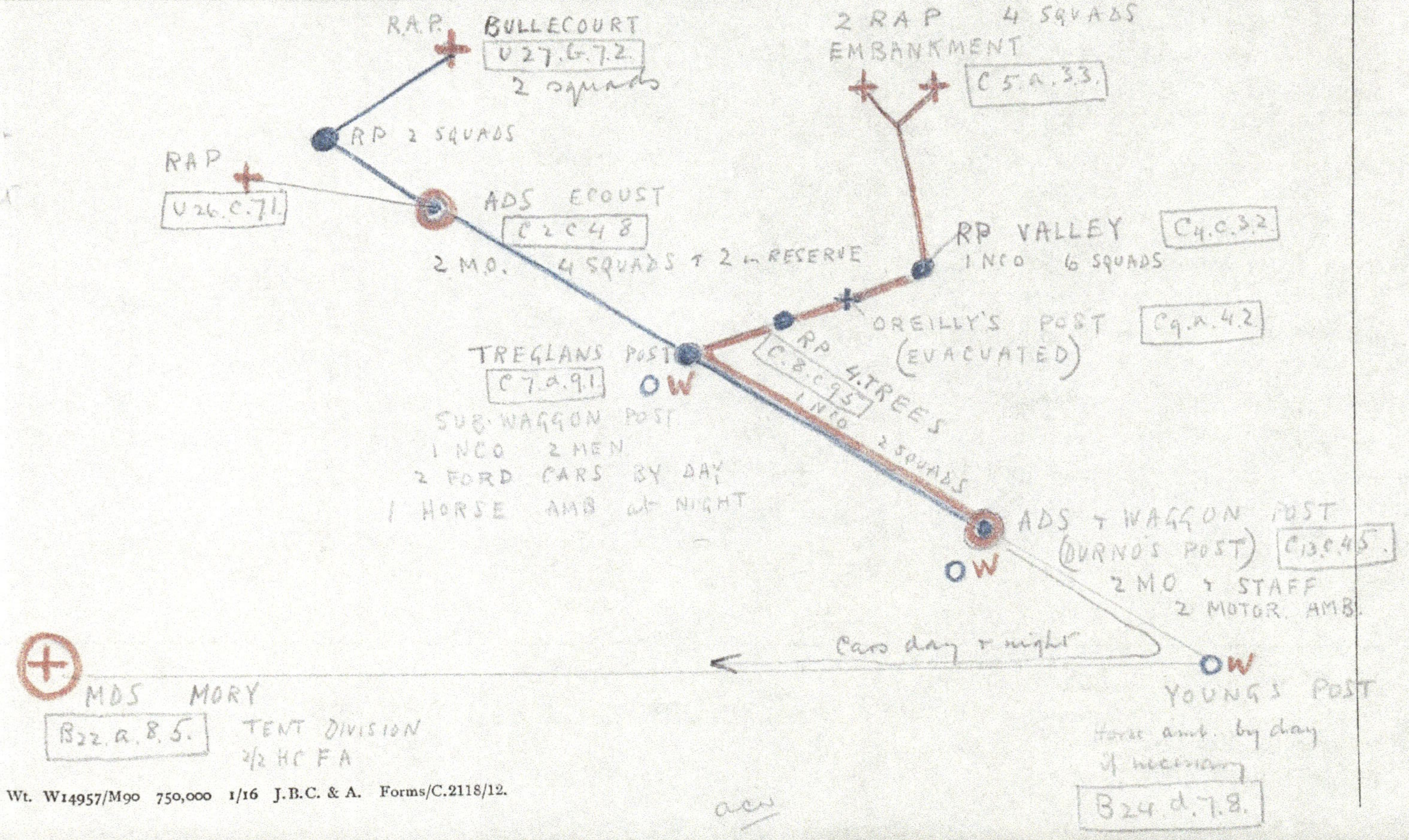

Army Form C. 2118.

WAR DIARY
or
INTELLIGENCE SUMMARY
(Erase heading not required.)

2/2 HOME COUNTIES FIELD AMBULANCE — MEDICAL

Instructions regarding War Diaries and Intelligence Summaries are contained in F.S. Regs., Part II. and the Staff Manual respectively. Title Pages will be prepared in manuscript.

Place	Date 1917	Hour	Summary of Events and Information	Remarks and references to Appendices
Reconnaissance park on May 23rd 1917			Reference Diagram on preceding page showing arrangements for evacuation made on May 23, 1917. **A. ROUTE** coloured blue is worked by 10 squads at a time. **B. ROUTE** coloured red is worked by 14 squads at a time. Each squad consist of 4 bearers. The No 4 of each squad is supplied with a card bearing the names of each man in his squad. The number of the squad, the name of the Post and the district stage on which the squad was posted. The squads of A Rout and B rout are relieved on alternate days. Specimen of Card supplied to each Squad. [Diagram: A — No. ___ Squad — Number & names of men 1___ 2___ 3___ 4___ POST___ DATE POSTED___ — Unit to which squad belongs]	

Army Form C. 2118.

2/2 HOME COUNTIES FIELD AMBULANCE

WAR DIARY or **INTELLIGENCE SUMMARY**

(Erase heading not required.)

MEDICAL
JC 5

Place	Date	Hour	Summary of Events and Information	Remarks and references to Appendices
MDS MORY (C.Albany) B22 a 85 ref map 57c	1917 May 26	12.30 pm	Lieut C. BAYLOR RAMC reported for duty at MDS in accordance with orders from ADMS 58th Divn. Wounded admissions from noon 25th to noon 26th — Officers 2 OR 33	ACW
MDS MORY	27th	2 pm	Capt HAYES SMITH RAMC 2/1 i/c reported his visit to the 2/3 H C F A MDS	
		11 a.m.	The DDMS V Corps visited the MDS	
			Wounded admissions from noon 26th to noon 27th Officers nil OR 32	RCW
MDS MORY	28th	3 pm	Wounded admissions from noon 27th to noon 28th Officers nil OR 29 Lieut DUTHIE returned to MDS from ADS ECOUST Lieut BAYLOR returned to MDS from ADS ECOUST	ACW

2/2 HOME COUNTIES FIELD AMBULANCE

Army Form C. 2118.

WAR DIARY or **INTELLIGENCE SUMMARY**

MEDICAL

Place	Date	Hour	Summary of Events and Information	Remarks and references to Appendices
MDS MORY (YMER-B)	1917 May 29	2 p.m.	Lieut W H ORTON RAMC (TC) of 2/1 HCFA reported at MDS for duty.	
Bn o 85		6.45 p.m.	Capt McKENZIE left to rejoin his own unit the 2/1 WRFA	
RAP 2/2			Capt KENWORTHY left to rejoin his own unit the 2/2 WRFA. Wounded admissions from noon 28th to noon 29th Officers nil OR 27	
MDS MORY	30th		Wounded admissions from noon 29th to noon 30th Officers nil OR 14 Capt GERATY left MDS at 9 p.m. to take over charge of medical 2/6 B" London Regt	
MDS MORY	31st		Wounded admissions from noon 30th to noon 31st Officers 4 OR 21	

2449 Wt. W14957/M90 750,000 1/16 J.B.C. & A. Forms/C.2118/12.

2/2nd Home Counties F.A.

COMMITTEE FOR THE
MEDICAL HISTORY OF THE WAR
Date -7 AUG.1917

Army Form C. 2118.

WAR DIARY
or
INTELLIGENCE SUMMARY

(Erase heading not required.)

2/2 HOME COUNTIES FIELD AMBULANCE

MEDICAL

Instructions regarding War Diaries and Intelligence Summaries are contained in F. S. Regs., Part II. and the Staff Manual respectively. Title Pages will be prepared in manuscript.

Place	Date	Hour	Summary of Events and Information	Remarks and references to Appendices
MDS MORY (Adinfer) Bar a 28.6 Map 57 c	June 1st		Wounded admissions from now May 31st to noon June 1st Officers 1 OR 11	
MDS MORY	2nd	2 p.m	LIEUT ORTON proceeded to A.D.S. Ecoust to relieve Capt SLATER	
		4.15	Capt SLATER reports for duty at MDS	
			Wounded admissions from noon June 1st to noon June 2nd Officers 2 OR 50	acu
			MAJOR DIXON. 4o 2/1 HCFA, RAMC reports at MDS for duty	acu

Army Form C. 2118.

2/2 Home Counties Field Ambulance

WAR DIARY or INTELLIGENCE SUMMARY

MEDICAL

(Erase heading not required.)

Instructions regarding War Diaries and Intelligence Summaries are contained in F.S. Regs., Part II. and the Staff Manual respectively. Title Pages will be prepared in manuscript.

Place	Date	Hour	Summary of Events and Information	Remarks and references to Appendices
MDS MORY	June 3rd 1917	9.00am	Read out on Parade the Divisional Commander's and G.O.C. annual pleasure in awarding the award of the MILITARY MEDAL to #95422 L/Cpl. L.G. GRAFT 2/2nd H.C. F.A./2nd Div. R.E. 451, June 3rd Ball.	
		9am	Capt. TURLE RAMC T.F. left MDS to relieve MO of 2/4 LONDON Regt and take over medical charge of that unit.	
Bee 85 Regt SLC			Denoted admissions from noon 2nd to noon 3rd 1 June Officers and O.R. 14	AEW
MDS MORY (Author)		1pm	Capt. J.S. WARD, RAMC T reports for duty at MDS and is posted on the strength of the 2/2 H.C.F.A.	
		2.0p	12 O.R. from Cyclists Base Depot, Rouen reported as reinforcements.	
		3 p.m	The MDS and immediate neighbourhood was shelled. The quartermaster's stores were partly demolished but no other important damage was done. No casualties occurred among the personnel of the unit.	
			Was done. No casualties occurred among the personnel of the unit. 2nd June & Officers and O.R. 17	AEW
			Donated admissions from noon 3rd to noon	

WAR DIARY
or
INTELLIGENCE SUMMARY

Army Form C. 2118.

MEDICAL

2/2 HOME COUNTIES FD AMBUL

Place	Date	Hour	Summary of Events and Information	Remarks and references to Appendices
M.D.S. JAURY	JUNE 1917			
B.22.a.5.5.	8th	1.30p	Capt. Hawkins left the M.D.S. on leave.	
		2.30pm	P.D.M.S. visited M.D.S. Division ordered above Major H. Fallon R.A.M.C.(T.F.) assuming the	
Rof map 57c		6.10p	G.O.C. visited M.D.S. acting pad. Lieut Colonel Tillott in command. A/iller Dulat 306.7	
			Wounded admissions now known Bustead Ambulance rate Officers 1 O.R. 14	
		10.30pm	The minority of the M.D.S. are skilled intermittently until 2.15 am the following day	
			but invited. Zero 0.5. 0.25. 0.50. 0.50 — present wounded to fractise.	
	9th	11.0	Court Marshal held at M.D.S. on Lieut C. Baylor R.M.S. (T.F.)	
CROISILLES B.13.d.1.6 Ref map 57c		5.0pm	M.D.S. transferred from MORY to ERVILLERS (Map 57c B.13.d.1.6) now left at NORY. Major J.H. Dixon R.A.M.C. (T.F.) holding point	
			Wounded admissions from June 6th & noon June 8th & noon June 7th 5 Officers 1 O.R. 7 Sick	
			" " " " " 7th " " 8th 2 " " O.R. 2	
	7th	12.0pm	Wounded admissions noon June 6th & noon June 7th 5 Officers 1 O.R. 7 Sick	
			" " " " " " " " " " " " " " O.R. 4	
"		4.0pm	Capt. S.K. McKee proceeded to A.D.S. ECOUST to relieve Capt. L. HADENGUEST	
"		6.30pm	Capt. L. HADENGUEST reported for duty at M.D.S. having handed over A.D.S. to Capt. McKee	

Army Form C. 2118.

MEDICAL

WAR DIARY
or
INTELLIGENCE SUMMARY

2/2 HOME COUNTIES 7TH AMBUL.

(Erase heading not required.)

Place	Date	Hour	Summary of Events and Information	Remarks and references to Appendices
ERVILLERS B13 d 16 Ref Map 57c	JUNE 8th	12.0 noon	Capt. SLATER & Capt. HUNT & 2.M. G. KNOWLES to Hospital Sick (2/3 H.C. 3rd Amb.) Wounded admissions none Jan 7.0.17 to noon Jan 8.17. Officers Nil O.R. 14 Sick " " " " " " " " " Nil O.R. 2	
	9th		Wounded admissions none 8th to noon June 9.17. Officers 1 O.R. 20 Sick " " " " " " " " " Nil OR 3	
	10th		Wounded " " " June 9th to noon June 10.17 — Nil OR 3 Sick " " " " " " " " " Nil OR Nil	
			Capt. Anstey reports from attached for temporary duty.	
			Major Hospital DIXON to dentist, reports to M.D.S. from MORY Amb, INCO & 6 OR at MORY.	
	11th		Wounded admissions noon June 10th to noon June 11.17. Officers Nil O.R. 9. Sick " " " " " " " " " Nil OR Nil	
	12th		" " " " " " 12th — " " " " " " " " Nil OR 8	
	13th		" " " " " " 13.17. Officers 1 OR 8	
			Capt. AUSTEN 2/M M.D.S. & reports for duty with 2/2 Bn Lond. Regt. (vice Capt. ATLEE Sick)	
	14th		Wounded admissions noon June 13rd " " " " " " 14.17 Officers 2 O.R. 35	
			Lieut Q.M.R reports for duty at M.D.S. from A.D.S. ECOUST	
			Capt. GUEST left M.D.S. & proceeded to A.D.S. Ecoust for duty. (vice Lieut ORTON)	
			Capt. McLARTY reported to A.D.S for duty with 2/2 H.C. 23 Amb.	
			D.D.M.S. visited M.D.S.	
	15th		School of Operation Orders by Col. HOUGHTON ADMS received HE 6/17 — Map Ref 57c NW 57b SW	
			1. 173rd Inf. Bde. will attack & capture HINDENBURG FRONT + SUPPORT LINES — U 14c C+D	
			2. Attack will be made in 154 phase 1st Phase early morning 15th June U 20 a	
			2nd Phase — 16th June	
			continued —	

Army Form C. 2118.

MEDICAL

WAR DIARY or INTELLIGENCE SUMMARY
(Erase heading not required.)

2/2 H.C. 9? Ambl.

Place	Date	Hour	Summary of Events and Information	Remarks and references to Appendices
ERVILLERS B.13.d.1.6. Map 57C	July 15th cont?		3. 2/1st Division on our left is also to attack with one of the Bns of 16th Bde in the second phase of capturing the HINDENBURG support Line from U.14.a.45.45 (inclusive) northwards.	
			4. O.C. 2/3 H.C. 9? A. will maintain the establishment of all existing Relay posts. Any further work of evacuation in accordance with scheme attached will firstly be additional. Stretcher bearer squads from R.A.P. U.19.d.7.7 when their posts is vacating the Bearer Squads will be the establishment of the Post U.13.d.1.6. to evacuate R.A.P. T.20.6.3.3. All such cases will be evacuated by 2/1st Division.	
			5. O.C. 2/2 H.C. 9? Amb will strengthen existing bearer posts of evacuation to the R.A.P of B.W. Frontl.	
			6. For such ambulances as the Division will require more than the one of No 9/11 O.9 3/2 HC9A at 10 pm 14/6/17 also will be responsible for conveyance of casualties from sidewalks. D.Slop. ad. ECOUST = St LEGER to the M.D.S.	
			7. O.C. ? HC9A will be detail one Bearer Sub Division 1 officer to O.C. 2/3 HC9A at 10 am 15/6/17 at A.D.S. ST LEGER. Remaining Bearer Sub Divis of 2/1 HC9?A will be held in reserve ready to move at horas notice.	
			8. Sub ??? ? Squads from sub amb will send 1 at A.D.S. ST LEGER to O.C. 2/3 HC9?A at 9 am 15/6/17.	
			MEDICAL ARRANGEMENTS as conclusion with Adm Ord? No 40 g 6/6/17 (dates of evacuation of wounded)	
			WALKING Bearers front by R.Q? S.B & R.A.P. U.19.D.7.7 (M.O + R.A.M.D Bearers) (Bearers by R.A.M.C Bearers) Relay posts & subsequent + R.A.P V.25.6.3.?	
			WALKING WOUNDED from V.25.6.3.3 passed along Evacuated to A.D.S. ECOUST - C.2.C.4.5 thence by ??Amb ambulances to M.D.S. ERVILLERS.	
			STRETCHER CASES by hand carriage through shelter along bearing ??? to A.D.S. ST LEGER (B.4.d.3.8) - at night a tram ambulance tank to A.B.S ST LEGER (B.4.d.3.8) by Front St??? track R? U. 25d. 4.6. thence from A.D.S. ST LEGER will be conveyed by Mot? Ambul to M.D.S ERVILLERS. cont/2

Army Form C. 2118.

MEDICAL

WAR DIARY or INTELLIGENCE SUMMARY

2/2 H.C. 90 Ambul

(Erase heading not required.)

Place	Date	Hour	Summary of Events and Information	Remarks and references to Appendices
ENVILLERS B.13.B.1.6 Map 57C	June 1918		LEFT ROUTE OF EVACUATION from Front to R.A.P. T.15.a.9.7. (CHALK PIT) & R.A.P. T.2q.b.3.3. (SUGAR FACTORY)	
			M.O. & R.A.M.C. Bearers moved back by Motor Amb. from Hex of Land correspt. to Railed CHILBOLTON & Relay Post, CROISILLES (T.23.d.2.6) thence by Motor Amb.l. A.M.D.S. ENVILLERS	
			RIGHT ROUTE OF EVACUATION via TIGER TRENCH & PELICAN AVENUE & SOUTHERN bank & Relay Post V.26.c.9.0 from V.26.c.q.0 by Land Carriage & Railed CHILBOLTON & A.D.S. ECOUST.	
			ECOUST by Mot. Amb. to M.D.S. BEVILLERS	
			ESTABLISHMENT of POSTS in connection with Divisional Plan No. 40	

POST	A.M.O.	Stretcher Squads (4 Bearers ea.) ZERO + 18 hours	M.O.	Stretcher Squads (4 Bearers ea.) ZERO + 18 hours
R.A.P. U.19.2.7.7		2	1 M.O.	10
RELAY POST U.25.a.7.6	1 M.O.	4	1 M.O.	10
R.A.P. U.25.0.3.13	2 M.O.	4	2 M.O.	10
RELAY POST V.13.d.6.6	1 N.C.O.	2	1 N.C.O.	2
R.A.P. T.24.6.3.3	1 M.O.	2	1 M.O.	2
RELAY POST T.30.a.3.c	1 N.C.O.	3	1 N.C.O.	3
RELAY POST B.S.F.N.6	1 N.C.O.	3	1 N.C.O.	3
A.D.S. ST LEGER	2 M.O.	5	2 M.O.	2
M.D.S. BEVILLERS	6 Medical Officers & Third Division			
RELAY POST V.25.c.9.1	1 N.C.O.	1	1 N.C.O.	2
RELAY POST V.29.c.4.6	1 N.C.O.	2	1 N.C.O.	2
R.A.P. V.29.6.7.2	1 M.O.	3	1 M.O.	3
R.A.P. C.F.A.3.3	1 M.O.	3	1 M.O.	3
A.D.S. ECOUST	2 M.O.	4	2 M.O.	4
BURNING POST C.13.a.5.2				

A.D.M.S. (Rail?) M.D. STAFF at 10.30 a.m.

WOUNDED admission from Noon June 24th & Noon June 25th. Officers 3. O.R. 67. (Died) Accid. O.R. 5. Germans 2.

Army Form C. 2118.
MEDICAL

WAR DIARY or INTELLIGENCE SUMMARY

2/2 Home Counties F.D. Ambul

(Erase heading not required.)

Place	Date	Hour	Summary of Events and Information	Remarks and references to Appendices
ERVILLERS B.13.a.1.6. Sh.51b57c	June 16th		Visit by D.D.M.S. & A.D.M.S. Transfer admissions from June 15th & noon June 16th:– Officers 12 O.R. 181 Germans 3 Evac " " " " – Nil O.R. 1 Capt. ROGERS attached for duty. Capt Jude reported back at MDS for duty. GCW	
ERVILLERS	17th	9 a.m.	Capt WATKIN returned from leave	
		9.30 a.m.	Maj DIXON left MDS to be temporarily attached to 2/3 H.C.F.A. for duty.	
		12 n.	Capt TURLE evacuated sick to 2/3 H.C.F.A	
		5 p.m.	Capt WARD left MDS to take over medical charge of the 2/10 Battn London Regt. Owing to shelling of the road between ECOUST and TREGLANS, POST at C.3.q.9.1., TREGLANS POST is reopened today and an N.C.O. and two men posted there. Ambulance waggons are to be stationed there and not to go further than [illegible] GCW	

2/2 HOME COUNTIES FIELD AMBULANCE WAR DIARY or INTELLIGENCE SUMMARY MEDICAL

Army Form C. 2118.

Place	Date	Hour	Summary of Events and Information	Remarks and references to Appendices
ERVILLERS B.13.d.1.6 Ref Map 57c	June 17		Nil of the present. Wounded admissions from noon June 16th to noon 17th Officers 9. O.R 376. Number of minor Sprains in line of evacuation returned by them. AEW	
		4pm	Capt ROGERS R.A.M.C. of the 2/3 HCFA reports at MDS for duty. Capt O. DE MUTH R.A.M.C attached to 2/3 HCFA awaiting military burn. (DRO 494) AEW	
ERVILLERS	June 18		Wounded admissions from noon June 17th to noon 18th - Officers 7. O.R. 105. Serum processed. AEW	
ERVILLERS	19th		Wounded admissions from noon June 18th to noon 19th Officers 3 O.R. 77	
		5pm	Major DIXON returned to his own unit the 2/1 HCFA for duty. Capt ROGERS returned to ADMS office for duty.	over

Army Form C. 2118.

2/2 Hom COUNTIES FIELD AMBULANCE

WAR DIARY
or
INTELLIGENCE SUMMARY

MEDICAL

(Erase heading not required.)

Place	Date 1917	Hour	Summary of Events and Information	Remarks and references to Appendices
ERVILLERS M.D.S. B13 d 16 Ref map 57ᵉ	June 19		Distribution of motor ambulances in lines of evacuation from divisional front to MDS as follows:- 1 Ford car at TREGLAWNS POST C7 d 9, by day and 2 by night. 3 Siddeley Deasy cars at BURNOS POST C13 c 45 day & night. 1 Ford car at St LEGER day & night. 4 S.D. cars at St LEGER at night and 3 by day. 6 S.D. cars at Main Dressing Station by day.	ACW
ERVILLERS	20ᵗʰ		Wounded admissions from June 19ᵗʰ to 20ᵗʰ Officers 1 OR 27	ACW

Army Form C. 2118.

2/2 HOME COUNTIES FIELD AMBULANCE

MEDICAL

WAR DIARY or INTELLIGENCE SUMMARY
(Erase heading not required.)

Instructions regarding War Diaries and Intelligence Summaries are contained in F. S. Regs., Part II. and the Staff Manual respectively. Title Pages will be prepared in manuscript.

Place	Date 1917	Hour	Summary of Events and Information	Remarks and references to Appendices
ERVILLERS	June 21	10 a.m.	Capt MCGILLIVRAY having been relieved by Lieut DUTHIE at BURNOUS POST left the unit for two days leave	
R13 d 16 R.y Map 57c		12 a.n.	Lieut KNOWLES returned to unit from hospital. Wounded admissions from noon June 20th to noon 21st Officer nil OR 20 ORs	
ERVILLERS	22nd		Wounded admissions from noon June 21st to noon 22nd Officer 1 OR 19 ORs	
ERVILLERS	23rd	12 n.n	The M.D.S. at ERVILLERS was handed over to O.C. 22nd Field Ambulance. The 22nd F.A. also took over the A.D.S. at ECOUST and all relay posts and collecting posts in charge of the 2/2 H.C.F.A. The personnel of 2/2 H.C.F.A. at the A.D.S. and other posts, on being relieved, rejoined the main body of the unit.	
		1.30 p.m.	Promulgation of sentence on Pte C BAYLOR RAMC who was tried by Field General Court martial on June 6th 1917 on a charge of drunkenness when on active service - He was found guilty and sentenced to be dismissed from His Majesty's Service. Sentence confirmed by F.M. D.HAIG 17.6.17. Sentence duly promulgated at ERVILLERS 23.6.17.	

2/2 HOME COUNTIES FIELD AMBULANCE

Army Form C. 2118.

MEDICAL

WAR DIARY
or
INTELLIGENCE SUMMARY
(Erase heading not required.)

Place	Date	Hour	Summary of Events and Information	Remarks and references to Appendices
COURCELLES LE COMTE B10 a 58 (sheet 57c)	23rd (continued)	2 pm	This unit marched out of the MDS ERVILLERS	
		4 pm	The unit took over the reception hospital at COURCELLES from the 2/1 H.C.F.A.	
			22nd Field Ambulance.	
		8/-	Capt DUTHIE left to rejoin his unit the 2/1 HCFA. Capt ROGERS left to report for duty at the ADMS Office. Wounded admissions from noon June 22nd to noon June 23rd Officers nil OR 10 Sick admissions for the same period - OR 6	ACW
COURCELLES	24th		The unit is to receive the sick of the Division. The 2/3 HCFA will evacuate all sick from Brigade areas in ABLAINZEVILLE and LOCUST WOOD and bring them to the 2/2 HCFA. The 2/2 HCTA will collect the sick in Brigade area at COURCELLES Wounded admissions from noon June 23rd to noon June 24th - Officers nil OR 2 Sick admissions from noon June 23rd to noon June 24th - Officers nil OR 2	ACW

Army Form C. 2118.

2/2 HOME COUNTIES FIELD AMBULANCE

WAR DIARY
or
INTELLIGENCE SUMMARY   MEDICAL

(Erase heading not required.)

Instructions regarding War Diaries and Intelligence Summaries are contained in F.S. Regs., Part II. and the Staff Manual respectively. Title Pages will be prepared in manuscript.

Place	Date	Hour	Summary of Events and Information	Remarks and references to Appendices
COURCELLES B21 a 58 (1 map 57c)	June 25		Sick admissions from noon June 24th to noon June 25th Officers nil OR 23	ACW
COURCELLES	26	3pm	Checking of antityphoid equipment is being carried out. A demonstration of sanitary appliances in the camp was given by Capt GUEST to RAMC Officers and NCOs & men of sanitary squads of the division (173rd Bde) Sick admissions from noon June 26th to noon June 26th Officers 1 OR 27	ACW
COURCELLES	27		Sick admissions from noon June 26th to noon 27th Officers 2 OR 22	ACW

Army Form C. 2118.

2/2nd HOME COUNTIES FIELD AMBULANCE

WAR DIARY
or
INTELLIGENCE SUMMARY   MEDICAL

(Erase heading not required.)

Instructions regarding War Diaries and Intelligence Summaries are contained in F. S. Regs., Part II. and the Staff Manual respectively. Title Pages will be prepared in manuscript.

Place	Date 1917	Hour	Summary of Events and Information	Remarks and references to Appendices
COURCELLES B21 a 5.8 Ruy Map 57c	June 28th	3 pm	A demonstration of sanitary appliances to Rank & File officers and orderlies appointed by 174th Brigade was given by Capt GUEST. Sick admissions from noon June 27th to noon 28th — Officers nil OR 30	ACW
COURCELLES	29th	7 pm	Sick admissions from noon June 27th to noon 29th — Officers nil OR 17 LIEUT T. M. DISHINGTON RAMC reported for duty and is Taken on the strength of the unit.	ACW
COURCELLES	30th		Demonstration of sanitary appliances to RAMC officers and orderlies appointed by 175th Brigade given by Capt GUEST in the camp. Sick admissions from noon June 29th to noon 30th — Officers 1 OR 21	ACW

2/2nd Home Counties F.A.

COMMITTEE FOR THE MEDICAL HISTORY OF THE WAR
Date 10 SEP. 1917

Army Form C. 2118.

2/2 HOME COUNTIES FIELD AMBULANCE RAMC T

WAR DIARY
or
INTELLIGENCE SUMMARY

(Erase heading not required.)

Place	Date 1917	Hour	Summary of Events and Information	Remarks and references to Appendices
COURCELLES LE COMTE				
A.S.C.72. (Rq Inf 570)	July 1st		Wounded Sick admissions from noon June 30th to noon July 1st — Officers nil O.R. 25	ACW
COURCELLES	" 2nd		Sick admissions from noon July 1st to noon July 2nd — Officers 4 O.R. 22	ACW
FOURCELLES	" 3rd		Sick admissions from noon July 2nd to noon July 3rd — Officers 2 O.R. 28	ACW
COURCELLES	" 4th	9am	Capt McGILLIVRAY returned from leave	
			Sick admissions from noon July 3rd to noon July 4th — Officers nil O.R. 43	ACW
COURCELLES	" 5th		Sick admissions from noon July 4th to noon July 5th — Officers nil O.R. 38	ACW
			Pte GUEST, Lieut KNOWLES + 6 other NCOs + men proceeded as advance party to MARICOURT	
FOURCELLES	" 6th		Sick admissions from noon July 5th to noon July 6th — Officers 1 O.R. 46	ACW
FOURCELLES	" 7th		Sick admissions from noon July 6th to noon July 7th — Officers 1 O.R. 45	ACW
			Lieut DISHINGTON RAMC left to take medical charge temporarily of the 58th Divisional Train. Capt W B GOURLAY RAMC reported for duty and in exchange thereof	ACW

2/2 Home Counties Field Ambulance

Army Form C. 2118.

WAR DIARY or INTELLIGENCE SUMMARY

MEDICAL

Place	Date	Hour	Summary of Events and Information	Remarks and references to Appendices
COURCELLES LE COMTE A15 C92 (ref map 57c)	July 7/17	8.30 a.m.	The out at COURCELLES having been handed over to a holding party of the 21st Field Ambulance and all patients having been evacuated or discharged, the unit paraded for moving to a new station. A & B sections in charge of the Officer Commanding Main moved out of the Camp to proceed to MARICOURT to take over the Capt Reston Station. C. Section under Capt McGILLIVRAY was ordered to stand by until 3 p.m. and accompany the 173rd Infantry Brigade Group on the moral to the new area.	
MARICOURT A21.c.4.8. (ref map 57c)		6 pm	A & B. sections arrived at MARICOURT and took over the Capt Rest Station from the 136th Field Ambulance. Orders received from ADMS 58 div that C section under Capt McGILLIVRAY will be temporarily attached for duty to the 2/3 H.C.F.A. on arrival in the new area. Sick admissions from noon July 7th to noon July 8th Officers nil O.R. 25	aew

Army Form C. 2118.

2/2 HOME COUNTIES FIELD AMBULANCE

WAR DIARY
or
INTELLIGENCE SUMMARY

MEDICAL

Instructions regarding War Diaries and Intelligence Summaries are contained in F.S. Regs., Part II. and the Staff Manual respectively. Title Pages will be prepared in manuscript.

(Erase heading not required.)

Place	Date	Hour	Summary of Events and Information	Remarks and references to Appendices
MARICOURT A 21 a 88 ref p 62c 1/40,000	July 9th 1917	12 noon	Corps Rest Station officially taken over from 135th Field Ambulance, and also Corps Scabies Hospital. Number of Cases taken over in C.R.S. Officers 7 O.R. 677 " " " " Corps Scabies Station - Officers nil O.R. 71	ACW
MARICOURT	July 10		Personnel of 135th Field Ambulance left MARICOURT. Capt PROCTOR R.A.M.C. and 51 N.C.Os & men of the 135th Field Ambulance remain behind to assist in running the Corps Rest Station and are temporarily attached to 2/2 H.C.F.A. Capt BRENTNALL R.A.M.C. 9th Bttn East Lancs C.P. ^ Field Ambulance and 19 other ranks are also attached. Admissions to C.R.S. from noon July 9 to noon 10th Officers nil O.R. 8 " " Corps Scabies Station " - - " Officers nil O.R. 4	ACW
MARICOURT	July 11		Admissions to C.R.S. from noon July 10th to noon 11th Officers nil O.R. 4 " " Corps Scabies Station from July 10th to noon 11th Officers nil O.R. 6	ACW

Army Form C. 2118.

WAR DIARY
or
INTELLIGENCE SUMMARY

(Erase heading not required.)

2/2 HOME COUNTIES FIELD AMBULANCE

MEDICAL

Instructions regarding War Diaries and Intelligence Summaries are contained in F.S. Regs., Part II. and the Staff Manual respectively. Title Pages will be prepared in manuscript.

Place	Date 1917	Hour	Summary of Events and Information	Remarks and references to Appendices
MARICOURT A21 a 8.8. ref map 62c 1/40,000	July 12th		Admissions to C.R.S. from noon July 11th to noon July 12th — Scabies station " " "	Officers 1 OR 26 Officers nil OR 2 men
MARICOURT	July 13th		Admissions to CRS from noon July 12th to noon July 13th Scabies Stn " " "	Officers 1 OR 82 Officers nil OR 8 men
MARICOURT	July 14th		Admissions to CRS from noon July 13th to noon July 14th Scabies Stn " " "	Officers nil OR 83 Officers nil OR 24 men
MARICOURT	July 15th		Admissions to CRS from noon July 14th to noon July 15th " Scabies Stn " " "	Officers nil OR 72 Officers nil OR 11 men
			Capt McLARTY left to wait for duty with the 241st Division and is struck off the strength accordingly.	
MARICOURT	July 16th		Admissions to CRS from noon July 15th to noon July 16th " Scabies Stn " " "	Officers nil OR 57 Officers nil OR 12 men
			Lieut KINGSTON RAMC and 30 O.R. of the 2/3rd NORTH MIDLAND FIELD AMBULANCE reported for duty.	

2/2 HOME COUNTIES FIELD AMBULANCE

Army Form C. 2118.

WAR DIARY or INTELLIGENCE SUMMARY

MEDICAL

(Erase heading not required.)

Place	Date	Hour	Summary of Events and Information	Remarks and references to Appendices
MARICOURT A21.a 88 ref map 62c 1/40000	July 17th	4PM	Admission to C.R.S. from noon July 16th to noon July 17th " " Section / other " " " " Captn L.H. GUEST detached for temporary duty with 2/1 H.C.F.A.	Officers and OR 73 Officers and OR 11 aon
MARICOURT	July 18		Admission to CRS from noon July 17th to noon July 18th " " Section / other " " " "	Officers and OR 59 Officers and OR 3 aon
MARICOURT	July 19th	12 noon	Capt. MCGILLIVRAY with 2 men from 2nd division N.C. Section having returned from 2/3 H.C.F.A. reported for duty. The tent subdivision C Section under Capt GOURLAY proceeded to number 29 C.C.S. at GREVILLERS BAPAUME for duty Admission to CRS from noon July 18th to noon 19th " " Section / other " " " "	Officers and OR 70 Officers and OR 5 aon
MARICOURT	July 20		Admission to CRS from noon July 19th to noon 20th " " Section / other " " " "	Officers 2 OR 46 Officers and OR 3 aon

2/2nd HOME COUNTIES FIELD AMBULANCE

Army Form C. 2118.

WAR DIARY
or
INTELLIGENCE SUMMARY

MEDICAL

(Erase heading not required.)

Instructions regarding War Diaries and Intelligence Summaries are contained in F. S. Regs., Part II. and the Staff Manual respectively. Title Pages will be prepared in manuscript.

Place	Date 1917	Hour	Summary of Events and Information	Remarks and references to Appendices
MARICOURT A21 a 8.8 (ref map 62c 1/40000)	July 21		Admissions to C.C.S. from noon 20th to noon 21st — Officers nil O.R. 62 " " Sedan hospital " " " " Officers nil O.R. 7	CCS CCS
MARICOURT	July 22		Admissions to C.C.S. from noon 21st to noon 22nd Officers nil O.R. 31 " " Sedan hospital " " " " " nil O.R. 8	CCS CCS
MARICOURT	" 23		Admissions to C.C.S. from noon 22nd to noon 23rd Officers nil O.R. 23 " " Sedan hosp " " " " " nil O.R. 4	CCS CCS
MARICOURT	" 24		Admissions to C.C.S. from noon 23rd to noon 24th Officers nil O.R. 15 " " Sedan St. " " " " " nil O.R. 5	CCS CCS
MARICOURT	" 25		Admissions to C.C.S. from noon 24th to noon 25th Officers nil O.R. 37 " " Sedan St. " " " " " 1 (Brevet indifferent) " 17	CCS CCS

Army Form C. 2118.

MEDICAL

2/2 HOME COUNTIES FIELD AMBULANCE

WAR DIARY or INTELLIGENCE SUMMARY

(Erase heading not required.)

Instructions regarding War Diaries and Intelligence Summaries are contained in F. S. Regs., Part II. and the Staff Manual respectively. Title Pages will be prepared in manuscript.

Place	Date (1917)	Hour	Summary of Events and Information	Remarks and references to Appendices
MARICOURT A 21 a 88 (ref map 62c) (40 OVP)	July 26		Admissions to CRS noon 25th to noon 26th Officers 1 OR 29 " Scabies Stn " " " " 0 OR 13	ACW
			Capt S. K. McKEE proceeded on leave from 26.7.17 to 5.8.17	
MARICOURT	" 27		Admissions to CRS noon 26th to noon 27th Officers nil OR 41 " Scabies Stn - 26 - - 27 " nil OR 2	ACW
MARICOURT	" 28		Admissions to CRS noon 27th to noon 28th Officers nil OR 24 " Scabies Stn 27th - - 28th Officers nil OR 11	
		12 noon	Capt Rest Station and Scabies hospital handed over to advance party of 2/8th Field Ambulance.	
			Capt GOURLAY and the last out division of C Section left no 29 CCS and proceeded to IZEL-LES-HAMEAU to advance party to take over site & new station from the 2/8th Field Ambulance	ACW

2/2 HOME COUNTIES
FIELD AMBULANCE

Army Form C. 2118.

WAR DIARY
or
INTELLIGENCE SUMMARY
(Erase heading not required.)

Instructions regarding War Diaries and Intelligence Summaries are contained in F. S. Regs., Part II. and the Staff Manual respectively. Title Pages will be prepared in manuscript.

MEDICAL

Place	Date	Hour	Summary of Events and Information	Remarks and references to Appendices
MARICOURT A.21.a.8.6 (ref map 62c 1/40000)	1917 July 29	9 a.m.	The unit marched out from camp at MARICOURT. Capt BRENTNALL with detachment of the 111th Field Ambulance left to join their own unit. Capt KINGSTON and personnel of 2/3 NORTH MIDLAND F.A. remained eating spare for the night	
		6 p.m.	Unit arrived at SAILLY-AU-BOIS and billetted for the night	
SAILLY-AU-BOIS J.1.8.6 (ref map 57d)	July 30	9 a.m.	The unit marched out from SAILLY-AU-BOIS	
		12 a.m.	The unit arrived at LA CAUCHIE and encamped at V.18.a.37 (ref map 57c)	
LA CAUCHIE V.18.a.3.7. (ref map 57c)	July 31	9 a.m.	The unit marched out from LA CAUCHIE	
		1 p.m.	The unit arrived at IZEL-LES-HAMEAU, J₂ central (ref map 57c) and the men were billetted in the village. Capt QUEST and LIEUT DISHINGTON returned to the unit for duty	

Year 1917

140/2304

War Diary
of
2/2nd H.C. Field Ambulance
for month of August 1917

M95/6948

A.D.M.S. 58th (LONDON) DIVISION

COMMITTEE FOR THE
MEDICAL HISTORY OF THE WAR
Date -1 OCT 1917

Aug 1917
1 Hospitals
4
5

2/2 HOME COUNTIES FIELD AMBULANCE

Army Form C. 2118.

WAR DIARY
or
INTELLIGENCE SUMMARY

(Erase heading not required.)

Instructions regarding War Diaries and Intelligence Summaries are contained in F.S. Regs., Part II. and the Staff Manual respectively. Title Pages will be prepared in manuscript.

[Stamp: 2nd HOME COUNTIES FIELD AMBULANCE, R.A.M.C. No. H526 Date 19-- MEDICAL]

Place	Date	Hour	Summary of Events and Information	Remarks and references to Appendices
IZEL-LES-HAMEAU (J.20.B.4)	1.8.17	8.45 a.m.	Capt. Q.C. WATKIN, one Sgt. one Cpl. and 1/Cpl. & 16 O.R. left to report to 5.C.C.S. for AGNEZ-LES-DUISANS for duty.	Map FRANCE 51c
		9.0 a.m.	Capt. McGILLIVRAY & one O.R. left to report to 29th Squadron R.F.C. for duty.	
		12.0 noon	Sick admitted – nil. Wounded nil.	
	2.8.17	9.15 a.m.	Programme of training drawn up. 7 to 7.30 am Squad drill. 9–12.30 Route March or Company Drill and Physical Training. Twice a week Route march at full Marching Order. 2–4.30 p.m. Sketch Drill or Route March.	
		12.0 noon	Sick & Wounded admitted – nil.	
	3.8.17	9.15 a.m.	Capt. W.B. GOURLAY granted leave until 17.8.17 (Contact Leave)	
		12.0 noon	Sick & Wounded admitted – nil.	
			Capt. McGILLIVRAY & one O.R. report remit from 29th R.F.C.	
	4.8.17	12.0 noon	Sick admitted since 12.0 noon 3.8.17 – Two (own personnel) Wounded – nil.	
	5.8.17	9.0 a.m.	Capt. L. HADEN GUEST granted 4 days leave to PARIS – 5.8.17 – 8.8.17.	
	6.8.17	12.0 noon	Sick admitted nil. Wounded nil	
	7.8.17	12.0 noon	Sick admitted since 12.0 noon 6.8.17 – Two (own personnel) Wounded nil.	
	8.8.17	11.0 a.m.	A.D.M.S. inspected unit on parade & presented to Merit Cards to 149422 L/Cpl. Croft J.D. 149589 Pte. Rickett J.H. 149095 Pte. Butcher L. 149549 Pte. Pike L. for gallant HQS422 L/Cpl. Bugg J.B.C.C. & A. Forms/C.2118/12 & NICOURT, for conduct to & devotion to duty & C.C.S. 149548 Pte. Marks E. 149596 Pte. Dimoff A.E. [...]	Wounded in action died from 17th Aug B.E. sent to R.F.C. (29) for employment, this Service & 2/1st H.C. F.A. at AVESNES-LE-COMTE.

Army Form C. 2118.

WAR DIARY
or
INTELLIGENCE SUMMARY

(Erase heading not required.)

2/2 HOME COUNTIES FIELD AMBULANCE

MEDICAL

Instructions regarding War Diaries and Intelligence Summaries are contained in F. S. Regs., Part II. and the Staff Manual respectively. Title Pages will be prepared in manuscript.

Place	Date	Hour	Summary of Events and Information	Remarks and references to Appendices
IZEL LES HAMEAU	9.8.17	12 noon	Sick & Wounded admitted — nil	Map Ref. 57C
Izel (M/51C)	10.8.17	12 noon	Capt L. HADENQUEST returned from leave to PARIS.	
			Sick & wounded admitted nil	
			Lieut. R. C. KNOWLES granted leave to 20.8.17	
"	11.8.17	12 noon	Sick & wounded admitted nil	
"	12.8.17	12 noon	Sick & wounded admitted 1	nil
"	13.8.17	12 noon	Sick wounded admitted 2	nil
"	14.8.17	12 noon	Sick wounded admitted nil	nil
"	15.8.17	12 noon	Sick wounded admitted 1	nil
"	16.8.17	12 noon	Sick wounded admitted nil	nil
"	17.8.17	12 noon	Sick wounded admitted nil	nil
"	18.8.17	12 noon	Sick wounded admitted nil	nil

Army Form C. 2118.

2/2 HOME COUNTIES FIELD AMBULANCE

WAR DIARY
or
INTELLIGENCE SUMMARY

MEDICAL

(Erase heading not required.)

Instructions regarding War Diaries and Intelligence Summaries are contained in F. S. Regs., Part II. and the Staff Manual respectively. Title Pages will be prepared in manuscript.

Place	Date 1917	Hour	Summary of Events and Information	Remarks and references to Appendices
IZEL-LES-HAMEAU (ref map 51C) J.a.8.4.	Aug 19th		Sick & wounded admissions 1	acw
"	" 20th		Sick & wounded admissions nil	acw
"	" 21		Sick & wounded admissions 1	acw
			Capt McGILLIVRAY, Sergt HOWSE and Pte LING left to proceed to WINNEZEELE	
			N.E. of CASSELL (ref map HAZEBROUCK 5a) with orders to report to Area Commandant Then on advance party	acw
			Lieut KNOWLES returned from leave	
"	" 22	6 pm	Capt WATKIN and tent subdivision N/B section reported back from no 8 C.C.S.	acw
		12 m	Sick & wounded admissions 1	
"	" 23		Sick & wounded admissions nil	acw

Army Form C. 2118.

2/2 HOME COUNTIES
FIELD AMBULANCE

MEDICAL

WAR DIARY
or
INTELLIGENCE SUMMARY

(Erase heading not required.)

Instructions regarding War Diaries and Intelligence Summaries are contained in F. S. Regs., Part II. and the Staff Manual respectively. Title Pages will be prepared in manuscript.

Place	Date 1917	Hour	Summary of Events and Information	Remarks and references to Appendices
IZEL-LES-HAMEAU Ia 84 (ref. map 51C)	Aug 24th	6.45 pm	The unit paraded ready to move off. Left all baggage packed	
		7 pm	The unit marched out of IZEL LES HAMEAU & proceed to AUBIGNY and bivouacked in a field	aew
		8.30	The unit arrived at AUBIGNY station to entrain motor cleared	
AUBIGNY .. 25		2.30 a.m.	The transport proceeded to AUBIGNY station to entrain and entrained.	
			O/c Lieut DISHINGTON	
		4.30 a.m.	Personnel marched to AUBIGNY	
		5.45 a.m	Train left AUBIGNY	
		2.30 pm	Train arrived at HOPOUTRE siding near POPERINGHE. The unit detrained and marched to GWENT FARM, A28 a 55 (ref. map Belgium & France sheet 28)	aew
			where it encamped.	
			Sick & wounded admissions nil	
GWENT FARM A28 a 55 (ref sheet 28)	,, 26		Capt GOURLAY, Lieut DISHINGTON and C Section tent sub division left to report to O.C. Advanced dressing station at C25 d 31 (ref sheet 28). Sick & wounded admissions nil. CAPT L H GUEST to A.D.M.S. office for duty	aew aew

2449 Wt. W14957/M90 750,000 1/16 J.B.C. & A. Forms/C.2118/12.

2/2 HOME COUNTIES FIELD AMBULANCE

Army Form C. 2118.

MEDICAL

WAR DIARY
or
INTELLIGENCE SUMMARY
(Erase heading not required.)

Instructions regarding War Diaries and Intelligence Summaries are contained in F.S. Regs., Part II. and the Staff Manual respectively. Title Pages will be prepared in manuscript.

Place	Date	Hour	Summary of Events and Information	Remarks and references to Appendices
GWENT FARM A28 a 55 Ref sheet 28 map of Belgium & France	1917 Aug 27th		Sick & wounded admissions — nil	acv
GWENT FARM A 28 a 55 (Ref Sheet 28)	Aug 28th	4:30 pm	CAPT. J.E.N. RYAN reported at Gwent Farm for duty. CAPT. A.C. WATKIN & B. Sec. Tent Subdivision reported at XVIII Corps W.M.C.P. for duty.	F.M.O.G.
GWENT FARM A28 a 55 (Ref Sheet 28)	Aug 29th	8:30 am	LT. COL. H. FULTON, two officers, & 21 O.R. proceeded to A.D.S. DUHALLOW C25 d 31 (Ref Sheet 28) & took over from 1/1 SOUTH MIDLAND Fd. AMB^{ce}. Sick & Wounded passed through A.D.S. for 24 hrs :- Wounded 5. Sick 12. 1 Sergt, 100 O.R. held in reserve at GWENT FARM, for bearer duty with 2/3rd H.C. F^d Ambce	F.M.O.G.
A.D.S. DUHALLOW C25 d 31 Sheet Ref 28	Aug 30th		CAPT. S.K. McKEE reported at A.D.S. DUHALLOW. C25 d 31 (Sheet ref 28) for duty. Sick & wounded passed through A.D.S. for 24 hrs :- Wounded 12; Sick 35	F.M.O.G.

Army Form C. 2118.

WAR DIARY
or
INTELLIGENCE SUMMARY
(Erase heading not required.)

Instructions regarding War Diaries and Intelligence Summaries are contained in F. S. Regs., Part II. and the Staff Manual respectively. Title Pages will be prepared in manuscript.

Place	Date	Hour	Summary of Events and Information	Remarks and references to Appendices
A.D.S. DUHALLOW C 25 d 31 (Sheet Ref. 28)	1914. Aug 31st		Sick and Wounded passing through A.D.S. for 24 hrs:— Wounded 21 Sick 29. G.H. McS.	

B.E.F.

SUMMARY OF MEDICAL WAR DIARIES OF 2/2nd H.C.F.A. 58th Div.
18th Corps 5th Army. (from 25/8/1917).

Western Front Operations - Aug.-Sept. 1917.

Officer Commanding - Lt.Col. H. Fulton.

SUMMARISED UNDER THE FOLLOWING HEADINGS:-

Phase "D" 1. - Passchendaele Operations, "July - Nov. 1917."
    (a) - Operations commencing July 1917.

B.E.F.   1.

2/2nd H.C.F.A. 58th Div.   Western Front.
18th Corps 5th Army.   Aug.-Sept. 1917.
Officer Commanding - Lt.Col. H. Fulton.

PHASE "D" 1. - Passchendaele Operations, "July-Nov.1917."

    (a) - Operations commencing July 1st 1917.

Headquarters at Gwent Farm. A28. a.5.5. (Sheet 28).

Aug. 25th.   Moves and Transfer.   Unit transferred with 58th Div. from 17th Corps III. Army to 18th Corps 5th Army and moved to Gwent Farm.

26th.   Moves. Deatachment.   2 & 1 T.S.D. to A.D.S. Duhallow C.25.d.3.1. for duty.

29th.   Moves. To A.D.S. Duhallow C.25.d.3.1. and took over from 1/1st S.M.F.A.

B.E.F. 1.

2/2nd H.C.F.A. 58th Div.   Western Front.
18th Corps 5th Army.   Aug.-Sept. 1917.
Officer Commanding - Lt.Col. H. Fulton.

PHASE "D" 1. - Passchendaele Operations, "July-Nov.1917."

(a) - Operations commencing July 1917.

Headquarters at Gwent Farm. A28. a.5.5. (Sheet 28).

Aug. 25th.   Moves and Transfer.   Unit transferred with 58th Div. from 17th Corps III. Army to 18th Corps 5th Army and moved to Gwent Farm.

26th.   Moves. Deatachment.   2 & 1 T.S.D. to A.D.S. Duhallow C.25.d.3.1. for duty.

20th.   Moves.   To A.D.S. Duhallow C.25.d.3.1. and took over from 1/1st S.M.F.A.

2/2nd Home Counties F.A.

14/2+38

COMMITTEE FOR THE
MEDICAL HISTORY OF THE WAR
Date -5 NOV. 1917

SECRET

Army Form C. 2118

WAR DIARY
or
INTELLIGENCE SUMMARY

(Erase heading not required.)

MEDICAL Vol 8

M95/948

WAR DIARY
of
2/2 H.C. Fd Amb
R.A.M.C (T)

From
1st Sept, 1917

To
30th Sept, 1917

30/9/17

Lt Col RAMC
OC 2/2 H.C.F.Amb
RAMC

Army Form C. 2118.

WAR DIARY
or
INTELLIGENCE SUMMARY
(Erase heading not required.)

Instructions regarding War Diaries and Intelligence Summaries are contained in F.S. Regs., Part II. and the Staff Manual respectively. Title Pages will be prepared in manuscript.

Place	Date	Hour	Summary of Events and Information	Remarks and references to Appendices
	1914			
A.D.S. DUHALLOW C.25.d.3.0. (Sheet 28)	Sept 1st		Sick & wounded passing through A.D.S. for 24 hrs :- {Wounded 20, Sick 31 G.M.M.S.	
A.D.S. DUHALLOW C.25.d.3.0. (Sheet 28)	Sept 2nd		Sick & wounded passing through A.D.S. for 24 hrs :- {Wounded 26, Sick 25. CAPT. J.E.N. RYAN attached to 2/3 H.C. F.AMB. for duty. G.M.M.S.	
A.D.S. DUHALLOW C.25.d.3.0 (Sheet 28)	Sept 3rd		Sick & wounded passing through A.D.S. for 24 hrs :- {Wounded 30, Sick 15. G.M.M.S.	
A.D.S. DUHALLOW C.25.d.3.0 (Sheet 28)	Sept 4th		Sick & Wounded passing through A.D.S. for 24 hrs :- {Wounded 34, Sick 16. G.M.M.S.	
A.D.S. DUHALLOW C.25.d.3.0 (Sheet 28)	Sept 5th		Sick & Wounded passing through A.D.S. for 24 hrs :- {Wounded 44, Sick 13. G.M.M.S.	

WAR DIARY or INTELLIGENCE SUMMARY

Army Form C. 2118.

Place	Date	Hour	Summary of Events and Information	Remarks and references to Appendices
A.D.S. DUHALLOW C.25 d.30 (Sheet Ref 28)	1917 Sept 6th	—	Sick & wounded passing through A.D.S. for 24 hrs. {Wounded 53, Sick 30} CAPT. J.E.N. RYAN evacuated Sect to O.S.C 5th XVIII Corps. F.M. M.S.	
A.D.S. DUHALLOW C.25 d.30 (Sheet Ref 28)	Sept 7th	—	Sick & wounded passing through A.D.S. for 24 hrs {Wounded 26, Sick 39} F.M. M.S.	
A.D.S. DUHALLOW C.25 d.30 (Sheet Ref 28)	Sept 8th	—	Sick & wounded passing through A.D.S. for 24 hrs {Wounded 49, Sick 5-6} F.M. M.S.	
A.D.S. DUHALLOW C.25 d.30 (Sheet Ref 28)	Sept 9th	—	Sick & wounded passing through A.D.S. for 24 hrs {Wounded 75, Sick 42} 1st LIEUT. K.P. FROST, M.O.R.C. U.S.A. reported to the unit for duty. F.M. M.S.	
A.D.S. DUHALLOW C.25 d.30 (Sheet Ref 28)	Sept 10th	—	Sick & wounded passing through A.D.S. for 24 hrs. {Wounded 130, Sick 38} F.M. M.S.	

WAR DIARY

INTELLIGENCE SUMMARY

(Erase heading not required.)

Army Form C. 2118.

Place	Date	Hour	Summary of Events and Information	Remarks and references to Appendices
A.D.S. DUHALLON C.25 d 30 (Sheet 28/N.W.)	1914 Sept 11th		Sick & wounded passing through A.D.S. for 24 hrs { Wounded 95, Sick 29. Lieut. T.M. DISHINGTON ordered to proceed to 2/3 Lincoln Regt. to duty as R.M.O. vice Capt. B.A. BULL killed in action at ST JULIEN. G. Mollison. G is struck off strength	
A.D.S. DUHALLON C.25 d 30 (Sheet 28/N.W.)	Sept 12th		Sick & wounded passing through A.D.S. for 24 hrs { Wounded 8-9, Sick 25. G. Mollison	
A.D.S. DUHALLON C.25 d 30 (Sheet 28/N.W.)	Sept 13th		Sick & wounded passing through A.D.S. for 24 hrs { Wounded 42, Sick 35. G. Mollison	
A.D.S. DUHALLON C.25 d 30 (Sheet 28/N.W.)	Sept 14th		Sick & Wounded passing through A.D.S. for 24 hrs { Wounded 50, Sick 32. G. Mollison	
A.D.S. DUHALLON C.25 d 30 (Sheet 28/N.W.)	Sept 15th		Sick & wounded passing through A.D.S. for 24 hrs { Wounded 39, Sick 19. G. Mollison	

Army Form C. 2118.

WAR DIARY
or
INTELLIGENCE SUMMARY

(Erase heading not required.)

Place	Date	Hour	Summary of Events and Information	Remarks and references to Appendices
	1916			
A.D.S. DUHALLOW C.25.d.30 (Sheet 28/28)	Sept 16th		Sick & wounded passing through A.D.S. for 24 hrs { Sick 50, Wounded 54 } Medical arrangements "58th" Division. M2563 received Sins detail of offensive Scheme including one Infantry Section Bearer & Relay Post work. From 7 Bde A.D.M.S. letter to be taken at A.D.S. DUHALLOW, also the H.Q. name is BRAKE CAMP.	
A.D.S. DUHALLOW C.25.d.30 (Sheet 28/28)	Sept 17th		Sick & wounded passing through A.D.S. for 24 hrs { Sick 26, Wounded 34 } LIEUT. L.G. MOORE. M.O.R.C. A.S.A. reported for duty. J.M.Willis.	
A.D.S. DUHALLOW C.25.d.30	Sept 18.	6 p	Sick passing through for previous 24 hours 39, wounded 35 LHS Medical arrangements 58th Division M2604 received shows Regt detailed for Bearer duties on Routes of Evacuation, one half in rear of R.A.Ps., one half in rear of REIGERSBURGH CAMP & carry wounded from area York, Bean Synd. & the Diebelli to detailed A.D.S. A Special tent of R.A.M.C. detailed for duty. R.P. SWITCH R.P. VANHEULE FARM R.P. TIN HUT. A.D.C.P. R.P. CANOPUS R.P. CROSS ROADS R. Div. Collect. Post. Captain L. HADEN GUEST rejoined on return from leave. LHS	

WAR DIARY or INTELLIGENCE SUMMARY

Army Form C. 2118.

Place	Date	Hour	Summary of Events and Information	Remarks and references to Appendices
A.D.S. DUHALLOW (C25 d 30) Sheet 28	Sept 19	6.0 p.m.	Sick passing through A.D.S. for previous 24 hours 141, Wounded, 73. Severe bombardment of German position opposite Divisional Frontier being carried out.	L.NS
"	Sept 20	5.40 a.m.	Capt L. HADEN GUEST detailed to report and act as Collecting Post for new 204/17 Capt. S. K. McKEE evacuated to C.C.S.	L.NS
"	"		Division attacked German position at HUBNER TRENCH and beyond. All objectives gained shortly after attack	L.NS
"	Sept 20	10 a.m.	No Record of Sick. Wounded since 6.0 p.m. previous night:— Officers: Stretcher, 1; Walking, 9. O.R.: Stretcher, 3; Walking, 34.	L.NS
"	Sept 20.	7.0 p.m.	No Record of Sick. Wounded. Officers: Stretcher, 15; Walking, 10. O.R: Stretcher, 129; Walking, 586. P.O.W.: Stretcher, 13; Walking, 47. = Total 900 + includes Other Formations.	L.NS
"	Sept 21	7.0 p.m	No Record of Sick. Wounded. Officers: Stretcher, 5; Walking, Nil. O.R: Stretcher, 128; Walking, 206. P.O.W.: Stretcher, 14; Walking, 7. = Total 358 includes Other Formations.	L.NS
"	Sept 22	7.0 p.m.	No Record of Sick. Wounded. Officers: Stretcher, 7; Walking, 4. O.R. Stretcher, 69; Walking, 122. P.O.W.: Stretcher, 18; Walking, 6. = Total 226 includes Other Formations.	L.NS

WAR DIARY
INTELLIGENCE SUMMARY

Army Form C. 2118

Place	Date	Hour	Summary of Events and Information	Remarks and references to Appendices
A.D.S. DUHALLOW (Sheet 28 C25d 3.0)	23.9.17	7.0 p.m.	Wounded passing through A.D.S. since 7.0 p.m. 22.9.17:— Officers Lying 1 Walking nil O.R. Lying 57 Walking 64 P.O.W. Lying 2 Walking nil. Total 114	L.H.S.
"	24.9.17	7.0 p.m.	Wounded passing through A.D.S. since 7.0 p.m. 23.9.17:— Officers Lying 7 Walking 1 O.R. Lying 36 Walking 64 P.O.W. Lying 1 Walking nil. Total 109	C.M.S.
	25.9.17	7.0 p.m.	Wounded passing through A.D.S. since 7.0 p.m. 24.9.17:— Officers Lying 4 Walking 1 O.R. Lying 38 Walking 25 P.O.W. nil. Total 68	L.H.S.
	26.9.17	7.0 p.m.	Wounded passing through A.D.S. since 7.0 p.m. 25.9.17:— Officers Lying 6 Walking 4 O.R. Lying 92 Walking 93 P.O.W. Lying 11 Walking 5. Total 211	L.H.S.
		8.0 p.m.	R.A.M.C. Operation Order No. 27 received 1 giving A.D.M.S. orders for move to relief of XIX Corps Rest Area	L.H.S.

WAR DIARY or INTELLIGENCE SUMMARY

Army Form C. 2118

Place	Date	Hour	Summary of Events and Information	Remarks and references to Appendices
A.D.S. DUHALLOW (Sheet 28 (DINND) (25.d.3.0)	27.9.17	5.0 p.m. 7.0 p.m.	Captain T. SCOTT FORREST R.A.M.C. T.C. reported for duty with 2/2 H.C.F.A. at Wagon Lines GWENT FARM Sheet 20 A22a.9.3). Wounded passing through the A.D.S. since 7.0 p.m. 26.9.17:— Officers Lying 7 Walking 1. O.R. Lying 108 Walking 47. P.O.W. Lying 3 Walking 1. Total 167	L.M.B. L.M.B. L.M.B.
"	28.9.17	2.0 p.m. 2.30 p.m. 3.30 p.m.	A.D.S. DUHALLOW handed over to 1/3 S. Midland F.A. Unit transport from A.D.S. moved off to GWENT FARM (Sheet 20 A22a.9.3) Personnel of unit entrained at A.D.S. on DECAUVILLE railway with bearers of 2/1 & 2/3 H.C.F.A. relieved from forward line & evacuated wounded to OESELHOEK. Lt. Colonel A. FULTON arrived GWENT FARM after Hospital. Personnel of unit arrived & Decauville Railway at OESELHOEK & marched to GWENT FARM	L.M.B. L.M.B. L.M.B. L.M.B.
GWENT FARM (Sheet 28 A22a.9.3)	29.9.17	4.30 5.30 9.0 a.m. 10.0 a.m.	Transport of unit under command of Captain McGILLIVRAY moved off from GWENT FARM to join Transport of 173 Bde at junction of Swift Ch. & POPERINGHE–VLAMERTINGHE Road & proceeded to XIX Corps Rest "AREA"– DESTINATION of 2/2 H.C.F.A. LIEQUES, PAS DE CALAIS, to take over Camp. Rest Site. Advance party in car & Motor Lorry left for C.R.S. L/C QUES under command of Captain L. HADDEN QUEST.	L.M.B. L.M.B.

1875 Wt. W593/826 1,000,000 4/15, J.B.C. & A. A.D.S.S./Forms/C. 2118.

Army Form C. 2118

WAR DIARY
or
INTELLIGENCE SUMMARY

(Erase heading not required.)

Instructions regarding War Diaries and Intelligence Summaries are contained in F. S. Regs., Part II. and the Staff Manual respectively. Title Pages will be prepared in manuscript.

Place	Date	Hour	Summary of Events and Information	Remarks and references to Appendices
GWENT FARM. (Sheet 28 A28a.9.9)	29.9.17	12:0 midnight	Severe Bombing by Enemy Aeroplanes took place during all surroundings are. No casualties.#19thF.Ambulance.	L.H.S.
"	30.9.17	4.0 a.m.	Bombing by E.A. ceased. 20 casualties in 2/2 W.C.F.A.	
		2.0 p.m	Convoy of Motor Ambulances despatched from GWENT FARM to XIX Corps Rest Station, LICQUES. Personnel of Ambulance waiting Entrain for Railhead AUDRICQUES at 12.30 a.m. Oct 1st 17.	L.H.S.

B.E.F.

SUMMARY OF MEDICAL WAR DIARIES OF 2/2nd H.C.F.A. 58th Div.
18th Corps 5th Army. (from 25/8/17).

Western Front Operations - Aug.-Sept. 1917.

Officer Commanding - Lt.Col. H. Fulton.

SUMMARISED UNDER THE FOLLOWING HEADINGS:-

Phase "D" 1. - Passchendaele Operations, "July - Nov. 1917."

(a) - Operations commencing July 1st 1917.

Sept. 1-19th.	Operations R.A.M.C. Routine at A.D.S.	
	Casualties. 1st-19th. Passed through A.D.S. 599 sick. 1004 wounded.	
20th.	Operations. 58th Division attacked enemy position Hubner Trench - all objectives gained.	
	Casualties. 35 and 852 wounded and 60 Prisoners of War wounded passed through.	
21st.	Casualties. 5 & 332 wounded and 21 P.O.W. wounded passed through.	
22nd.	11 & 191 " and 24 " " "	
23rd/		

B.E.F.

2/2nd H.C.F.A.   58th Div.   Western Front.
18th Corps 5th Army.   Aug.-Sept. 1917.

Officer Commanding - Lt.Col. H. Fulton.

19th Corps 5th Army from 30th Sept.

PHASE "D" 1. - Passchendale Operations,"July-Nov. 1917."
 (a) - Operations commencing July 1st 1917.

Headquarters at Gwent Farm A.28.a.5.5. (Sheet 28).

Sept. 23rd. Casualties.   1 & 111 wounded and 2 P. of W. wounded passed
                                                              through.

  24th.   "   8 & 100 wounded and 1 "   "   "   "

  25th.   "   5 & 63 wounded passed through.

  26th.   "   10 and 185 and 16 wounded P. of W. passed
                                                              through.

  27th.   "   8 and 155 wounded and 4 wounded P. of W.
                                                        passed through.

  28th. Medical Arrangements. A.D.S. handed over to 1/3rd S.M.F.A.

        Moves. To Gwent Farm A28. a. 9.9. (Sheet 28).

  30th. Moves and Transfer. To 19th Corps, 5th Army and moved to
        Licques.

Sept. 1-19th.	Operations R.A.M.C. Routine at A.D.S.	
	Casualties. 1st-19th. Passed through A.D.S. 599 sick. 1004 wounded.	
20th.	Operations. 58th Division attacked enemy position. Hubner Trench - all objectives gained.	
	Casualties. 35 and 852 wounded and 60 Prisoners of War wounded passed through.	
21st.	Casualties. 15 & 332 wounded and 21 P.O.W. wounded passed through.	
22nd.	11 & 191 " and 24 " " "	

B.E.F.

2.

2/2nd N.C.F.A. 59th Div.　　　Western Front.
18th Corps 5th Army.　　　Aug.-Sept. 1917.

Officer Commanding - Lt.Col. H. Fulton.

19th Corps 5th Army from 30th Sept.

PHASE "D" 1. - Passchendale Operations,"July-Nov. 1917."
　　(a) - Operations commencing July 1917.

Headquarters at Gwent Farm A.28.a.5.5. (Sheet 28).

Sept. 23rd.　Casualties.　1 & 111 wounded and 2 P. of W. wounded passed through.

　24th.　　"　　8 & 100 wounded and 1 "　　"　"　"

　25th.　　"　　5 & 63 wounded passed through.

　26th.　　"　　10 and 185 and 16 wounded P. of W. passed through.

　27th.　　"　　8 and 155 wounded and 4 wounded P. of W. passed through.

　28th.　Medical Arrangements. A.D.S. handed over to 1/3rd S.M.F.A.

　　　Moves. To Gwent Farm A28.a.9.9. (Sheet 28).

　30th.　Moves and Transfer. To 19th Corps 5th Army and moved to Licques.

Army Form C. 2118

WAR DIARY
or
INTELLIGENCE SUMMARY
(Erase heading not required.)

MEDICAL

140/499

CONFIDENTIAL.

War Diary
of
2/2nd H.C. Fd. Amb. R.A.M.C.(T)

From October 1st, 1917, to October 31st, 1917.

[Signature]
Lt. Col. R.A.M.C.(T) O.C.
2/2nd H.C. FLD. AMB.

COMMITTEE FOR THE
MEDICAL HISTORY OF THE WAR
Date -8 DEC. 1917

2/2ND
HOME COUNTIES
FIELD AMBULANCE
No. 41536
Date. 31/10/1917

Army Form C. 2118

WAR DIARY
or
INTELLIGENCE SUMMARY
(Erase heading not required.)

Instructions regarding War Diaries and Intelligence Summaries are contained in F. S. Regs., Part II. and the Staff Manual respectively. Title Pages will be prepared in manuscript.

Place	Date	Hour	Summary of Events and Information	Remarks and references to Appendices
LICQUES PAS DE CALAIS, FRANCE.	Oct. 1st, 1917.	9.00 a.m.	XIXth Corps Rest Station at LE VIEUX CHATEAU, LICQUES, taken over and opened.	Maps: HAZEBROUCK 5a & CALAIS 13
"	"	5.30 p.m.	Transport Column under Capt. McGILLIVRAY, G.M., arrived at LICQUES	L.H.A.
"	"	6.00 p.m.	Admissions to C.R.S. from 9 a.m. - Wounded Nil. Sick, 19 Other Ranks.	
"	"	7.00 p.m.	Main Body of Unit arrived at LICQUES. Journey from PESELHOEK to AUDRICQ having been delayed by bombing by enemy aircraft and congestion of line.	
"	Oct. 2nd	12.00 Noon	Admissions from 12 noon, Oct 1st - Wounded, Nil. Sick, 24 Other Ranks. Capt. Scott - FORREST, R.A.M.C. detd. for duty with D.D.M.S. XIXth Corps.	L.H.A.
"	Oct. 3rd	12.00 Noon	Admissions from 12 noon, Oct 2nd - Wounded, Nil. Sick, 13 Other Ranks. 8 Reinforcements arrived from Base, one a prisoner undergoing Field Punishment No 2.	L.H.A.
"	Oct. 4th	12.00 Noon	Admissions from 12 noon, Oct 3rd - Wounded, Nil. Sick, 2 Officers, 14 Other Ranks.	L.H.A.
"	"	4.00 p.m.	Out of S^{ding} List by Lt. Col. FULTON, O.C. 2/2 H.C.F.A.M.S., enquiring into the absence of No 3369 Pte BARLOW, J., a prisoner undergoing sentence of Field Punishment No 2. President Capt. L. HADEN GUEST. Members, Capt. G.M. McGILLIVRAY. No other Officers available.	
"	Oct. 5th	9.00 a.m.	Lt. Col. FULTON, R.A.M.C. proceeded to BOULOGNE on leave for England. Command handed to Capt. L. HADEN GUEST	L.H.A.
"	"	12.00 Noon	Admissions since 12 noon, Oct 4th - Wounded, Nil. Sick, 1 Officer, 17 Other Ranks	
"	Oct. 6th	12.00 Noon	Admissions since 12 noon, Oct 5th - Wounded, Nil. Sick, 11 Other Ranks	L.H.A.
"	Oct. 7th	12.00 Noon	Admissions since 12 noon, Oct 6th - Wounded, Nil. Sick, 1 Officer, 7 Other Ranks	L.H.A.
"	"	5.00 p.m.	Capt. G.M. McGILLIVRAY admitted Hospital and at "P.U.O."	

WAR DIARY or INTELLIGENCE SUMMARY

Army Form C. 2118

(Erase heading not required.)

Instructions regarding War Diaries and Intelligence Summaries are contained in F.S. Regs., Part II. and the Staff Manual respectively. Title Pages will be prepared in manuscript.

Place	Date	Hour	Summary of Events and Information	Remarks and references to Appendices
LICQUES, PAS DE CALAIS. FRANCE.	Oct. 8th	9.00 a.m.	Party of 9 Other Ranks proceeded to XI Army Rest Camp	L.J.R.
"	"	11.00 a.m.	D.D.M.S. and Officer of Camp R.E. called and inspected building. Left conducted Billets for non Com. & "A" Section. Horses now found more standings in CHATEAU grounds stabling. "C" Section at LICQUES and COURTEBOURNE. Main of "B" Section moved to Billets in LICQUES and May "B" Edn. "C" Section to Billets in COURTEBOURNE. D.A.D.O.S. called re tents & C.R.S.	
"	"	12.00 Noon.	Admissions since 12.00 Noon. Oct. 7th. 1 Wounded N.C.O. Sick, 1 Officer, 11 Other Ranks. Capt. SCOTT-FORREST attached off strength reporting as M.O. i/c Chinese Labour Coy.	
"	Oct. 9th	11.00 a.m.	Brigadier General MOIR, D.A.A.9 Q.M.G. XX Corps called and inspected premises and went afterwards with view to collection of XX Corps Rest Station by order of A/SSEN FOND. Rear Officer XX Corps called re meeting of CHATEAU in lieu of RELAY.	L.J.R.
"	"	2.00 Noon.	Admissions since 12.00 Noon. Oct. 8th 1Wounded N.C.O. Sick, 3 Officers, 13 Other Ranks.	
"	Oct. 10th	11.00 a.m.	D.D.M.S. called & inspected C.R.S.	L.J.R.
"	"	12.00 Noon.	Admissions since 12.00 Noon. Oct. 9th. Wounded, N.C.O. Sick, 2 Officers, 3 Other Ranks.	
"	"	2.00 p.m.	D.A.D.O.S. called re Ordnance Stores for Hospital.	
"	"	4.00 p.m.	Lieut. & Q.M. G. KNOWLES ½ H.C.F.AMB. admitted to Hospital with "P.U.O."	L.J.R.
"	Oct. 11th	10.50 a.m.	D.A.D.M.S. inspected Hospital. Lieut. BLAIR ½ H.C.F.AMB. reported for duty as temporarily attached Officer.	
"	"	12.00 Noon.	Admissions since 12.00 Noon D.G.1011. 1Wounded N.C.O. Sick, 4 Other Ranks	
"	Oct. 12th	12.00 Noon.	Admissions since 12.00 Noon. Oct. 11th. 1Wounded N.C.O. Sick, 1 Officer, 6 Other Ranks	L.J.R.
"	"	3.30 p.m.	Lieut. & Q.M. G. KNOWLES ½ H.C.F.AMB invalided to C.C.S. with "P.U.O."	

Army Form C. 2118

WAR DIARY
or
INTELLIGENCE SUMMARY
(Erase heading not required.)

Instructions regarding War Diaries and Intelligence Summaries are contained in F. S. Regs., Part II. and the Staff Manual respectively. Title Pages will be prepared in manuscript.

Place	Date	Hour	Summary of Events and Information	Remarks and references to Appendices
LIGQUES PAS DE CALAIS FRANCE	Oct. 13th	11.00 a.m.	D.D.M.S. inspected Hospital.	L.H.
		12.00 Noon	Admissions since 12.00 Noon, Oct 12th, Wounded, Nil. Sick, 1 Officer, 6 Other Ranks	L.H.
		2.00 p.m.	Capt. GOURLAY, R.A.M.C., returned to Unit from detached duty with D.D.M.S. XIX Corps. and reported for duty.	
"	Oct. 14th	10.30 a.m.	A.D.M.S. inspected Hospital. Lieut. K.P. FROST, M.O.R.C. U.S.A., returned from duty with 48th Division at A.D.S., DUNALLON, and reported for duty.	L.H.
"	"	12.00 Noon.	Admissions since 12.00 Noon, Oct 13th Wounded, Nil. Sick, 1 Officer, 1 Other Ranks.	L.H.
"	Oct. 15th	12.00 Noon.	Admissions since 12.00 Noon, Oct 14th Wounded Nil. Sick, 2 Officers, 5 Other Ranks	L.H.
"	"	6.00 p.m.	Lt. Col. FULTON, R.A.M.C., returned from leave and resumed command of Unit.	
"	Oct. 16th	9.00 a.m.	Capt. W.B. GOURLAY, R.A.M.C., detailed for duty as M.O. of 2/9 Border Regt.	L.H.
"	"	12.00 Noon	Admissions since 12.00 Noon, Oct 15th Wounded Nil. Sick, 15 Other Ranks	
"	Oct. 17th	12.00 Noon	Admissions since 12.00 Noon, Oct 16th Wounded, Nil. Sick, 8 Other Ranks.	
"	Oct. 18th	9.00 a.m.	Capt. A.C. WATKIN, R.A.M.C., detailed for temporary duty as M.O. of 2/6th Border Regt. Lieut BLAIR detailed by A.D.M.S. to be sent for duty to 2/9 Border Regt.	L.H.
"	"	12.00 Noon	Admissions since 12.00 Noon, Oct 17th Wounded Nil. Sick, 17 Other Ranks	L.H.
"	Oct. 19th	3.45 a.m.	Transport of Unit, under Lieut K.P. FROST, moved off en route for POPERINGHE.	
"	"	12.00 Noon	Admissions since 12.00 Noon, Oct 18th, Wounded Nil. Sick, 16 Other Ranks.	
"	Oct. 20th	4.30 p.m.	C.R.S. books closed. C.O. with transferred sick to 9/3 H.B.F.A. on march to C.C.S.	L.H.
"	"	5.5 p.m.	Embussing portion of Ambulance with one G.S. limber and 2 Half limbers moved off to entrain at ALBANY under command of Capt. L. HADEN GUEST.	
"	"	7.00 p.m.	Transport of Unit arrived at POPERINGHE and marched to Horse lines at L.11.6. S.S. Sheet 28.	

1875 Wt W593/326 1,000,000 4/15 J.B.C. & A. A.D.S.S./Forms/C. 2118.

WAR DIARY
or
INTELLIGENCE SUMMARY
(Erase heading not required).

Army Form C. 2118

Instructions regarding War Diaries and Intelligence Summaries are contained in F. S. Regs., Part II. and the Staff Manual respectively. Title Pages will be prepared in manuscript.

Place	Date	Hour	Summary of Events and Information	Remarks and references to Appendices
AUDRICQ	Oct. 21.	12.30 a.m.	Marching Portion of Unit entrained to proceed to POPERINGHE.	L.H.B.
POPERINGHE	"	7.00 a.m.	Marching Portion of Unit detrained at HOPOUTRE SIDING and marched to billets at POPERINGHE	Sheet 28
GWENT FARM	Oct. 22.	2.30 p.m.	Unit marched from POPERINGHE to GWENT FARM occupying Farm House, Huts & Horselines.	L.H.B.
"	"	5.30 p.m.	Capt. H.C. WOODYATT, R.A.M.C., Capt. M.A. MACKINNON, R.A.M.C., and Capt. P.J. LYDEN, R.A.M.C., reported for duty.	
"	Oct. 23	10.00 a.m.	Lt. Col. FULTON, R.A.M.C., and Capt. L. HADEN GUEST, R.A.M.C., attended at A.D.M.S. 58 Div Office in POPERINGHE. Instructions received to proceed to A.D.S. MINTY FARM, and DIVISIONAL DRESSING STATION, ESSEX FARM, which are to be taken over by 2/2 H.C.F.A. in relief of Ambulances of 18th DIVISION	L.H.B.
MINTY FARM	Oct. 24	10.00 a.m.	Advance Party of 2/2 N.C.F.A. under Capt. H.C. WOODYATT, Capt. L. HADEN GUEST, and Capt. H.C. WOODYATT, R.A.M.C., and 20 Other Ranks, arrived at A.D.S. MINTY FARM, and proceeded to take over from Officer Commanding, Fd. Amb., 18th Div. Accommodation at A.D.S. consists of one Elephant iron shelter with sandbagged roof, for dressing wounded; one wooden shelter for Medical and Quartermaster Stores, N.C. Os Quarters and Orderly Room; Two ventilated shelters for wounded awaiting dressing and also used as Quarters for personnel; one shelter for personnel accommodating 15 Other Ranks, one [redacted] MESS shelter for Officers, Quarters and bunks for 6; small shelter for men's cookhouse and kitchen and Officers' kitchen.	L.H.B.
"	"	10.30 a.m.	Bombs from aeroplane dropped immediately behind and immediately in front of A.D.S. About 26 wounds and 2 Killed. 4/Cpl BRISTOW E. and L/Cpl ARTHUR W.R. 2/2 to 2/2 H.C.F.A., wounded by bombs One Medical Officer of F.A. 1st Div. (LIEUT. COBRAN), wounded in legs inside Dressing Room whilst

Army Form C. 2118

WAR DIARY
INTELLIGENCE SUMMARY
(Erase heading not required)

Instructions regarding War Diaries and Intelligence Summaries are contained in F. S. Regs., Part II. and the Staff Manual respectively. Title Pages will be prepared in manuscript.

Place	Date	Hour	Summary of Events and Information	Remarks and references to Appendices
			at 2.1.2 further cot from door. E.A. presumably not bombing Brewery Station, but Light Railway adjacent. MINTY FARM had only been an A.D.S. two days. Surroundings are very dirty. Ambulance Bore-car approach A.D.S. below further obscuring pillbox. Exists in front. Several sanitary arrears of pannier, bad.	
MINTY FARM	Oct 24	12.00 Noon	Party of 6 other ranks taken over to RUDOLPH FARM (Map 28, C.21.d.33) the DIVISIONAL WALKING WOUNDED COLLECTING POST, by Capt. L. HADEN GUEST and station taken over from 2/2 H.C.F.A.	L.H.G.
"	"	7.00 p.m	Station formerly taken over by Capt. L. HADEN GUEST for 2/2 N.C.F.A. Headquarters of Ambulance established at ESSEX FARM (Map Reference Sheet 28, C19 c.3.0) Transport Lines remain at GWENT FARM	
"	Oct 25	9.00 a.m	A.D.S. MINTY FARM inspected by A.D.M.S. 58 Div. and O.C. 2/2 H.C.F.A and 2/3 H.C.F. Ambulances. O.C. Bearers in the line, Capt. LEESON R.A.M.C. 2/3 H.C.F.A. conducted his Headquarters at MINTY FARM	L.H.G.
ESSEX FARM MINTY FARM	"	"	Capt A.C. WATKIN returned to Headquarters, ESSEX FARM and reported for duty.	
"	"	7.00 p.m	Wounded passed through since 7.00 pm 2nd Oct. 1917: 58 Div. Officers 2, O.R. 68; Other formations Officers 3, O.R. 66 Casualties. Pte Lennon C.E. G.S.W. (Shell) Pte Bressey 8f. G.S.W. (Shell) Buttock	L.H.G.
"	Oct 26	9.00 a.m	Work begun on erection of English shelter alongside existing structure, work being carried out by 503 Fd Coy R.E. assisted by R.A.M.C. Personnel. Shelter to be protected by overhead cover, blanketed up by heavy beams and sandbags.	
"	"	12.00 Noon	Heavy storm of enemies all night and morning, a considerable number very bad. Batteries and camps in neighbourhood also attacked. Two medical officers required to cope with cases at RUDOLPHE FARM.	

1875 Wt. W593/826 1,000,000 4/15 J.B.C. & A. A.D.S.S./Forms/C. 2118.

WAR DIARY or INTELLIGENCE SUMMARY

Army Form C. 2118

Instructions regarding War Diaries and Intelligence Summaries are contained in F. S. Regs., Part II. and the Staff Manual respectively. Title Pages will be prepared in manuscript.

Place	Date	Hour	Summary of Events and Information	Remarks and references to Appendices
MINTY FARM	Oct 26th	7.00 p.m.	Wounded passed through since 7.0 p.m. 25/10/17: 58 Div., Officers 1, O.R. 236; Other formations, Officers 1, O.R. 54. Unit Casualties: O.R. 5 (1 N.Y.D. Gas Poisoning). Medical Staff required in addition to O.O., A.D.S. Two Medical Officers for day duty and one for night at MINTY FARM, one for day and one for night at RUDOLPH FARM.	
"	"	7.30 p.m.	Infantry action by 173rd Bde ended but (not) very satisfactory completing this morning. Wounded are now beginning to arrive.	
"	Oct 27th	9.00 a.m.	Progress being made with Brg. Rd. shelter, the room 1 which was erected and boarded and in use as a Dressing room has enlarged party completed.	L 118
"	"	7.00 p.m.	Wounded passing through since 7 p.m. 26/10/17. 58 Div., Officers 1, O.R. 101; Other formations Officers 2, O.R. 36. Unit Casualties O.R. 10 (N.Y.D. Gas Poisoning) Walking Wounded opened at RUDOLPH FARM.	
"	"	8.00 p.m.	Soup Kitchen for Troops and Walking Wounded opened used chiefly during the day however.	
"	Oct 28th	8.00 a.m.	Work of erecting extra shelter accommodation in part of old German communication trench "Gurne Yane Garry" begun. Trench to be floored and trench barricade roofed with English shelter curved iron. Conference being improved. Space in front of A.D.S. where cars draw up being cleared, cleaned and covered with heavy joinders. Space in front and round shelter being trench board covered.	L 118
"	"	12.00 Noon	Steady stream of wounded passing through.	
"	"	7.00 p.m.	Wounded passed through since 7.00 p.m. 27/10/17. 58 Div., Officers 2, O.R. 62; Other formations Officers 1, O.R. 35. Unit Casualties O.R. 4 (3 G.S.W., 1 N.Y.D. Gas Poisoning).	

1875 Wt. W593/826 1,000,000 4/15 J.B.C. & A. A.D.S.S./Forms/C. 2118.

WAR DIARY or INTELLIGENCE SUMMARY

Army Form C. 2118

Place	Date	Hour	Summary of Events and Information	Remarks and references to Appendices
MINTY FARM	Oct 28th	10 pm	The Company came. Volunteer party of 2 N.C.O. proceeded to TRACAS FARM in front line to clear wounded.	L.18
"	Oct 29th	8.0 am	Structural improvements to A.D.S. continue to be carried out. Boarding of standing for Ambulance Cars in front of A.D.S. laid down. Volunteer party returned from TRACAS FARM. Capt. L. HADEN GUEST remaining at TRACAS FARM to dress cases.	L.
"	"	7.0 pm	Wounded passing through A.D.S. since 28/10/17. 58th Div. Officers 1, O.R. 69. Other Formations, Officers 4, O.R. 93. Unit casualties: O.R. 6 (Inc. 3 killed in action, 3 G.S.W.). Local shelling more marked than usual.	
"	Oct 30th	1.30 am	Capt. L. HADEN GUEST returned from TRACAS FARM to secure bearer party who had not returned to clear to Mebus.	L.18
"	"	5.00 am	Heavy attack by 9th Battn. this morning. Attack in portions of enemy including NOBLES FARM, CAMERON HOUSES and MORAY HOUSE. Zero hour 5.50. No wounded yet arrived.	
"	"	12.00 Noon	Heavy wounded just beginning to arrive.	
"	"	7.00 pm	Wounded passing through since 10 p.m. 29/10/17. 58 Div. Officers 4, O.R. 153. Other Formations, Officers 5, O.R. 72. Unit casualties N.I.L. Shelling less than normal.	L.H.R.
"	Oct 31st	8.00 am	Large part of structural improvement of road & standing for cars much hampered by enemy shelling. Shelter, Cookhouse, and laying of English stable of formation of Greek stone trench completed.	
"	"	12.00 Noon	Wounded passing through slowly but are mostly cases which have been lying in town for days.	
"	"	7.00 pm	Wounded passing through since 10 p.m. 30/10/17. 58 Div. Officers N.I.L. O.R. 105. Other Formations Officers 2, O.R. 26. Unit casualties Nil.	L.H.R.

Army Form C. 2118

MEDICAL Vol 10

WAR DIARY

or

INTELLIGENCE SUMMARY

(Erase heading not required.)

CONFIDENTIAL

War Diary

of

2/2ND H.C. FD. AMB., R.A.M.C.(T)

FROM 1-11-1917 TO 30-11-1917.

COMMITTEE FOR THE
MEDICAL HISTORY OF THE WAR
Date 17 JAN. 1918

2/2ND
HOME COUNTIES
FIELD AMBULANCE.
No.
Date 1-12-1917

Lt.Col. R.A.M.C.(T)
O.C.
2/2ND H.C. FLD. AMB.

Place	Date	Hour	Summary of Events and Information	Remarks and references to Appendices
	Nov 1917			

Army Form C. 2118.

WAR DIARY
or
INTELLIGENCE SUMMARY.
(Erase heading not required.)

Instructions regarding War Diaries and Intelligence Summaries are contained in F.S. Regs., Part II. and the Staff Manual respectively. Title pages will be prepared in manuscript.

Place	Date	Hour	Summary of Events and Information	Remarks and references to Appendices
ESSEX FARM (Sheet 28 - C.19.c.3.0.) and A.D.S. NINTY FARM (Sheet 28 - C.10.c.3.6.)	1/11/17	—	Letter received from A.D.M.S. forwarding following letters received from C.R.E., 58 Div. and G.S.O.1, 58 Div. as follows:—	
			"58 Div., G.S.1182.	
			"29-10-17.	
			"G. 58 Div. — I should like to acknowledge the very valuable assistance which has been given by the R.A.M.C. stretcher-Bearers to the Field Companies in getting out stuck lorries in the last ten days. These men in addition to their own turbo-tour carried forward a large number of stores for us and helped us in a big way. The O.C. 2/3rd Field Ambulance has also helped with transport."	
			"(Sd.) W. HYDE - KELLY, Lt.Col., R.E., C.R.E., 58 Div., 29-10-17."	
			"58 Div., G.S.1182.	
			"A.D.M.S. — In forwarding the attached report the G.O.C. wishes to say how much he appreciates the entirely voluntary and useful work done by the R.A.M.C. Stretcher-Bearers and Transport. He wishes one to add that the spirit of co-operation shown by all ranks have at heart the success of the Division in the common cause."	
			"(Sd.) J.E. TURNER, Lt.Col., Gen. Staff, 58 (Lond.) Div., 30-10-17." L.H.Q.	

Army Form C. 2118.

WAR DIARY
INTELLIGENCE SUMMARY.
(Erase heading not required.)

Instructions regarding War Diaries and Intelligence Summaries are contained in F. S. Regs., Part II. and the Staff Manual respectively. Title pages will be prepared in manuscript.

Place	Date	Hour	Summary of Events and Information	Remarks and references to Appendices
ESSEX FARM and A.D.S. MINTY	1/11/17	6 p.m.	1 Wounded passing through A.D.S. MINTY for 24 hours to 6 p.m. 1/11/17:–	
			ALL FORMATIONS – Lying – Officers 2 Other Ranks 59 58 DIV. ONLY – Other Ranks 24	
			(INCLUDING 58TH Walking – Do. – 1 Do. do. 39 Do. do. 20	
			DIV.) 3 98 44	
		6.15 p.m.	Extract from Progress Report by Capt. A.C. WATKIN from A.D.S. MINTY.	
			"The work on new shelters etc. is being continued."	
			Weather: Dull.	L.H.G.
Do. do.	2/11/17	10 a.m.	Shelling very heavy in the morning at the A.D.S. MINTY and Working Party was sent back	
			to ESSEX FARM. Shelling slackened in the afternoon.	
" "	"	6 p.m.	Wounded passing through A.D.S. MINTY, for 24 hours to 6 p.m. 2/11/17:–	
			ALL FORMATIONS – Lying – Officers – Other Ranks 28 58 DIV. ONLY – Other Ranks 15	
			(INCLUDING 58TH Walking – Do. – – Do. do. 24 Do. do. 10	
			DIV.) – 52 25	
" "	"	6 p.m.	Extract from Progress Report by Capt. L. HADEN GUEST from A.D.S. MINTY;	
			"Standing for Cars – A party have gone out to collect planks to improve Roadway in	L.H.G.

Army Form C. 2118.

WAR DIARY
or
INTELLIGENCE SUMMARY.
(Erase heading not required.)

Instructions regarding War Diaries and Intelligence Summaries are contained in F. S. Regs., Part II. and the Staff Manual respectively. Title pages will be prepared in manuscript.

Place	Date	Hour	Summary of Events and Information	Remarks and references to Appendices
			Front of A.D.S.	
			Weather: Dull with drizzling intervals	L.W.R.
ESSEX FARM	3/11/17		D.D.M.S., II. Corps visited ESSEX FARM during morning	
and A.D.S. MINTY	"	6 p.m.	Wounded passing through A.D.S. MINTY for 24 hrs. to 6p.m. 3/11/17	
			ALL FORMATIONS lying — Officers 6 Other Ranks 23 / 58 DIV only — Officers 3 Other Ranks 14 (Including 58 Div) Walking — Do. — Do. do. 30 Do. do. 13	
			— 6 53 3 27	
		6 p.m.	Extract from Progress Report by Capt. A.C. WATKIN from A.D.S. MINTY:— "Owing to continued shelling the work has been delayed"	L.W.R.
			2 Other Ranks, 2/2nd H.C.F. Amb., reported "N.Y.D. Gas Poisoning". Removed to Duty.	
"	4/11/17		Extract from C/O of LT. GEN. SIR IVOR MAXSE, K.C.B, C.V.O, D.S.O, Commanding XVIII Corps. read for information of all Ranks:—	
			"1st November 1917	
			"To-day I have been so busy handing over that I could not make an opportunity of calling personally upon you and your Brigadiers to express to them and to all Ranks my appreciation of the splendid work they have put in throughout the month	L.W.R.

WAR DIARY
or
INTELLIGENCE SUMMARY.
(Erase heading not required.)

Army Form C. 2118.

Instructions regarding War Diaries and Intelligence Summaries are contained in F.S. Regs., Part II. and the Staff Manual respectively. Title pages will be prepared in manuscript.

Place	Date	Hour	Summary of Events and Information	Remarks and references to Appendices
			"they have been in this Corps. Their spirit has been magnificent throughout. On the 20th September they won the best battle yet fought in this Corps and we have had 13 Casttles in FLANDERS. I consider the 20th September as the Birthday of the Corps and the capture of WURST FARM was a real feat of arms – never than 1000. Having captured that ridge the 58th Division not only held its ground but they defeated no less than five fresh battalions which counter-attacked them during the afternoon. They & the 51st Division were highly tried on that day, and the army owes to battles that he has never once counter-attacked up in strength save that half I by Jonnick casey to your people has greatly I have appreciated their service and loyal support. I bid them farewell."	L.H.R.
ESSEX FARM and AD SPINT FARM	6/11/17		Letter by D.A. & Q.M.G. I army on the Medical Service also part of information of I.C.C. "Special Order by General Sir H. de la GOUGH, K.C.B., K.C.V.O. Commanding Fifth Army 30th October, 1917 "MEDICAL SERVICES." "The Army Commander desires to express his appreciation of the excellent work which has been, and is still being done by the Medical Services in con–	L.H.G.

WAR DIARY
or
INTELLIGENCE SUMMARY.
(Erase heading not required.)

Army Form C. 2118.

Place	Date	Hour	Summary of Events and Information	Remarks and references to Appendices
ESSEX FARM and A.D.S. MINTY FARM.	4/11/17	Noon	In action with the active operations on this front. The casualties are moderate in which there has been performed effects the greatest credit on all concerned. The evacuation of the sick and wounded from the front to the Casualty Clearing Stations has been most carefully organised and success fully carried out, while the preventive cabill and attention displayed at the Casualty Clearing Stations, together with the increased comfort provided for the patients has led to highly satisfactory results being obtained. "H.N. SARGENT, Major-General, D.A. & Q.M.G. XVth Army."	L.M.S.
"	"	"	The IInd Corps Walking Wounded Collecting Post, where "C" Section Tent Sub-Division was doing duty closed at Noon at the Irish Farm and moved to DUHALLOW M.D.S.	
"	"	6pm	Wounded passing through A.D.S. MINTY FARM for 24 hrs. ending 6pm:—	
			AMPLIFICATIONS: Lying— Officers 5 | Other Ranks 18 | 55 Division: Other Ranks 1	
			(INCLUDING 58 Walking Do — Do do 15 Do do 6	
			Div) — 5 36 7	
"	"	6.5pm	Extract from Progress Report by Capt. L. HADEN GUEST from A.D.S., MINTY FARM:—	
			"Very few wounded are coming through. All communications are intact. There is very"	L.H.G.

WAR DIARY
or
INTELLIGENCE SUMMARY.
(Erase heading not required.)

Army Form C. 2118.

Place	Date	Hour	Summary of Events and Information	Remarks and references to Appendices
			Cold & shelling	L.I.B.
			Weather turned changeable	
ESSEX FARM and A.D.S. MINTY FARM.	5/11/17	—	Capt. G.M. McGillivray granted leave from 5-11-17 to 19-11-17.	
"	"	2 p.m.	The wheeled transport to Kempton Park to carry out 48 hrs gas & anti gas course from the line.	
"	"	6 p.m.	Wounded passing through A.D.S. Minty Farm for 24 hrs ending 6 p.m.:—	
			ALL FORMATIONS :— Lying — Officers — Other Ranks 20 ‖ 58 DIV. ONLY: Other Ranks 17	
			(INCLUDING 58 DIV.) Walking Do. 2 Do. do. 17 Do. do. 15	
			2 37 32	
"	"	6 p.m.	Extract from Progress Report by Capt. L. HADEN GUEST for 24 hrs ending 6 p.m.:— "Considerable work in hand, new latrine erected. English Shelter for our Corporals being built up of No. 3 Shelter nearly complete. Body of Capt. G.D.G. ELTON, G.S.O.(2), 58 Div. distp. in charge of Q.M.S. QVR. & D.H.Q. Very few wounded and	
"	"	—	back and situation quiet."	
"	"	—	1 Reinforcement (Sergt.) taken on Strength.	
"	"	—	1 Other Rank, 2/5 B. C.R. Limb reported "N.Y.D. Gas Poisoning" — Evacuated.	L.I.B.

Army Form C. 2118.

WAR DIARY
or
INTELLIGENCE SUMMARY.
(Erase heading not required.)

Instructions regarding War Diaries and Intelligence Summaries are contained in F. S. Regs., Part II. and the Staff Manual respectively. Title pages will be prepared in manuscript.

Place	Date	Hour	Summary of Events and Information	Remarks and references to Appendices
ESSEX FARM and A.D.S. MINTY FARM	6/11/17	9 a.m.	Capt. M.A. MACKINNON detailed for duty with the 47th H.A. Group and struck off strength.	
"	"	"	1st Lieut. J.A. LESS, M.O.R.C., U.S.A. reported for duty and was taken on the strength. (Auth: A.N.125 6/11/17)	
"	"	"	1st Lieut. R.B. CRAIN, M.O.R.C., U.S.A. temporarily attached to unit for duty (Auth A.M 124 6/11/17)	
"	"	6 p.m.	1 Other Rank, M.T., A.S.C. granted 30 days' leave to England for purpose of ploughing. Tractor and land confirmed by Agricultural Committee.	
"	"	"	Wounded passing through A.D.S. MINTY FARM, for 24 hrs. ending 6 p.m.	
			ALL FORMATIONS – Lying – Officers 1 Other Ranks 8 58 DIV ONLY – Other Ranks 5	
			(INCLUDING 58 DIV.) Walking Do. – Do. do. 24 Do. do. 8	
			1 32 13	
"	"	6.15 p.m.	Contract Event Program Report by Capt. L. HADEN GUEST, from A.D.S. MINTY FARM :–	
			"Constructional Work :– Shelter 3 is complete. Trench Shelter nearly complete. Kick"	
			"Shelter :– R.E. Party is proceeding with this tomorrow. General Situation – Very few wounded"	
			"very little shelling."	
			"Weather: Rain/fine intermittently."	L.H.R.
"	7/11/17	6 p.m.	Wounded passing through A.D.S. MINTY FARM for 24 hrs. ending 6 p.m. :–	
			ALL FORMATIONS :– Lying – Other Ranks 10 58 DIV. ONLY – Other Ranks 10	
			(INCLUDING 58 DIV.) Walking Do. do. 19 Do. do. 17 No Casualties in Officers	
			29 27	L.H.R.

Army Form C. 2118.

WAR DIARY
or
INTELLIGENCE SUMMARY.
(Erase heading not required.)

Instructions regarding War Diaries and Intelligence Summaries are contained in F. S. Regs., Part II. and the Staff Manual respectively. Title pages will be prepared in manuscript.

Place	Date	Hour	Summary of Events and Information	Remarks and references to Appendices
ESSEX FARM and A.D.S. MINTY FARM.	7/11/17	6 p.m.	Extract from Progress Report by Capt. A.C. WATKIN from A.D.S. MINTY FARM:- "Working Parties:- R.E. Party has been at work constructing Kitchen Drainage & foot at the back of A.D.S. has been carried on as far as possible. General Situation:- Very few casualties and very little shelling." A Quiet War Day.	L.H.S.
" " "	8/11/17	6 p.m.	Wounded passing through A.D.S. MINTY FARM, for 24 hrs, ending 6 p.m.:- ALL FORMATIONS Lying - Other Ranks 6	58 DIV. only Other Ranks 3 (INCLUDING 58 DIV.) Walking Do. do. 14	Do. do. 14 =20 / =17 =26	
" " "	"	6 p.m.	Extract from Progress Report by Capt. A.C. WATKIN from A.D.S. MINTY FARM:- "General Situation: Quiet. Working Parties:- Work continued as in yesterday's report." Three enemy batteries fell before evening.	L.H.S.
" " "	9/11/17	6 p.m.	Wounded passing through A.D.S. MINTY FARM, for 24 hrs, ending 6 p.m.:- ALL FORMATIONS: Lying - Officers - Other Ranks 9	58 DIV. only Officers - Other Ranks 2 (INCLUDING 58 DIV.) Walking Do. 1	Do. do. 22	Do. 1	Do. do. 11 =1/=31 =1/=13	L.H.S.

WAR DIARY
or
INTELLIGENCE SUMMARY.
(Erase heading not required.)

Army Form C. 2118.

Place	Date	Hour	Summary of Events and Information	Remarks and references to Appendices
ESSEX FARM and A.D.S. MINTY FARM	9/11/17	6 p.m.	Extract from Progress Report by Capt. A.C. WATKIN from A.D.S. MINTY FARM:— "The Cooks commenced using the New Cookhouse this afternoon. Cabart is being made for the next Circuit. The row of graves near the Cemetery has been railed off. Work has been commenced in roofing over the passage to Officers' Mess. General Situation. No. of I.V. cases accumulation for invalid."	
"	"		"Quiet. A wet day." Medical Arrangements — Div. Corps. M.S. 1/4/17 et 8/4/17 recd. Army General Staff for obtaining of casualties disposed of patients etc.	L.H.S.
"	10/4/17	6 p.m.	Wounded passing through A.D.S. MINTY for 24 hours ending 6 p.m.:—	
			ALL FORMATIONS:— Lying — Officers — Other Ranks 10 53 DIV. ONLY. Other Ranks 4 (INCLUDING 58 DIV.) Walking Do — Do do 35 Do do 11 ———— ———— 45 15	
"	"	6.30 p.m.	Extract from Progress Report by Capt. A.C. WATKIN from A.D.S. MINTY FARM:— "Working Parties:— Work has been continued as per yesterday's report. General Situation:— Very few wounded. Have passed through. The Main Latrine was partially stove in by enemy shelling."	
"	"		1 Other Rank of 2/Bn. B.G.H. Rank reported "N.Y.D. Gas Poisoning. Removed at Duty." (Later evacuated).	L.H.S.

Army Form C. 2118.

WAR DIARY
or
INTELLIGENCE SUMMARY.
(Erase heading not required.)

Instructions regarding War Diaries and Intelligence Summaries are contained in F. S. Regs., Part II. and the Staff Manual respectively. Title pages will be prepared in manuscript.

Place	Date	Hour	Summary of Events and Information	Remarks and references to Appendices
ESSEX FARM and A.D.S. MINTY FARM.	10/11/17	—	Rain fell practically all day	L.H.G.
	11/11/17	6 p.m.	Wounded passing through A.D.S., MINTY FARM, for 24 hours ending 6 p.m.:—	
			ALL FORMATIONS:— Lying – Officers 1 Other Ranks 16 | 58 DIV. ONLY:— Officers Other Ranks 7	
			(INCLUDING 58 DIV.) Walking. Do. do. 20 | Do. 1 Do. do. 11	
			$\overline{1}$ $\overline{36}$ $\overline{1}$ $\overline{18}$	
"	"	6 p.m.	Extract from Progress Report by Capt. L. HADEN GUEST, from A.D.S. MINTY FARM:—	
			"Roofing of passage way to Officers' Mess with English Shelter ones is being completed"	
			"and well be camouflaged. Kitchen is completed. Old Shelter at RUDOLPH FARM are	
			"now in order and sandbagged. Drainage of pond at back of A.D.S. is completed"	
			"and let bags filled to wall earth and rubble. Shelling normal."	
"	"	"	Notification received of 1 Other Ranks dying in Hospital from wounds received in action 30/4/17	L.H.G.
"	12/11/17	6 p.m.	Wounded passing through A.D.S. MINTY FARM for 24 hours ending 6 p.m.:—	
			ALL FORMATIONS:— Lying – Other Ranks 6 | 58 DIV. ONLY:— Other Ranks 2	
			(INCLUDING 58 DIV.) Walking. Do. do. 21 | Do. do. 4	
			$\overline{27}$ $\overline{6}$	
"	"	6 p.m.	Extract from Progress Report by Capt. L. HADEN GUEST, from A.D.S. MINTY FARM:—	L.H.G.

Army Form C. 2118.

WAR DIARY
or
INTELLIGENCE SUMMARY.
(Erase heading not required.)

Instructions regarding War Diaries and Intelligence Summaries are contained in F. S. Regs., Part II. and the Staff Manual respectively. Title pages will be prepared in manuscript.

Place	Date	Hour	Summary of Events and Information	Remarks and references to Appendices
ESSEX FARM and A.D.S. MINTY FARM	12/11/17	—	"Wounded - Very few cases are passing through. Shelling - Local Shelling Severe.	
"	"		"Casualties" Results of fine Sorts Bombs during the afternoon"	
"	"		Extract from 58th Div R.Os. of 12/11/17. No. 870.	
"	"		"The Divisional Commander has much pleasure in announcing the following awards	
"	"		"to the undermentioned N.C.Os and Men" - 495412 Sgt. W.A. NOWERS, R.A.M.C. (Military Medal).	
"	"		"495360 Sgt. A. KIMBERLEY, R.A.M.C. (Military Medal), 495466 Pte. W.T. BAILEY, R.A.M.C. (Military	
"	"		"Medal), 495268 Pte. V. ROGERS, R.A.M.C. (Military Medal) - (all of 2/1st N.B.T.Amb.)	L.H.S.
"	13/11/17	9 am	Capt. H.C. WOODYATT detailed for duty with 290 Bde. R.F.A.	
"	"	Noon	Lieut. R. WARD (R.A.M.C-T.C.) reported forcibly and taken in charge. (Auth. A.24/69). Re-	
"	"		tailed for duty as A.D.S. MINTY.	
"	"	2 p.m	Lieut. R.B. CRAIN, M.O.R.C. U.S.A. returned to Division to-day. 2/Lt. J.O.B.T.Club	
"	"	6 p.m	Extract from Progress Report by Capt. L. HADEN GUEST:-	
"	"		"Constructional Work: The paths to Quartos taken over from gunners is partly completed	
"	"		"and culverts being blocked in by sandbags. Water Tanks are sandbagged	
"	"		"Work in roadway filled up and clearing operations continued.	
"	"		"Shelling: There has been considerable shelling by heavies (presumably 5.9 and	
"	"		"H.V.S.) for last hour and this is continuing at Canadian Artillery.	L.H.S.

WAR DIARY or INTELLIGENCE SUMMARY.

Army Form C. 2118.

(Erase heading not required.)

Place	Date	Hour	Summary of Events and Information	Remarks and references to Appendices
ESSEX FARM and A.D.S. MINTY FARM.	14/11/17	8.30am	2/3rd H.C.F.Amb. Headquarters moved from ESSEX FARM. Bearers in Line before an charge of O.B. 2/2nd H.C.F.Amb	L.H.B.
"	"	6.0pm	Wounded passing through A.D.S., MINTY FARM for 24 hours, ending 6 p.m:—	
			ALL FORMATIONS:— Lying - Other Ranks 22 58 Div any Other Ranks 1	
			(INCLUDING 58 Walking Do. do. 55 Do. do. 10	
			DIV.) 77 11	
"	"	6.15pm	Extract from Progress Report by Capt. L. HADEN GUEST from A.D.S., MINTY FARM:—	
			"Constructional Work:— The pathway to new Officers' Quarters is about completed and	
			"camouflaged, the old entrance on to the road is sandbagged and overhead cover	
			"provided for new passage way. Beds in No. 3 Shelter are completed, except for	
			"inter-netting which is to be fixed tomorrow. Shelling - busy in the forenoon and	
			"until about 12.30, since then normal."	
"	"		New arrangements No. 9 by A.D.M.S. 58 DIV., for PROVEN Area received	
"	"		Administrative Instructions issued relative to 58 DIV. ORDER No. 69. (Train Table for Trains and	
			Lorries). Issued by A.D.M.S., 58 DIV.	
"	"		Administrative Orders in connection with 17th Bde. Order No. 56. received from 17th B.H.Q. Units to HERZEELE)	L.H.B.

WAR DIARY
or
INTELLIGENCE SUMMARY.
(Erase heading not required.)

Army Form C. 2118.

Place	Date	Hour	Summary of Events and Information	Remarks and references to Appendices
ESSEX FARM and A.D.S. MINTY FARM	15/11/17	2.30pm	Detachment of 1 Officer and 19 Other Ranks of Unit left C.W.W.C.P. and marched to GWENT FARM.	
" "	"	6pm	Wounded passing through A.D.S., MINTY FARM, for 24 hrs, ending 6pm:—	
			ALL FORMATIONS:— Lying — Officers — Other Ranks 7 58 DIV only: Officers — Other Ranks 3	
			(INCLUDING 58 DIV.) Do. do 16 Do. do 2	
			Walking Do. 1 Do. —	
			— — — —	
			1 23 1 5	
" "	"	6.30pm	Extract from Progress Report from Capt L. HADEN GUEST, from A.D.S., MINTY FARM:—	
			"Constructional Works:— (1) New Officers' and Men's Quarters are now completed, paths duckboarded and rubbish cleared out. (2) Bell or Number 3 Shelter are made. (3) RUDOLPH FARM was inspected today and is in good order. (4) All is ready for handing over here and at RUDOLPH FARM. (5) Dressing Room has been busy all day but at no time has there been pressure. (6) Sleeping arrival, weather sunny and dry."	
" "	"		Lieut. KNOWLES, G., Quartermaster, returned to Unit and retaken on its strength.	
" "	"		Message of appreciation of the work of the M.T., A.S.C. attached received from Capt. J. BUCKLEY, R.A.M.C., O.C. 31 M.A.C. Passed for information to all concerned as follows:—	L.H.G.

WAR DIARY or INTELLIGENCE SUMMARY

Army Form C. 2118.

Place	Date	Hour	Summary of Events and Information	Remarks and references to Appendices
ESSEX FARM and A.D.S. MINTY FARM	16/11/17	Noon	"To A.D.M.S. 56 DIV :- Allow me to say a few words of appreciation on the work put in by our N.C.O's and Men of the Mechanical Transport Section of the Field Ambulance of your Division, attached to the 31st M.A.C. have done themselves. They were entirely responsible for clearing the left sector of the line from MINTY FARM and during the whole time they have been under my charge there has never been any complaint made. I have also at all times been down to carry on their duties unarmed all conditions even of exposure to very much the way they have done their duty.— (Sd) J. BUCKLEY Capt. R.A.M.C. O.C. 31 M.A.C. Dated 15-11-17."	L.K.G.
"	"	Noon	21 Reinforcements arrived at ESSEX FARM	
"	"	4 p.m	Two Motorcars (C95368 O4/Cpl HERBERT C and M95482 P/R RAYWORTH P.I.) returned to Unit from KEMPTON PARK. Standing in following Report of work done :-	
			Dr.G. Batt. Cpy. Trenches. No. of M.B.	
			Nov. 8 - 2/9 - AB.C.&D. Message - 350) proceeding to	
			" 10 - 2/6 - " " - 420) Line	
			" 12 - 2/5 - B. - " " - 78 from Line	
			" 13 - 2/1 - A&C. Message - 165) proceeding to	
			" 14 - 2/1 - D. " - 60) Line	
			In addition to above, approx. 100 walking wounded cases forwarded parade.	
"	"	9 p.m	Advance Party u/c of Capt WATKIN left GWENT FARM for HERZEELE (PHILIPPO FARM)	L.K.G.

Army Form C. 2118.

WAR DIARY
or
INTELLIGENCE SUMMARY.
(Erase heading not required.)

Instructions regarding War Diaries and Intelligence Summaries are contained in F. S. Regs., Part II. and the Staff Manual respectively. Title pages will be prepared in manuscript.

Place	Date	Hour	Summary of Events and Information	Remarks and references to Appendices
ESSEX FARM and A.D.S. MINTY FARM.	16/11/17	7 p.m.	Relief of Staff at A.D.S., MINTY FARM and Bearers on the line effected in accordance with O.O. and 58 Division Operation Order No. 30. Bearers sent to GWENT FARM.	L.H.S.
"	"		No.342182 Pte. RATCLIFF C. killed during relief by H.E. shell.	
"	17/11/17	4.30 a.m.	Party in charge of S. Maj. DARLEY A.E. proceeded up the line to bring body of Pte Ratcliff down to Dynamon A.D.S. Headquarters moved to HERZEELE from ESSEX FARM, the whole body of the Unit marching in mass.	
PHILLIPPO FARM, HERZEELE.	"	Noon	from GWENT FARM for same destination. Headquarters arrived at HERZEELE at Noon.	
"	"	3 p.m.	rest of the Unit arriving at 3 p.m.	L.H.S.
"	"	5 p.m.	Medical Inspection Tent open for the reception of sick from the 174th Bde.	L.H.S.
PHILLIPPO FARM, HERZEELE.	18/11/17		Capt. L. HADEN GUEST granted leave from 18th to 24th inst. to Paris.	
PHILLIPPO FARM, HERZEELE.	19/11/17		1st Lieut K.P. FROST. M.O.R.C. + U.S.A. detailed to take over Medical charge of the 2/4th London Regt. Unit at rest all strength	L.H.S.
PHILLIPPO FARM, HERZEELE.	20/11/17	7.30 p.m.	Capt. A.G. EAST reported and taken on strength.	
"	"		Telegram from 58 Div. received as follows :- "A.1840 AL 20/11/17. Sanction has been obtained for you to have LE VAL RESTANT as a Divisional Rest Station"	
"	"		D.A.A.G. 58 Div. Letter of 20-11-17 states that in the probable distribution of the Division in the BLEQUIN Area the 2/2nd & 2/3rd will be at ECURE or LE VAL RESTANT	
"	"		174 Inf. Bde. Letter of G.S/3017 of 20/11/17, an Advance Party. Allotment of Billets in New	L.H.S.

WAR DIARY
or
INTELLIGENCE SUMMARY.
(Erase heading not required.)

Army Form C. 2118.

Place	Date	Hour	Summary of Events and Information	Remarks and references to Appendices
PHILLIPPO FARM, HERZEELE	21/11/17	—	Orders issued to be at ECURE.	L.H.S.
" "	"	—	A.D.M.S. 58 Div. M/3112 of 21/11/17. Warning Order that 2/3746 Field Amb will be situated at ECOUIRE in New Area.	
" "	"	—	A.A. & Q.M.G. 58 Div. No. Q.77/7100 of 21/11/17. States that none of the Division will probably be in place on the 26th inst.	
" "	"	—	A.D.M.S. 58 Div. Telegram M.1809 of 21/11/17 states "Reference Warning Order M.3112, for ECURE read LE VAL RESTANT."	L.H.S.
PHILLIPPO FARM, HERZEELE	22/11/17	7 a.m.	Advance Party etc. of Capt. A.C. WATKIN left by lorry with Stores for ECURE.	
" "	"	2 p.m.	1 Other Ranks 2/2 H.B.T. Amb, placed in Battle Casualty Clearing to go after Conf Pieaney.	
" "	"	—	A.A. & Q.M.G. 58 Div. No. Q.787/700 of 22/11/17 states these will probably move on 26th.	L.H.S.
PHILLIPPO FARM, HERZEELE	23/11/17	—	A.D.M.S. 58 Div. M/3112 of 23/11/17 cancels M/3112 of 21/11/17 states that Division will probably move in early date to an area north of the BLEQUIN Area.	
" "	"	—	Telegram rec'd from Capt. A.C. WATKIN: "W.I. 04- 23/11/17. "Under orders from Acting Staff Captain 174 Bde. I am also moving to LUMBRES leaving Sgt. NOWERS + 5 Men etc in charge of Stores at ECOUIRE, can Billeting area for Amb. changed to VIEIL MOULIER"	
" "	"	—	"am Am forwarding these tomorrow morning."	L.H.S.

Army Form C. 2118.

WAR DIARY
or
INTELLIGENCE SUMMARY.
(Erase heading not required.)

Instructions regarding War Diaries and Intelligence Summaries are contained in F. S. Regs., Part II. and the Staff Manual respectively. Title pages will be prepared in manuscript.

Place	Date	Hour	Summary of Events and Information	Remarks and references to Appendices
PHILIPPO FARM HERZEELE	23/11/17	—	174 Inf Bde Warning Order B.M/7/48, stating that Bde would move to LUMBRES shortly. Tactical trains on 26th inst.	LH8
PHILIPPO FARM HERZEELE	24/11/17	—	Capn. A.G. EAST goes on 14 days' leave to England.	
"	"	—	Telegram went from 174 Inf Bde of 24/11/17 cancelling all leave of B.E.Os, as per Q.79/307. Further instructions to be issued. (S.C.T. 254).	
"	"	—	174 Inf Bde Telegram S.C.T. 254, of 24/11/17, advising that that units who take over PARLIAMENT CAMP PROVEN, on the arrival from 87th I.C.Bank.	
"	"	—	174 Inf Bde Order No. 57, of 24/11/17, re move by rail and march route from the HERZEELE AREA to LE LUMBRES AREA. Transport to proceed by March route. Units to entrain at PROVEN and detrain at WIZERNES. Also embracing messing arrangements &c.	
"	"	—	174 Inf Bde B.M/7/48 81 confirming in detail B.M/7/48, of 23/11/17.	
"	"	—	174 Inf Bde Movement Order Q.79/385, of 24/11/17, giving particulars of move.	
"	"	—	174 Inf Bde Telegram — Q.D. 572, of 24/11/17, giving details for transport march to PROVEN, received.	
"	"	—	of 24/11/17, giving details for march to PROVEN, received.	
"	"	—	A.A. & Q.M.G. Administrative instructions issued in accordance with 58th Div Order No. 72, and Distribution of Units in New Area, of 24/11/17, filed under A.D.M.S. M.3112.	LH8

Army Form C. 2118.

WAR DIARY
or
INTELLIGENCE SUMMARY.
(Erase heading not required.)

Instructions regarding War Diaries and Intelligence
Summaries are contained in F. S. Regs., Part II.
and the Staff Manual respectively. Title pages
will be prepared in manuscript.

Place	Date	Hour	Summary of Events and Information	Remarks and references to Appendices
PHILLIPPO FARM	25/11/17	9.30am	Unit marched off to Neir Station destination for the night being PARLIAMENT CAMP.	
HENZEELE	"			
PARLIAMENT CAMP	"	9 pm	Unit arrived at PARLIAMENT CAMP.	
"	"		17th M.I.Bde. S.C.T. 270. of 25/11/17 giving disposition of Units in LUMBRES' Area for 26/11/17. "A" H.Q.A.C.R.	
"	"		17th M.I.Bde. Q.79/3/85 of 25/11/17 showing composition of Units on the final area "A/2 Sqdn. 6th C.A. LART."	
"	"		VIEIL MOULIER." marching to	
"	"		17th M.I.Bde. B.M.17/28p. of 25/11/17 forwarding particulars of entraining points	L.H.G.
"	"		17th M.I.Bde. Entraining Orders in connection with B.C.No.57.	
PARLIAMENT CAMP	26/11/17	9 am	Unit marched to PROVEN STATION, entraining there, & leaving at 1 pm.	
WIZERNES	"	4.30pm	Unit arrived at WIZERNES and march commenced to LART.	L.H.G.
LART	"	11.30pm	LART reached after a trying march under unfavourable climatic conditions	
LART	27/11/17	10am	March to VIEIL MOULIER commenced	
VIEIL MOULIER	"	1.30pm	Unit arrived at LE VIEIL MOULIER.	L.H.G.
"	"		Medical Arrangements for LUMBRES Area fixed under a Dressing Station No.10. of 26/11/17 received.	
VIEIL MOULIER	28/11/17		Capt. WATKIN proceeded on Halfpay-leave to England	L.H.G.
"	"	9.45am	Motor Ambulances collected sick of 17th Bde.	

WAR DIARY
INTELLIGENCE SUMMARY.
(Erase heading not required.)

Army Form C. 2118.

Place	Date	Hour	Summary of Events and Information	Remarks and references to Appendices
VIEIL MOULIER	28/4/17	2 p.m.	Capt. P.T. LYDON proceeded to 2nd A.H.Q. for Cypher duty	L.M.L.
VIEIL MOULIER	29/4/17	—	Work for the general improvement of the sanitation of the Billeting Area proceeded with	
"	"	—	Fire gully and fan continues placed at Sperry. All water supplies tested	
"	"	—	Administrative Orders for LUMBRES AREA, SUB AREA B of 29/4/17 received from 17th Inf. Bde.	L.M.L.
"	"	—	Material for incinerators indented for	
VIEIL MOULIER	30/4/17	—	Letter from Surgeon General, D.M.S. II Army, received as follows:—	
			"MESSAGE TO MEDICAL CORPS.— On the occasion of my handing over the Medical Administration of the Second Army, I wish to convey my best thanks to all Officers, Nursing Sisters and Other Ranks of the R.A.M.C., A.A.M.C., & C.A.M.C., for the valuable services which they have always rendered, and the zeal and energy with which they have invariably carried out the various duties which have attracted the Medical efforts of the Second Army have been due to the magnificent work and co-operation of all concerned. I regret that I am not permitted to express my thanks personally to all Ranks." Army M.O. 274-17.	
			Work of Improving the sanitation of the Billeting Area continued	L.M.L.

Vol 11

MEDICAL

COMMITTEE FOR THE
MEDICAL HISTORY OF THE WAR
Date —1 FEB. 1918

40/26/6

2/2ND
HOME COUNTIES
FIELD AMBULANCE.
No. H.C. 10.
Date 1.1.18.

Confidential

WAR DIARY
—of—

2/2 H.C. Fd Amb. R.A.M.C.(T)

FROM 1-12-17 TO 31-12-17.

Robert Rilemer O.C.
2/2ND H.C. FLD. AMB.

Army Form C. 2118.

WAR DIARY
or
INTELLIGENCE SUMMARY.
(Erase heading not required.)

Instructions regarding War Diaries and Intelligence Summaries are contained in F. S. Regs., Part II. and the Staff Manual respectively. Title pages will be prepared in manuscript.

Place	Date	Hour	Summary of Events and Information	Remarks and references to Appendices
LE VIEIL MOUTIER	1/12/17	—	Work of inspecting sanitation of Billeting Area continued	
NIELLE LES BLEQUIN	"	2.30pm	Meeting of the 58th Divisional Medical Society at A.D.M.S. Office.	
LE VIEIL MOUTIER	2/12/17	—	Improvement of sanitation continued.	
"	"	—	1 O.R. (Reinforcement) reported from Calais Base Depôt.	
LE VIEIL MOUTIER	3/12/17	2pm	174th Fd.Amb. Order B.M./7/52. 4 - 3/12/17 received. To move to DIRTY BUCKET Camp — Bac. by rail and Transport by road.	
"	"	6pm	Telegram Q.D.628 from 174 Bde received, cancelling B.M./7/52. Transport to go to ST JAN-TER-BIEZEN. Personnel to entrain at WIZERNES and detrain at ELVERDINGHE.	
LE VIEIL MOUTIER	4/12/17	8pm	A.D.M.S. M3219 forwarding Secret Administrative Instructions in accordance with 58th Divisional Order No. 73.	
"	"	11pm	Administrative Instructions in connection with 174 Infantry Bde. O.O. No. 58. Wire M.1336 from A.D.M.S. to detail 2 Medical Officers to report to O.C. 2/3rd H.A.C. Amb. by 3pm 5th Dec. for temporary duty.	

Army Form C. 2118.

WAR DIARY
or
INTELLIGENCE SUMMARY.
(Erase heading not required.)

Instructions regarding War Diaries and Intelligence Summaries are contained in F. S. Regs., Part II. and the Staff Manual respectively. Title pages will be prepared in manuscript.

Place	Date	Hour	Summary of Events and Information	Remarks and references to Appendices
LE VIEIL MOUTIER	6/12/17	2.30p.m.	Lt. Col. H. FULTON attended conference at A.D.M.S. Office	
"	"	3 p.m.	LIEUT. R. WARD and LIEUT. J. A. LEAS (M.O.R.C. U.S.A) reported to O.C. 34th N.G.F. Amb.	10
"	"		for temporary duty	
"	"		17th L. of Bde Orders - No 56, d/- 5/12/17 received	
"	"		A.D.M.S. O.O. No. 32, d/- 8/12/17 received: The Relief of 35th Division in Left Sector of	
"	"		II Corps front by 58th Div. The Relief to be completed by 6 a.m. 9th Dec. Details given	
"	"		as to location of Bearers, One Tent Sub Divisions at MINTY FARM A.D.S. and	
"	"		CEMENT HOUSE A.D.S. Also instructions concerning collection and evacuation	
"	"		of casualties.	
"	"		Amended Administrative Instructions received.	
"	"		Wire from Commanding Officer received: "Get ready 2 Tent Sub-Divisions	
"	"		Have 3 squads to move tonight."	
"	"		8 p.m. Two Tent Sub Divisions and 3 squads of Stretcher Bearers left for to reports to	
"	"		O.C. 2/3rd N.G. F. Amb.	
LE VIEIL MOUTIER	6/12/17	8.30 a.m.	Unit Transport moved off to ST. MOMELIN.	11

Army Form C. 2118.

WAR DIARY
or
INTELLIGENCE SUMMARY.
(Erase heading not required.)

Instructions regarding War Diaries and Intelligence Summaries are contained in F. S. Regs., Part II. and the Staff Manual respectively. Title pages will be prepared in manuscript.

Place	Date	Hour	Summary of Events and Information	Remarks and references to Appendices
LE VIEIL MOUTIER	6/12/17	—	A.D.M.S. M.3233 of 6/12/17 re II Corps Medical Arrangements received	H
LE VIEIL MOUTIER	7/12/17	8.45 a.m.	Dismounted portion of Unit marched off for LART.	H
LART	"	1 p.m.	Arrived.	H
"	"	—	A.D.M.S. M.3233 re 35th Div R.A.M.C. O.O. No. 32 received for information	H
LART	9/12/17	6.30 a.m.	Dismounted portion of Unit left for march to WIZERNES for entraining for ELVERDINGHE.	H
GWENT FARM	11/12/17	2 a.m.	Dismounted portion of Unit arrived after marching from ELVERDINGHE	H
ESSEX FARM	"	5 a.m.	Tent sub-divisions opened One Tent Sub-Division already in occupation at each of the A.D.S's. — MINTY FARM and CEMENT HOUSE.	H
"	"	4 p.m.	2 O.R's detailed for duty as carpenters at II Corps Rest Station	H
MINTY FARM	"	6 p.m.	Evening Report by O.C. A.D.S. MINTY FARM (Lieut. R. WARD): "General situation very quiet. The railway track road below PHEASANT TRENCH shelled evening between 4 & 5 p.m. The following casualties have been attended and	H

D. D. & L., London, E.C.
(A7883) Wt. W809/M1673 350,000 4/17 **Sch. 92a.** Forms/C/2118/14

Army Form C. 2118.

WAR DIARY
or
INTELLIGENCE SUMMARY.
(Erase heading not required.)

Instructions regarding War Diaries and Intelligence Summaries are contained in F. S. Regs., Part II. and the Staff Manual respectively. Title pages will be prepared in manuscript.

Place	Date	Hour	Summary of Events and Information	Remarks and references to Appendices
MINTY FARM	9/12/17	—	Evacuated from here to C.M.D.S. — WOUNDED — Officers — lying 1; O.R. lying 1; sitting 4.	
ESSEX FARM	10/12/17	—	A.D.M.S. O.O. No. 33 of 10/12/17 received.	
MINTY FARM	"	6 p.m.	Extract from Evening Report. "General situation very quiet. Great aerial activity this afternoon. Principal shelling in RUDOLPH Area. Water cart tins have been carried out, and the floors cleared up. Progress has been made in the erection of new kitchen, and wood has been collected for boarding the floor."	
MINTY FARM & CEMENT HOUSE	"	6 p.m.	Continued excavations for shelters ending to-am! — ALL FORMATIONS — MINTY FARM — Officers Nil, O.R. lying 2, Walking 1. CEMENT HOUSE — Officers Nil, O.R. Walking 2. 58th DIVISION — MINTY FARM — O.R. lying 1, Walking 1. CEMENT HOUSE — O.R. Walking 1.	

WAR DIARY
or
INTELLIGENCE SUMMARY.

(Erase heading not required.)

Army Form C. 2118.

Place	Date	Hour	Summary of Events and Information	Remarks and references to Appendices
ESSEX FARM	11/12/17	6p.m.	Capt. L. HADEN GUEST leaves for England upon termination of contract	
MINTY FARM	"	"	Extract from Progress Report:- "General situation very little change, Gas alarm last evening. I saw Staff Captain 175 Brigade this afternoon with reference to Scrap Kitchen. It was decided to place it in Brigade "Canteen". Progress has been made with the new kitchen."	
CEMENT HOUSE	"	"	Capt. G.M. McGILLIVRAY reports taking over of A.D.S. CEMENT HOUSE from 2/3rd S.M.B. at 4.30 p.m. 11/12/17. Enemy shelled / Evacuations for 24 hours ended 6 p.m. ALL FORMATIONS - MINTY FARM - Officers Nil; O.R. lying 10. 5th 8 Walking 9; CEMENT HOUSE - Officers Nil; O.R. lying 12, Walking 10. 58th DIVISION - MINTY FARM - Officers Nil; O.R. lying 6; Walking 7; CEMENT HOUSE - Officers Nil; O.R. lying 9; Walking 6.	
MINTY FARM	12/12/17	6p.m.	Extract from Report: "Very little shelling in neighbourhood of MINTY FARM last evening. Heavy shelling round KEMPTON PARK and FERDINAND FARM. Aerial battles this evening at 9; two GOTHAS brought down. The new kitchen is now completed and in use. The new drying room is ready for the evening of a stove." The	

Army Form C. 2118.

WAR DIARY
or
INTELLIGENCE SUMMARY.
(Erase heading not required.)

Instructions regarding War Diaries and Intelligence Summaries are contained in F. S. Regs., Part II. and the Staff Manual respectively. Title pages will be prepared in manuscript.

Place	Date	Hour	Summary of Events and Information	Remarks and references to Appendices
MINTY FARM	12/12/17	—	"Soup Kitchen at KEMPTON PARK is now in use."	
"	"	6 p.m.	Evacuations (Wounded) for 24 hrs ending 6 p.m. ALL FORMATIONS — MINTY FARM — Officers,	
			Nil; O.R. Lying 5, Walking 12; CEMENT HOUSE — Officers Nil; O.R. Lying 2, Walking	
CEMENT HOUSE	"	"	15. 53rd DIVISION — Officers Nil; O.R. Walking 5, from MINTY FARM; CEMENT HOUSE	
			— Officers Nil; O.R. Lying 2, Walking 14.	
MINTY FARM	13/12/17	6 p.m.	Extract from Report: "A number of gasshells were sent over, causing a	
			number of high explosive shells burst over KEMPTON PARK. There was fairly	
			heavy shelling between FERDINAND and HAANIXBEEK FARM. There has been	
			very little shelling today."	
CEMENT HOUSE	"	"	Extract from Report: "Heavy shelling with H.E. and gas shells at intervals during	
			the night."	
			Wounded evacuations for 24 hrs ending 6 p.m.: ALL FORMATIONS — MINTY FARM — Officers Nil;	
			O.R. Lying 6, Walking 2; CEMENT HOUSE — Officers Nil; O.R. Lying 2, Walking	
			10. 53rd DIVISION — MINTY FARM — Officers Nil; O.R. Lying 6, Walking 2; CEMENT	
			HOUSE — Officers Nil; O.R. Walking 9.	

WAR DIARY or INTELLIGENCE SUMMARY.

Army Form C. 2118.

Place	Date	Hour	Summary of Events and Information	Remarks and references to Appendices
ESSEX FARM	14/12/17	—	3 O.R. classified as "P.B." & sent to Cyclist Base Depôt by order of A.D.M.S., 58 Div.	
MINTY FARM	"	6 p.m	Evening Report: – "Very little shelling."	
CEMENT HOUSE	"	"	Evening Report: – "A large number of gas shells fell in the vicinity of the A.D.S. during the night. Morning very quiet. Since 2 p.m. a considerable number of H.E. shells have been falling between PIG and WHISTLE & this A.D.S."	
			Wounded Evacuations for 24 hrs ending 6 p.m. ≠ ALL FORMATIONS – MINTY FARM – Officers Nil, O.R. Lying 5, Walking 4; CEMENT HOUSE – Officers Nil, O.R. Lying 2, Walking 4, 58 DIVISION – Officers Nil, O.R. Lying 4, Walking 1 through MINTY FARM; CEMENT HOUSE – Officers Nil, O.R. Walking 4.	
CEMENT HOUSE ~~MINTY FARM~~	15/12/17	6 p.m	Evening Report: "I have found a very suitable site for a Soup Kitchen about 100 yards behind the post & close to the duckboard track. . . . I have marked the site "Reserved for E.H.N. Soup Kitchen." "A few H.E. & Shrapnel shells fell from time to time during the day."	
MINTY FARM	"	"	Evening Report: "Very little shelling during the past 24 hrs . . . The railway track was smashed beyond RUDOLPH this afternoon . . . The soup kitchen of	

WAR DIARY
or
INTELLIGENCE SUMMARY.
(Erase heading not required.)

Army Form C. 2118.

Place	Date	Hour	Summary of Events and Information	Remarks and references to Appendices
MINTY FARM	15/2/17		"RUDOLPH and KEMPTON PARK have been inspected and found satisfactory." The "Post inspection room at KEMPTON PARK has been inspected and is satisfactory." "Progress has been made in flooring No 1 shelter." Evacuation (Wounded) for 24 hrs ending 6 p.m.: ALL FORMATIONS – MINTY FARM – Officers, Nil; O.R. lying 2. Working 2; CEMENT HOUSE – Working 4; 58th DIV. – Officers, Nil; O.R. Working 2. MINTY FARM – Officers, Nil; O.R. Working 1; CEMENT HOUSE Working 2.	
MINTY FARM	16/2/17	6 p.m.	Evening Report: General situation very quiet. The enemy shelled at RUDOLPH "A KEMPTON PARK & Post-inspection room are satisfactory. The light railway is now running at 9 a.m. this morning." Evening Report: "Considerable amount of shelling with H.E. guns shelled in bursts on dusty through Friiz quiet trip." Evacuation (Wounded) for 24 hrs. ending 6 p.m.: ALL FORMATIONS – MINTY FARM – Officers, Nil; O.R. Lying 2. Working 2; CEMENT HOUSE – Officers, Nil; O.R. Lying 1. Working 4. 63 DIV. – MINTY FARM – Officers, Nil; O.R. Lying 2. Working	
CEMENT HOUSE	"		1. CEMENT HOUSE – Officers, Nil; O.R. Lying 1. Working 4.	

Army Form C. 2118.

WAR DIARY
or
INTELLIGENCE SUMMARY.
(Erase heading not required.)

Instructions regarding War Diaries and Intelligence Summaries are contained in F. S. Regs., Part II. and the Staff Manual respectively. Title pages will be prepared in manuscript.

Place	Date	Hour	Summary of Events and Information	Remarks and references to Appendices
ESSEX FARM	17/12/17	—	A.D.M.S. M.3988 of 17/12/17 received notifying that from the 20th inst., the forward Scout Army will be assigned to the Fourth Army.	
MINTY FARM	"	6 p.m.	Evening Report: "General situation very quiet. The flooring of No. 1 Shelter now complete... The driveway now has been lined & thoroughly cleaned."	
CEMENT HOUSE	"	"	Evening Report: "Usual shelling much gas shells & H.E. during the night." ALL FORMATIONS — MINTY FARM — Wounded Evacuations from 24 hours ending 6 p.m.: CEMENT HOUSE — Officers, Walking 5. Officers, Lying 1; O.R., Lying 6; Walking 6. 58th DIV. — MINTY FARM — Officers, Lying 1; Walking 1; O.R., 1; O.R., Lying 2; Walking 2; O.R., Lying 2; Walking 5. Lying 6. Walking 3. CEMENT HOUSE — Officers, Walking 1; O.R. Lying 2; Walking 5.	
ESSEX FARM	18/12/17	—	A.D.M.S. M/3332 of 18/12/17 re collection of sick from each side of the Canal Bank by Horse & Foot Ambs. received.	
MINTY FARM	"	6 p.m.	Evening Report: "General situation very quiet... The Tent Sub Divisions Treatment Rooms at RUDOLPH and MINTY FARM are now nearly furnished. Men have been detailed to look after the Rooms..."	
CEMENT HOUSE	"	6 p.m.	Evening Report: "Several shrapnel burst closely over this A.D.S. between 10 am & 11 am. Otherwise the situation is fairly quiet."	

WAR DIARY
or
INTELLIGENCE SUMMARY.
(Erase heading not required.)

Army Form C. 2118.

Place	Date	Hour	Summary of Events and Information	Remarks and references to Appendices
MINTY FARM CEMENT HOUSE	18/12/17	6 p.m.	Mounted Evacuations for 24 hrs ending 6 p.m. ALL FORMATIONS — MINTY FARM — Officers Lying 1, O.R. Lying 2, Walking 4. CEMENT HOUSE — Officers Nil, O.R. Lying 1, Walking 7. 53rd DIVISION — MINTY FARM — Officers Nil, O.R. Lying 1, Walking 2. CEMENT HOUSE — Officers Nil, O.R. Lying 1, Walking 1. 1 O.R. 2/3rd R.F. Aus — wounded & returned to duty. Daily Report of No.s of Men to have received treatment for the Removal of Frost Bite at CEMENT HOUSE, RUDOLPH FARM, MINTY FARM, KEMPTON PARK (Sheet II), MARSUIN FARM, BATHS (B.16 & 96 — Sheet 28) summary.	
MINTY FARM	19/12/17	6 p.m.	Enemy Report: "General situation very quiet."	
CEMENT HOUSE	"	"	Enemy Report: "Numerous H.E. Shrapnel & Gas Shells falling in the vicinity during the night. Everything comparatively quiet today."	
"	"	"	Mounted Evacuations for 24 hrs ending 6 p.m. ALL FORMATIONS — MINTY FARM — Officers Nil, O.R. Lying 1, Walking 1. CEMENT HOUSE — Nil. 53rd DIV. — Sie MINTY FARM — O.R. Walking 1.	

Army Form C. 2118.

WAR DIARY
or
INTELLIGENCE SUMMARY.
(Erase heading not required.)

Instructions regarding War Diaries and Intelligence Summaries are contained in F. S. Regs., Part II. and the Staff Manual respectively. Title pages will be prepared in manuscript.

Place	Date	Hour	Summary of Events and Information	Remarks and references to Appendices
ESSEX FARM	20/12/17	—	Capt. A.C. WATKIN returned from leave. O.R. had been out. Truck 15 19/12/17	
MINTY FARM	"	6 p.m.	Evening Report: "General situation in front"	
CEMENT HOUSE	"	"	Evening Report: "A large number of grenades fell close to this O.P.S. Battery fire. Gunfire died to an roar." Everything quiet today.	
"	"	6 p.m.	Returned Evacuations for 24 hrs. 2 nd.y 6 p.m. — ALL FORMATIONS — MINTY FARM — Officers Nil, O.R. lying 5; Walking 3. CEMENT HOUSE — Nil. 58th DIV — MINTY FARM — Officers Nil; O.R. lying W. Walking 3. CEMENT HOUSE — Nil	
MINTY FARM	21/12/17	6 p.m.	Evening Report: "General and a Seamay quiet."	A
CEMENT HOUSE	"	"	Evening Report: "Usual shelling on the Ypres Salient & H.E. during the night. Everything quiet today."	V
"	"	6 p.m.	Returned Evacuations for 24 hrs. 2 nd.y 6 p.m. — ALL FORMATIONS — MINTY FARM — Officers Nil; O.R. lying W. Walking 10. CEMENT HOUSE — Officers Nil; O.R. Walking 1. acc.t. of fog during a.m. 58th DIV	V
ESSEX FARM	22/12/17	—	173 Inf. Bde. Administrative Instructions No. 23, issued in consequence of 173 Inf. Bde. Order No. 51.	A

Army Form C. 2118.

WAR DIARY
or
INTELLIGENCE SUMMARY.
(Erase heading not required.)

Instructions regarding War Diaries and Intelligence Summaries are contained in F. S. Regs., Part II, and the Staff Manual respectively. Title pages will be prepared in manuscript.

Place	Date	Hour	Summary of Events and Information	Remarks and references to Appendices
MINTY FARM	22/12/17	6p.m	Enemy Report: "General situation very quiet."	
CEMENT HOUSE	"	"	Enemy Report: "Everything quiet, no firing"	
"	"	"	Wounded Evacuations for 24 hrs ending 6 p.m. — ALL FORMATIONS — MINTY FARM — Officers Lying 1, O.R. Lying 3, Walking 3. CEMENT HOUSE — Officers Nil, O.R. Lying 1.	
"	"	"	58th DIV — Officers Lying 1, O.R. Lying 1, Walking 1 at MINTY FARM. CEMENT HOUSE — Officers Nil, O.R. Lying 1.	
MINTY FARM	23/12/17	6p.m	Enemy Report: "General situation very quiet." "German Barrage from 5 to 5.15 p.m. 22/12/17."	
CEMENT HOUSE	"	"	Enemy Report: "Heavy enemy barrage along the front canal sector 5 p.m. to 5 p.m. yesterday and lasted for about 2 hours." "Occupied day."	
"	"	"	Wounded Evacuations for 24 hrs ending 6 p.m. — ALL FORMATIONS — MINTY FARM — Officers Walking 1, O.R. Lying 11, Walking 21. CEMENT HOUSE — Officers Nil, O.R. Lying 7, Walking 12. 58 DIV — MINTY FARM — Officers Nil, O.R. Lying 2, Walking 9. CEMENT HOUSE — Officers Nil, O.R. Lying 6, Walking 11.	
ESSEX FARM	24/12/17	—	1 Sgt. H.T., A.S.C. (Reinforcement) taken on strength.	

Army Form C. 2118.

WAR DIARY
or
INTELLIGENCE SUMMARY.
(Erase heading not required.)

Instructions regarding War Diaries and Intelligence Summaries are contained in F. S. Regs., Part II. and the Staff Manual respectively. Title pages will be prepared in manuscript.

Place	Date	Hour	Summary of Events and Information	Remarks and references to Appendices
MINTY FARM	24/9/17	6 p.m.	Evening Report: "General situation very quiet."	
CEMENT HOUSE	"	"	Evening Report: "Several grenades fired close to A.D.S. last night. Nothing further to report."	
"	"	"	Mounted Evacuations for 24 hrs. ending 6 p.m. — ALL FORMATIONS — MINTY FARM — Officers	
			Nil, O.R. Walking 4. CEMENT HOUSE — Officers Nil, O.R. Lying 1, Walking 1. 58th DIV. —	
			MINTY FARM — O.R. Walking 3. CEMENT HOUSE — O.R. Lying 1, Walking 1.	
MINTY FARM	25/9/17	6 p.m.	Evening Report: "General situation quiet."	
CEMENT HOUSE	"	"	Evening Report: "Have all day ... fairly quiet stay."	
"	"	"	Mounted Evacuations for 24 hrs. ending 6 p.m. — ALL FORMATIONS — MINTY FARM — Officers	
			Nil, O.R. Lying 6, Walking 6. CEMENT HOUSE — Officers Nil, O.R. Lying 1, Walking 2.	
			58th DIV. — MINTY FARM — O.R. Lying 6, Walking 6. CEMENT HOUSE — O.R. Lying 6, Walking 2.	
ESSEX FARM	26/9/17	8.30 a.m.	Capt. A.C.WATKIN took over medical charge of 2/2 Lond Rgt. (Temp.) releiving Lt. C.E. DUNAWAY, M.R.C.S.	
"	"	3.30 p.m.	Parade of N.C.Os. under Divisional Sanitary Officer for training in Anti gas drill (sick).	
MINTY FARM	"	6 p.m.	Evening Report: "General situation very quiet."	
CEMENT HOUSE	"	"	Evening Report: "Fairly quiet at the present stay."	
			Mounted Evacuations for 24 hrs. ending 6 p.m. — ALL FORMATIONS — MINTY FARM — Officer	

WAR DIARY
or
INTELLIGENCE SUMMARY.

(Erase heading not required.)

Army Form C. 2118.

Place	Date	Hour	Summary of Events and Information	Remarks and references to Appendices
MINTY FARM & CEMENT HOUSE	26/12/17	"	Nil. O.R. Dying 1. Wounding 2. CEMENT HOUSE — Officers Nil. O.R. Lying 3. Wounding 2.	
"	"	"	55th DIV — MINTY FARM — O.R. Lying 2. Wounding 2. CEMENT HOUSE — O.R. Lying 2. Wounding 2.	
MINTY FARM	27/12/17	6 p.m.	Enemy Report: "General situation very quiet."	
CEMENT HOUSE	"	"	Enemy Report: "Enemy shells on the vicinity during the night."	
"	"	"	Wounded Evacuations for 24 hrs ending 6 p.m. — ALL FORMATIONS — MINTY FARM —	
"	"	"	Officers Nil. O.R. Lying 1. Wounding 7. CEMENT HOUSE — Officers Nil. O.R. Lying 2. Wounding 2. 55th DIV. — MINTY FARM — O.R. Lying Nil. Wounding 7. CEMENT HOUSE — O.R. Lying 2. Wounding 2.	
MINTY FARM	28/12/17	6 p.m.	Enemy Report: "General situation very quiet."	
CEMENT HOUSE	"	"	Enemy Report: "Enemy aeroplanes very active all day long."	
"	"	"	Wounded Evacuations for 24 hrs ending 6 p.m. — ALL FORMATIONS — MINTY FARM — Officers	
"	"	"	Nil. O.R. Lying 2. Wounding 6. CEMENT HOUSE — Officers Nil. O.R. Lying 1. Wounding 5.	
"	"	"	55th DIV. — MINTY FARM — O.R. Wounding 4. CEMENT HOUSE — O.R. Lying 1. Wounding 5.	

WAR DIARY
or
INTELLIGENCE SUMMARY.
(Erase heading not required.)

Army Form C. 2118.

Place	Date	Hour	Summary of Events and Information	Remarks and references to Appendices
ESSEX FARM	28/12/17	—	Capt. A.A.Watson, R.A.M.C.(T.C.) Lieut. F.E.Clay, R.A.M.C.(T.C.) taken on the strength	
MINTY FARM	"	6pm	Evening Report: "General situation very quiet."	
CEMENT HOUSE	"	"	Evening Report: "Fairly heavy shelling during the late afternoon and evening."	
			Wounded evacuations for 24 hrs ending 6 p.m. — ALL FORMATIONS — MINTY FARM — Officers Nil, O.R. Lying Nil, Walking 8. CEMENT HOUSE — Officers Nil, O.R. Lying 1, Walking 1. 55th DIV. — MINTY FARM — O.R. Walking 6; CEMENT HOUSE — Nil.	
MINTY FARM	30/12/17	6pm	Capt. Watson, who has taken over duties of O.C. A.D.S. reports: "General situation quiet. General Sir H. Rawlinson paid a visit this afternoon and made enquiries about the first treatment with which he was satisfied."	
CEMENT HOUSE	"	"	Evening report: "Everything quiet today and Reconnoitering tonight."	
			Wounded evacuations for 24 hrs ending 6 p.m. — ALL FORMATIONS — MINTY FARM — Officers Nil, O.R. Lying 1, Walking 1; CEMENT HOUSE — Officers Nil, O.R. Lying 1, 55th DIV. — MINTY FARM — O.R. Walking 1, CEMENT HOUSE — Nil.	
MINTY FARM	31/12/17	6pm	Evening report: "General Situation — Considerable artillery fire on right."	

WAR DIARY
or
INTELLIGENCE SUMMARY.

Army Form C. 2118.

Place	Date	Hour	Summary of Events and Information	Remarks and references to Appendices
CEMENT HOUSE	3/12/17	6 p.m.	Evening report: "Conditions normal. Nothing to report."	
			Weather excellent for 24 hrs ending 6 p.m. — All Formations — Minty Farm — Officers	
			Nil, O.R. lying 1. Wadeleng 5. Cement House — Officers, Nil, O.R. lying 1. 58th Div.—	
			Minty Farm — O.R. lying 1, Wadeleng 5. Cement House — O.R. lying 1.	

CONFIDENTIAL.

Army Form C. 2118.

Instructions regarding War Diaries and Intelligence
Summaries are contained in F. S. Regs., Part II.
and the Staff Manual respectively. Title pages
will be prepared in manuscript.

WAR DIARY
or
INTELLIGENCE SUMMARY.
(Erase heading not required.)

MEDICAL

WAR DIARY
of
2/2ND H.C. FD. AMB. R.A.M.C.(T)

From 1/1/1918.
To 31/1/1918.

140/2695.

COMMITTEE FOR THE
MEDICAL HISTORY OF THE WAR
Date —4 MAR 1918

2/2ND
HOME COUNTIES
FIELD AMBULANCE.
No. HC311
Date 1/3/1915

O.C.
2/2ND H.C. FLD. AMB.

WAR DIARY or INTELLIGENCE SUMMARY

Army Form C. 2118.

Place	Date	Hour	Summary of Events and Information	Remarks and references to Appendices
Sheet 28				
H.Q. ESSEX FARM (C.19.c.4.0.)	1/1/18	10 a.m.	Lieut CLAY, F.E., R.A.M.C. detailed to take over temporarily the Medical charge of 295th Bde. R.F.A.	
"	"	"	Sick collected from Units on CANAL BANK by Horse Ambulance & evacuated to 58th D.R.S.	
MINTY FARM (C.20.c.7.6.)	"	6 p.m.	CANADA FARM. Extract from Progress Report by Cpl. WATSON, A.E., from A.D.S.:— "Essex & Indus Engineers quiet."	
"	"	"	CEMENT HOUSE. Extract from Progress Report. — ALL FORMATIONS — O.R. Sick 9, Wounded 6, 53rd DIV. — O.R. Sick 5.	
CEMENT HOUSE (U.26.C.2.2.)	"	"	Extract from Progress Report by Capt. McGILLIVRAY, G.M., from A.D.S.:— "Considerable activity by enemy aeroplanes then morning. Some shelling with H.E. & gas during the night. Otherwise normal."	
"	"	"	Evacuation for 24 hrs ending 6 p.m. – ALL FORMATIONS – O.R. Sick 3, Wounded 1, 53rd DIV. — O.R. Sick 61.	
ESSEX FARM	2/1/18	—	No. 495009 Sigmn & Mjr. DARLEY, A.E. transferred to 2/3rd N.C.F. Amb. R.A.M.C.(T)	
"	"	"	Sick collected from Units on CANAL BANK & evacuated to 58th D.R.S.	
MINTY FARM	"	6 p.m.	Extract from Progress Report:— General situation quiet.	
"	"	"	Evacuation for previous 24 hrs. — ALL FORMATIONS — O.R. Sick 9, Wounded 1, 53rd DIV. — O.R. Sick 8.	
CEMENT HOUSE	"	"	Extract from Progress Report: "Shelling between 8 p.m. & 10 p.m. on Battery on left of junction of Roads in front. O.O. & 9 mis. Strong."	
"	"	"	Evacuation for previous 24 hrs. : – 58th DIV. — Officer Sick 1, O.R. Sick 2, Wounded 2.	
ESSEX FARM	3/1/18	—	Sick collected from Units on CANAL BANK & evacuated to D.R.S.	

Army Form C. 2118.

WAR DIARY
or
INTELLIGENCE SUMMARY.
(Erase heading not required.)

Instructions regarding War Diaries and Intelligence Summaries are contained in F. S. Regs., Part II. and the Staff Manual respectively. Title pages will be prepared in manuscript.

Place	Date	Hour	Summary of Events and Information	Remarks and references to Appendices
MINTY FARM	3/1/18	6 p.m.	Extract from Progress Report:— "General Situation moderately quiet."	
"	"		Enemy Gun fire in our 24 hrs:— All FORMATIONS:— Officers Sick 1; O.R. Sick 7; Wounded 4; 58th DIV., Officers Sick 1; O.R. Sick 5.	
CEMENT HOUSE	"		Extract from Progress Report:— "Considerable activity by enemy artillery in the morning. Shelling by H.E. & Shrapnel on our S.P. Line & on Bn. Hqrs. & on F.C. from 12 to 1.30 p.m."	
"	"		Enemy Gun fire in our 24 hrs:— All FORMATIONS:— O.R. Wounded 3; 58th DIV. O.R. Wounded 3.	
MINTY FARM	4/1/18	6 p.m.	Extract from Progress Report:— "General situation quiet."	
"	"		Enemy Gun fire in our 24 hrs:— All FORMATIONS:— O.R. Sick 7; Wounded 5; 58th DIV:— O.R. Sick 5; Wounded 6.	
CEMENT HOUSE	"		Extract from Progress Report:— "During the morning the enemy heavily shelled fire on this Farm. H.E. Shrapnel & Gas. Between 7 p.m. & 12 midnight he again heavily shelled this area with gas shells all round the A.D.S. many of them within a few yards of the building."	
"	"		Enemy Gun fire in our 24 hrs:— All FORMATIONS:— O.R. Sick 1; Wounded in 58th DIV:— O.R. Sick 1; Wounded 2.	
MINTY FARM	5/1/16	6 p.m.	Extract from Progress Report:— "General situation very quiet."	
"	"		Enemy Gun fire in our 24 hrs:— 58th DIV:— O.R. Sick 4; Wounded 3.	
CEMENT HOUSE	"		Extract from Progress Report by Capt. A.C. WATKIN:— "No Shelling in the neighbourhood during last 24 hrs:— Work on trench continued on the main letter for post-mortem." "7.15 P.M. took over charge of the A.D.S. from Capt. McSULIVAN of 2/5th M. Sanitary..."	

WAR DIARY or INTELLIGENCE SUMMARY

Army Form C. 2118.

Place	Date	Hour	Summary of Events and Information	Remarks and references to Appendices
CEMENT HOUSE	5/1/18	6 p.m.	Evacuations for 24 hours. 58th Div:- O.R. Sick 6, Wounded 4.	
ESSEX FARM	6/1/18	3.30 p.m.	A.D.M.S. O.O. No 34, 4.6.1.18 issued in accordance with 58th Div O. No 89.: "The Division (less Artillery) will be relieved by the 35th Division (less Artillery) commencing the 7th Inst. & complete 11th Inst. 11 Corps Battle Area" & "The Young "H.C.F. Amb. will be transferred on the 8th Inst. by 06.108 p.m. to 3/2nd H.C.F. Amb. "which will proceed to PROVEN where the Officer Commanding 3/2nd H.C.F. Amb. will take over the School & Camp site as the Rest Station " for the Division. The Officer Commanding 3/2nd H.C.F. Amb will "make the necessary arrangements with the Officer i/c Rest Station to be responsible for the "collection & treatment of the sick of the 174th Infy Bde Group. "in addition to instructions already issued. General arrangements by 9uide"	
"	"	6 p.m.	Report from Officers i/c Units:- "General" returns very quiet.	
CEMENT HOUSE	"	"	Evacuations for 24 hours:- ALL FORMATIONS:- Officers Wounded 1, O.R. Sick 4, Wounded 6. 58th Div:- Officers Wounded 1, O.R. Sick 1, Wounded 5. Evacuation 2/3 H.C.F. Amb 03 Sick 4, O.R. Wounded 4, Sight Shoot forth.	
"	"	"	End of Col Hot bricks 24 hrs. ALL FORMATIONS:- Officers Sick 1, O.R. Sick 2, Wounded 4: 58th Div:- Officers Sick 1, O.R. Sick 2, Wounded 2.	
ESSEX FARM	7/1/18	12 a.m.	Admin Instruction No 18, 17th/18th Base Order No 87 issued.	
"	"	2.30 p.m.	Advance Party under Capt. McGILLIVRAY proceeded to PROVEN to take over REST STATION from 106 Fd. Amb.	
"	"	"	Capt. WATSON attached at MINTY FARM A.D.S. & reported at ESSEX FARM before proceeding to Divt. of Posts.	
MINTY FARM	"	6 p.m.	Report from Progress Report by Lt WARD: "General situation very quiet."	
"	"	"	Evacuations for Previous 24 hrs. :- ALL FORMATIONS:- O.R. Sick 5, Wounded 10. 58th Div:- O.R. Sick 1, Wounded 4.	

Army Form C. 2118.

WAR DIARY
or
INTELLIGENCE SUMMARY.
(Erase heading not required.)

Instructions regarding War Diaries and Intelligence Summaries are contained in F. S. Regs., Part II. and the Staff Manual respectively. Title pages will be prepared in manuscript.

Place	Date	Hour	Summary of Events and Information	Remarks and references to Appendices
CEMENT HOUSE	7/1/18	6 p.m.	Extensive Gas Progress Report: "No Shelling in immediate Neighbourhood ... Work on site near Shelter for first treatment so styling continues.	
"	"		Enemy Gas firing various Shells. - ALL FORMATIONS - Officers Wounded 2, O.R. Wounded 2.	
GREAT FARM	8/1/18	10 a.m.	Detach: 1 St. Officer, Bearers of Unit marched off to New Station at PROVEN. Capt. WATSON in chg.	
MINTY FARM	"	1 p.m.	Relief of Staff at MINTY FARM A.D.S. effected by 106th Fd. Amb. Staff returned to ESSEX FARM. Evacuation to time of leaving: ALL FORMATIONS: O.R. Sick 12, O.R. Wounded 4. 58 DIV. - O.R. Sick 7	
CEMENT HOUSE	"	4 p.m.	Relief of Staff at CEMENT HOUSE A.D.S. effected by 106th Fd. Amb. Staff returned to ESSEX FARM. Evacuation to time of leaving: ALL FORMATIONS: O.R. Wounded 11, 58 DIV.; O.R. Wounded 2.	
ESSEX FARM	"	2.30 p.m.	Remainder of Unit moved by road to PROVEN. Transport moved off from ISLAY FARM.	
PROVEN	"	6 p.m.	Reconnaissance of approach & Transport road with difficulty. Unit arrived at New Station. REST STATION at SCHOOL taken over. 55 patients of 352nd Div. left behind by outgoing unit.	
DIV. REST STATION PROVEN	9/1/18	Noon	HOSPITAL Noon State: Cavalry 4; Army 4.	
" "	10/1/18	"	HOSPITAL Noon State: Remd. 4; Actnd. 10; Evacd. 3; Rmg. 11. 4 Died.	
" "	11/1/18	"	HOSPITAL Noon State: Remd. 11; Actnd. 31; Evacd. 13; Rmg. 29. 4 Died.	
" "	12/1/18	"	HOSPITAL Noon State: Remd. 29; Actnd. 14; Evacd. 10; Rmg. 33. 4 Died.	
" "	"	5 p.m.	Capt. WATSON, A.A., & Lieut. WARD, R., left on temporary duty with D.D.M.S. XIX Corps.	
" "	13/1/18	Noon	HOSPITAL Noon State: Remd. 33; Actnd. 17; Evacd. 3; Rmg. 37. 4 Died.	
" "	14/1/18	Noon	HOSPITAL Noon State: Remd. 37; Actnd. 18; Evacd. 7; Rmg. 48.	

WAR DIARY
or
INTELLIGENCE SUMMARY.
(Erase heading not required.)

Army Form C. 2118.

Place	Date	Hour	Summary of Events and Information	Remarks and references to Appendices
DIV. REST STATION PROVEN	14/1/18	—	Letter from A.A. & Q.M.G., 58th Div. (No. A/22/689 df. 12/1/18) quoted for information of Lt. Col. Boulos: "I am desired to inform you that at the parade for the decoration of uniors & choir singing the Corps Commander expressed his gratitude to the amount of work that had been done by the Division under his command. He hoped that he officers & men would be made known in everything in the Division. He spoke in the most flattering way of the very fine spirit & gallant behaviour that had been shown on all occasions in the Line by the 58th Division. He said also he felt quite sure that it would continue to uphold the high standard it had always maintained during the time it had been in FRANCE. He paid a very high tribute to the way in which Londoners had fought during the past. He hoped that all would be able to see the red fighting spirit read out of the gallant deeds performed. He was about to proceed further. He knew how difficult it would make them feel having to the Off. who he imagined the importance of the night that had to be carried out by Platoon Commanders. He said he had never known an action to fail without the Platoon Commanders had made it their business to keep in close touch with & to study the ground they were going to fight over. The usual hour Riffley plans had been arranged & signed & that not enough care was taken along the ground by the Platoon or Company commanders in the Line. Before going to fight any operation, every advantage should be taken or in the view, if any, along the Division, by reading the correspondence of every subaltern in the line, I am specially congratulate them all on the very fine part they have played during the D.Vision, by reading all Inf. formerly of 58 Div in Fifth Army. Trans have been attached." (Sd) A. McNulty, Lt.Col., A.A. & Q.M.G, 58 Div. 14/1/18	17
"	"	2.30pm	Actg. D.D.M.S., II Corps visited the Rest Station	
"	15/1/18	Noon	HOSPITAL NOM. STATE. Remt. 48; Actual 22; Daily Disch. 16; Remg Sm.	
"	"	1.30pm	A.D.M.S. M.3250 df. 15/1/18 read re detailing Advance Party to VILLERS BRETONNEUX 16/1/18	
"	"	2.0pm	MEM. S.C. 20/3943 df. 15/1/18 amending M3250 received	
"	"	7.30pm	174 INF. BDE. S.C. 20/3943 df. 15/1/18 re Ref. that in connection with B.M./7/6.39 Q.S./19/95 received	18
"	"	9.25pm	A.D.P.S. M3250 forwarding Ad.Instr. for move of 58 Div. to FIFTH ARMY. Train tables attached.	

WAR DIARY
or
INTELLIGENCE SUMMARY.
(Erase heading not required.)

Army Form C. 2118.

Instructions regarding War Diaries and Intelligence Summaries are contained in F. S. Regs., Part II. and the Staff Manual respectively. Title pages will be prepared in manuscript.

Place	Date	Hour	Summary of Events and Information	Remarks and references to Appendices
Div Rest Station PROVEN	16/1/18	4am	Capt. A.C. WATKIN and 6 O.R. proceeded to POPERINGHE as Advance Party for journey & entraining to VILLERS BRETONNEUX for March to MOREUIL.	
"	"	Noon	HOSPITAL Noon State. Remd. 54; Admd. 14; Evac. & Disch. 10; Reng 58.	
"	"	1.10pm	Adm. Inst. No. 2 for Move of 174th INF BDE recd. also Transport Arrangements in connection with same.	17
"	"	10.29pm	A.D.M.S. M. 3520 forwarding amendment to Train Table. A.D.M.S. O.O. No. 35. of. 16/1/18.	
"	17/1/18	Noon	HOSPITAL Noon State. Remd. 58; Admd. 17; Evac. 45; Duty 14; Reng. 16.	17
"	"	5 am	Lieut. LEAS reported for duty with 58 Div R.E's (conformity)	
"	18/1/18	9am	174 INF BDE. Order No. 60 of. 17/1/18 recd.	
"	"	Noon	HOSPITAL Noon State. Remd. 16; Admd. 25; Evac. 18; Duty 1; Reng. 22.	17
"	"	7.48pm	Capt. WATKINS wire reporting arrival recd. "Arrived MOREUIL 3pm, 18th Jan. aaa Billets secured aaa No police available at present for D.R.S."	
"	19/1/18	Noon	HOSPITAL Noon State. Remd. 22; Admd. 18; Evac. 20; Duty 1; Reng 19. (Closd of to 134 Fd AMB).	18
"	"	12.30pm 3.30pm	Unit entrained at Station for entrainment for VILLERS BRETONNEUX Train left. Travelled all night.	
VILLERS BRETONNEUX	20/1/18	5.30am	Unit arrived. Billets taken over. Sanitary conditions found to be very unsatisfactory.	
MOREUIL	"	Noon	Unit arrived. March to MOREUIL.	17

Army Form C. 2118.

WAR DIARY
or
INTELLIGENCE SUMMARY.
(Erase heading not required.)

Place	Date	Hour	Summary of Events and Information	Remarks and references to Appendices
MONEUX	21/1/18	3 am	Capt. WATSON & Lieut. WARD reported their return from duties with XIX Corps	
"	"	Noon	Noon State: Rand. Nil; Admd 1; Reng 1.	
"	22/1/18	Noon	State: Rand 1; Admd 6; Evacd 1; Reng 6.	
"	23/1/18	11 am	Capt. WATSON A.A. attached for temporary duty with 2/10 Bn. London Rgt.	
"	"	Noon	Noon State: Rand 6; Admd 7; Evacd 1; Reng 12	
"	24/1/18	12 noon	Lieut. WARD R. detached for temporary duty with 2/10 Bn. London Rgt.	
"	"	Noon	Noon State: Rand 12; Admd 12; Evacd 5; Reng 19.	
"	25/1/18	—	Hon. Capt. Q.O.M. KNOWLES, G., granted Leave 9/2/17	
"	"	Noon	Noon State: Rand 19; Admd 12; Evacd 4; Reng 27	
"	26/1/18	Noon	Noon State: Rand 27; Admd 8; Evacd 4; Duty 1; Reng. 30.	
"	27/1/18	Noon	Noon State: Rand 30; Admd 18; Evacd 12; Duty 2; Reng 34.	
"	28/1/18	Noon	Noon State: Rand 34; Admd 10; Evacd 18; Duty 2; Reng 24.	
"	29/1/18	10 am	Capt. PALMER R.A.M.C. reported for duty with unit on disposal of 2/5 Bn. Hand Rgt. to whom he was acting as R.M.O.	
"	"	Noon	Noon State: Rand 24; Admd 20; Evacd 10; Reng 34.	
"	"	—	R.A.M.C. Personal of Unit nursing by be doing it with exception of 1 N.C.O. & 3 Pts. was present at "A" Coy. for Colonel Service.	

Army Form C. 2118.

WAR DIARY
or
INTELLIGENCE SUMMARY.

(Erase heading not required.)

Place	Date	Hour	Summary of Events and Information	Remarks and references to Appendices
MARSEILLES	30/1/18	10.30 a.m.	Unit paraded for March to FRENCH HOSPITAL LESPINOY, where accommodation was lent by courtesy of FRENCH Authorities. Arrangements in readiness while Unit was to be billeted at EASTERN Hospital.	
FRENCH HOSP. LESPINOY	"	11 a.m.	Unit arrived at New Station. H.T. personnel & Horses billeted at CASTEL Wagon Parties at Hospital. Hospital prepared for reception of parties brought from MARSEILLES.	
" " "	"	Noon	Noon State, Rank 34; Oth.Rk 11; E.rpen 22; Duty 8; Reng. 16.	##
" " "	31/1/18	Noon	Noon State, Rank 16; Oth.Rk 5; E.rpen Nil; Duty 2; Reng. 18.	##

Army Form C. 2118.

WAR DIARY
or
INTELLIGENCE SUMMARY.

(Erase heading not required.)

CONFIDENTIAL

WAR DIARY

of

2/2 H.C. F. Amb. R.A.M.C. (T)

1st FEBRUARY 1918 — 28th FEBRUARY 1918

COMMITTEE FOR THE
MEDICAL HISTORY OF THE WAR
Date — 8 APR. 1918

MEDICAL

O.C.
Lt. Col. R.A.M.C. (T)
2/2nd H. C. FLD. AMB.

2/2nd
HOME COUNTIES
FIELD AMBULANCE.
No. H.C. 702
Date. 1/3/18

WAR DIARY
or
INTELLIGENCE SUMMARY

Army Form C. 2118.

(Erase heading not required.)

Place	Date	Hour	Summary of Events and Information	Remarks and references to Appendices
French Camp LESPINOY	1/2/18	Noon	Daily State. Reng. 18; Admit 7; Evac 6; Duty 3; Reng 16	
"	"	6 pm	2 O.R. R.A.M.C. returned to Unit after being detached as carpenters by order of D.M.S. XIX Corps	[struck off Strength]
French Hosp. LESPINOY	2/2/18	9 am	1 O.R. R.A.M.C. sent to No. 3 Mob. Dental Unit for duty as Dental Mechanic	[struck off Strength]
"	"	Noon	Daily State. Reng 16; Admit 15; Evac Hy Duty 1; Reng 26	
French Hosp. LESPINOY	3/2/18	8.7 am	Administrative instructions in connection with 174 Inf. Bde. Order D.M./746, A.Q.314/1/15 recd. Relin. Administrative Instructions in accordance with standing Order No. G.S. 85 (Sunday). A.D.M.S. 3653 (Sy. 1-2-18)	
"	"	"	30th Divn Medical Arrangements Location Table. M.921/18, A.D.M.S. 30th Divn. of 31/1/18 recd	
"	"	10.30 am	A.D.M.S. 58 Divn. O.O. 36 of 2/2/18 recd	
"	"	Noon	Daily State. Reng 26; Admit 9; Evac 18; Duty 1; Reng 16	
French Hosp. LESPINOY	4/2/18	10.45 am	Bapt WATKIN and 6 O.R. Left as advanced Party for CHAUNY	
"	"	"	Extract from Letter by Brig. Genl. Commanding II Corps 2/H.5/59/15 of 25-1-18 forwarded in Daily Orders. Reference my 2/H.R./3/15 of 13/1/18 - The Military Medal awarded to No. 49520b. Sergt W. A. NOWERS 7th H.C.F.Amb, should read "Bar to Military Medal"	
"	"	Noon	Daily State. Reng 16; Admit 5; Evac 11; Duty 0; Reng 10	

Army Form C. 2118.

WAR DIARY
or
INTELLIGENCE SUMMARY.
(Erase heading not required.)

Instructions regarding War Diaries and Intelligence Summaries are contained in F. S. Regs., Part II. and the Staff Manual respectively. Title pages will be prepared in manuscript.

Place	Date	Hour	Summary of Events and Information	Remarks and references to Appendices
French Camp LESPINOY	5/2/18	Noon	Daily State. Reinf 10, Admd 10, Evac 10, Duty 2, Reinf 8.	
		6.30pm	A.D.M.S. to 36th showing collection of sick location of troops in New Area recd	
			Camouflage notes ref 58 Div. Order No 98/cf 4/2/18, recd	
			Administrative Instructions No 140 (Part II) recd	
French Camp LESPINOY	6/2/18	Noon	Daily State: Reinf 8, Admd 18, Evac 16, Reinf 10	
			174 Inf Bde Order No 62/cf 5/2/18 with more Tables, recd	
French Camp LESPINOY	7/2/18	Noon	Corps + 2 O.B. R.A.M.C. war Subject 25 Londs bn reported as disposal of that	
			Initial + Return on Strength (Anti. Aircraft, A.B. 3rd Echelon)	
			Daily Sick. Reinf 10, Admd 9, Evac 9, Reinf 10	
French Camp LESPINOY	8/2/18	5.40am	Daily State. Reinf 10, Admd 18, Evac 20, Duty 3, Reinf 5.	
			Orders. Unit marched to entraining Station VILLERS BRETONNEUX	
VILLERS BRETONNEUX	"	11am	Unit entrained	
SINCENY-Shueyed Cie	"	11am	A.D.S. + posts of night section, taken over by Advance Party + N.C.O.s + R.A.M.C. wagon Orderlies	
APPILLY	"	3.30pm	Unit detrained + marched to CHAUNY	
Steel YOD CHAUNY Cat. at 6	"	4.30pm	Unit arrived at new H.Q. (St Charles Institute CHAUNY.)	

WAR DIARY
or
INTELLIGENCE SUMMARY.
(Erase heading not required.)

Army Form C. 2118.

Place	Date	Hour	Summary of Events and Information	Remarks and references to Appendices
CHAUNY	9/2/18	—	Lieut. F. E. CLAY, R.A.M.C. posted to 390 A Bac. F.A. as from 16/1/18	
"	"	Noon	Daily stats: Comp 5, Admd 28, Evac NLK, Comp 33	
"	10/2/18	10:00 a.m.	1/Lieut. D. W. KRAMER, 1/Lieut. C. C. ELEBASH, 1/Lieut. R. LONG, M.O.R.C., U.S.A. reported for duty & taken on strength as from 9/5/18	
"	"	"	Capt. J. B. Mc KEE reported for duty & taken on Strength of Unit	
"	"	Noon	Daily stats Comp 33, Admd 21, Evac NK, Comp 54	
"	11/2/18	11 a.m.	Capt. A. A. WATSON att. for temporary duty and 8th Sn London Regt 23 O.R. of 2/4th H.C.F. Amb. and 23 O.R. of 4th Sn Lonks attached temporarily for duty. W.O.R. arrived as reinforcements, taken on strength.	
"	"	"	Capt Scabies Station Established (3 O.R. M.S.M. W.O. to 6387/12 of 10/2/18)	
"	"	Noon	Daily stats Comp 54, Admd 11, Evac 75, Comp 50	
"	1/2/18	Noon	Daily stats Comp 50, Admd 24, Evac 35, Comp 39	

Army Form C. 2118.

WAR DIARY
or
INTELLIGENCE SUMMARY.
(Erase heading not required.)

Instructions regarding War Diaries and Intelligence Summaries are contained in F. S. Regs., Part II. and the Staff Manual respectively. Title pages will be prepared in manuscript.

Place	Date	Hour	Summary of Events and Information	Remarks and references to Appendices
CHAUNY	1/2/18	9 a.m.	1/Lieut D. W. KRAMER 1/Lieut C.C. ELBASH, of the M.O.R.C., U.S.A. sent to report to	
"	"	Noon	A.D.M.S. XIV Corps + struck off Strength. Daily State: Remg 39; Adm 53; Evac 36; Remg 56	
"	12/2/18	Noon	Daily State: Remg 56; Adm 22; Evac 11; Remg 67	
"	13/2/18	9 a.m.	S.C.R. from 32 C.C.S. posted as reinforcements, arrived + taken on strength. (Auth: A.R.S.2001, 75/C/F/1=6, 9/2/18)	
"	"		Capt. T.B. MC KEE relieved Capt. WATSON who returned to G.Q. + was admd. to Hosbital.	
"	"	Noon	Daily State: Remg 67; Adm 14; Evac 4; Remg 77	
"	14/2/18		Capt. WATSON evacuated to No.6 C.C.S.	
"	"	Noon	Daily State: Remg 77; Adm 13; Evac 9; Remg 83	
"	"		Capt. H.S. PALMER granted leave to 3/3/18	
"	15/2/18	Noon	Daily State: Remg 83; Adm 21; Evac 16; Remg 88	
"	"	3.30 pm	Capt. H.H. LEESON, M.C. reported for duty at G.Q. + proceeded to 8th Bn London Regt. in relief of Capt. MC KEE	

Army Form C. 2118.

WAR DIARY
or
INTELLIGENCE SUMMARY.
(Erase heading not required.)

Instructions regarding War Diaries and Intelligence Summaries are contained in F. S. Regs., Part II. and the Staff Manual respectively. Title pages will be prepared in manuscript.

Place	Date	Hour	Summary of Events and Information	Remarks and references to Appendices
CHAUNY	18/2/18	Noon	Daily State. Reinf 88, Attd 15, Evac 22, Enemy 81	
"			Capt. J.B. McKEE returned to the 8th Bn London Regt in relief of Capt LEESON who proceeded to A.D.M.S. Office, 58th Div, & then returned to H.Q.	
"	19/2/18	9 am	16 O.R. from Battalions on the 14th Feb reported at H.Q. to pursue a course of 14 days training in "Chiropody" conducted by Sergt A.C. WATKIN	
"	"	Noon	Daily State. Reinf 81, Attd 17, Evac 28, Enemy 70	
"	20/2/18	Noon	Daily State. Reinf 70, Attd 20, Evac 13, Enemy 77	
"	"	2 pm	D.M.S. V Army made a tour of inspection of the Institute	
"	21/2/18	Noon	Daily State. Reinf 77, Attd 14, Evac 21, Enemy 70.	
"	"	2.30 pm	R.W. Band gave a concert in the theatre at the Institute	
"	22/2/18	Noon	Daily State. Reinf 70, Attd 25, Evac 8, Enemy 85	

Army Form C. 2118.

WAR DIARY
or
INTELLIGENCE SUMMARY.
(Erase heading not required.)

Instructions regarding War Diaries and Intelligence Summaries are contained in F. S. Regs., Part II. and the Staff Manual respectively. Title pages will be prepared in manuscript.

Place	Date	Hour	Summary of Events and Information	Remarks and references to Appendices
CHAUNY	23/2/18	Noon	Daily State. Rang 85; Comd 14; Evac 16; Rang 83	
			495422 Corporal CRAFT, L.G. detailed to attend "B"Course at M.Corps Gas School from 25/2/18 to 4/3/18	
"	24/2/18	Noon	Daily State. Rang 83; Cmd 14; Evac 9; Rang 88.	
"	25/2/18	Noon	Daily State. Rang 88; Cmd 13; Evac 17; Rang 84	
		6 p.m.	Officers & Personnel of 2/3 4.6.Y.A. & 2 MACs at A.D.S. FARGNIERS, R.P., & R.A.P. of centre water when under command of O.B. 2/2 4.6.Y.A. (A.N.6.Z.) (A.D.M.S. Operation Order No 37 of 24/2/18)	
"	26/2/18	Noon	Daily State. Rang 84; Cmd 34; Evac 30; Rang 97	
"	27/2/18	Noon	Daily State. Eng 97; Cmd 10; Evac 21; Rang 86	
"	28/2/18	Noon	Daily State. Rang 86; Cmd 18; Evac 15; Rang 89	
		9 p.m.	23 M.C.I. Amb a(A.D.L.G.Z.) took over A.D.S. at FARGNIERS & relay posts on left route of evacuation from 2/3 M.C.Y Amb. (Auth. A.D.M.S. M3947 of 28/2/18)	

Army Form C. 2118.

WAR DIARY
or
INTELLIGENCE SUMMARY.
(Erase heading not required.)

Instructions regarding War Diaries and Intelligence Summaries are contained in F. S. Regs., Part II. and the Staff Manual respectively. Title pages will be prepared in manuscript.

Place	Date	Hour	Summary of Events and Information	Remarks and references to Appendices
CHAUNY	28/2/18	2.00p	A.D.M.S. 58 Div. M.3828/385/A Qu. dd. 28/2/18 Rec'd. containing instructions to take precautionary action. Report to be made when all arrangements are completed & Unit in readiness to move.	
"	"	2.35p	O.C. reported to A.D.M.S. "Action taken"	
"	"	7.30p	A.D.M.S. 58 DIV. M262 rec'd amending M3828/385/A dd.28/2/18. Qu. "Troops will now be ready to move at one hour's notice instead of 15 minutes as previously ordered."	

Army Form C. 2118.

MEDICAL Vol 14

WAR DIARY
or
INTELLIGENCE SUMMARY.
(Erase heading not required.)

Summary of Events and Information

CONFIDENTIAL

War Diary

of

2/2nd Home Counties Field Amb,
R.A.M.C.(T)

from 1/3/1918
to 31/3/1918.

Lt. Col. R.A.M.C.(T) O.C.
2/2ND H. C. FLD. AMB.

COMMITTEE FOR THE
MEDICAL HISTORY OF THE WAR
Date 12 MAY 1918

2/2ND
HOME COUNTIES
FIELD AMBULANCE.

Place	Date	Hour										Remarks and references to Appendices
	1 Mar 1918											

Army Form C. 2118.

WAR DIARY
or
INTELLIGENCE SUMMARY.
(Erase heading not required.)

Place	Date	Hour	Summary of Events and Information	Remarks and references to Appendices
SHEET 70.D. (H.Q.) CHAUNY. A.26.a.2.6.	1/3/18	11.a.m.	A.D.M.S. W.264. of 1/3/18. Turning III Opo conv. "Standing by at one hour's notice cancelled." Worked parties & other duties as usual.	R.A.P. B.27b.7.4. H.9b.39. H.28.8.9.
" " "	"	Noon	Daily State: SICK: Remd. 1 Off.16 O.R's; Admd. 12 O.R's; Evacd.10 Off., 13 O.R's; Remg. 3 O.R.	Evacuation Post G.14.a.9.6
" " "	"	"	" " SCABIES: " 2 Off., 92 " ; Admd. 8 " ; Dis. 2 O.R's; Remg. 2 Off., 88 O.R's	
" " "	2/3/18	Noon	Daily State: SICK: Remd. 3 O.R's; Admd. 2 Off., 20 O.R's; Evacd. 2 Off., 20 O.R's; Remg. 3 O.R.	R.P's B.28.c.1.1. H.27.b.30.
" " "	"	"	" " SCABIES: Remd. 2 Off., 88 O.R's; Admd. 10 O.R's; Evacd. 2 O.R's; Disch. 1 O.R; Remg. 2 Off., 95 O.R's	A.D.S. G.10.c.68.
" " "	3/3/18	9.a.m	Lt. Col. J. BARKLEY. R.A.M.C.(T) (C.C.2/3 H.C.F.AMB.) assumed temporary Command of the Unit in the absence of Lt. Col. H. FULTON. R.A.M.C.(T) on leave.	H.G. A.26.a.2.6. Mgas Post H.27/3 (M. Fact.)
" " "	"	Noon	Daily State: SICK: Remd. 3 O.R's; Admd. 2 Off., 9 O.R's; Evacd. 9 O.R's; Remg. 2 Off., 3 O.R's.	
" " "	"	"	" " SCABIES: " 2 Off., 95 O.R's; Admd. 7 O.R's; Disch. 10 Off., 8 O.R's; Remg. 10 Off., 94 O.R's.	
(A.D.S.) SINCENY G.10.C.6.8.	"	3.p.m.	Situation Report from Capt. G.L. McGILLIVRAY. O.C. A.D.S. forwarding report from R.G.O. 7th Bn. LOND Regt as follows: "The present R.A.P. is very much under observation as well as the Road leading to it & from it. Evacuation of stretcher cases by road in the day time is as well under observation of the enemy. A trench is being dug for a Group for stretcher cases. I am sending a report to O.C. 7th Bn. LOND Regt, and asking to (1) getting an R.A.P. established in a more suitable position or (2) having the present position improved."	(Map Ref.) R.A.P.: 7th Bn. H.28.a.8.9.)
(H.Q.) CHAUNY A.26.a.2.6.	4/3/18	4.a.m.	Lt. Col. FULTON granted leave until 18/3/18.	
" " "	"	Noon	Daily State: SICK: Remd. 2 Off., 3 O.R's; Admd. 2 Off., 10 O.R's; Evacd. 10 O.R's; Remg. 4 Off., 3 O.R's	
" " "	"	"	" " SCABIES: " 1 Off., 94 O.R's; " 9 O.R's; Evacd. 1 O.R; Died. 1 Off., 6 O.R's; "	
(A.D.S.) SINCENY G.10.C.6.8.	"	3.p.m.	Situation Report from O.C. A.D.S. includes report from 7th Bn. LOND Regt M.O. as follows: "I will endeavour to send cases down to A.D.S. by day-time as far as possible. As it is now expected to have a sickparade at about this expense (in the expense (in the R.A.P. in full view of the enemy) I may be compelled to send home sick cases very late in the evening."	

Army Form C. 2118.

WAR DIARY
INTELLIGENCE SUMMARY

(Erase heading not required.)

Instructions regarding War Diaries and Intelligence Summaries are contained in F. S. Regs., Part II. and the Staff Manual respectively. Title pages will be prepared in manuscript.

Place	Date	Hour	Summary of Events and Information	Remarks and references to Appendices
SHEET 70 D. (H.Q.) CHAUNY A.26.a.2.6.	5/3/18	10 a.m.	Arrangements to Med. Arr. in connection with III CORPS DEFENCE SCHEME received	
		Noon	Daily State: SICK: Rend. to Off.; 3 O.R's; Admd. 4 Off.; 8 O.R's.; Evacd. 1 Off.; 8 O.R's; Disch. 1 O.R's.; Reng. 7 Off.; 96 O.R's. WOUNDED: Admd. 1 O.R.; Reng. 1 O.R.	
			SCABIES: " 96 O.R's.; Admd. 8 O.R's.; Disch. 11 O.R's.; Reng. 93 O.R's.	
(A.D.S.) SINCENY G.10.c.6.8.	"	3 p.m.	Report from M.O. 7th Bn. LOND. REGT. forwarded: "The site of the R.A.P. is to be changed but until a new place is constructed we will continue to occupy this post. The D.A.D.M.S. has personally fixed a new site."	
			Lieut J.A. LEAS. M.O.R.C. (already detached) posted to 58 D.A.C. Struck off Unit strength.	
(H.Q.) CHAUNY A.26.a.2.6.	6/3/18	Noon	Daily State: { WOUNDED: Rend. 1 O.R.; Admd. 1 O.R.; Reng. 2 O.R. SICK: Rend. 7 Off.; 2 O.R's; Admd. 2 Off., 4 O.R's.; Evacd. 3 Off., 4 O.R's. Reng. 6 Off., 2 O.R's.	
			" SCABIES: " 93 O.R's.; Admd. 13 O.R's.; Evacd. 1 O.R.; Disch. 6 O.R's.; Reng. 99 O.R's.	
(A.D.S.) SINCENY G.10.c.6.8.	"	3 p.m.	Report from M.O. 7th Bn. LOND. REGT. Re: R.A.P. "I sent you a special report today on the likely position for a R.A.P. I understand the Battalion Commdy. Officer has also sent in a report recommending one of the two positions viz. 'Quarry near Bn. H.Q.' I have also written to the B. Spads Sub. Officer to ask his assistance in making the Relay Post in BARESIS mileage gap safe. This Relay Post is being established in accordance with instructions from the D.A.D.M.S."	
(H.Q.) CHAUNY A.26.a.2.6.	7/3/18	Noon	Daily State: SICK: Rend. 6 Off., 2 O.R's; Admd. 11 O.R.; Evacd. 1 Off., 11 O.R.; Reng. 5 Off., 2 O.R.	
" "	"	"	" WOUNDED: " 2 O.R's.; Admd. 1 O.R.; Reng. 3 O.R.	
" "	"	"	" SCABIES: " 99 O.R's.; Admd. 8 O.R'; Evacd. 2 O.R.; Disch. 18 O.R.; Reng. 92 O.R.	
" "	"	2.30 p.m.	Capt. H.H. LEESON, M.O., evacuated to No. 46 C.C.S. (Sick.)	
" "	"	3 p.m.	MDME. GOURKO, wife of famous RUSSIAN General visited & inspected the foremen in company with the A.D.M.S. 58 DIV.	
(A.D.S.) SINCENY G.10.c.6.8.	"	3 p.m.	Report from M.O. 7th Bn. LOND. REGT. forwarded: "The R.A.P. has been changed from H.28.a.8.9 to H.27.6.7.1. I visited the site at H.28.a.8.9 yesterday and in company with the C.O. it is being become untenable from enemy shelling. I consulted the C.O. before withdrawing + he approves of self change of site. I have your letter dealing with this matter. I will do what I can to get a proper R.A.P constructed."	

WAR DIARY
INTELLIGENCE SUMMARY
(Erase heading not required.)

Army Form C. 2118.

Instructions regarding War Diaries and Intelligence Summaries are contained in F. S. Regs., Part II. and the Staff Manual respectively. Title pages will be prepared in manuscript.

Place	Date	Hour	Summary of Events and Information	Remarks and references to Appendices
SHEET 70D. (H.Q.) CHAUNY A.26.a.2.6.	8/3/18	10.30am	Conference at H.Q. Instructions received re C.C. to coopts "Keupo" + to be prepared to man same.	x Includes 11 Italians
" "	"	Noon.	Daily State: Sick: Recd. 5 Off. 2 O.R.; Adnd. 2 Off. 18 O.R.; Evacd. 2 Off. 5 O.R.; Reng. 5 Off. 20 Off. 11 Italians	
" "	"	"	" " Wounded: Recd. 3 O.R.; Reng. 3 O.R.	
" "	"	"	" " Scabies: Recd. 92 O.R.; Adnd. 1 Off. 14 O.R.; Evacd. 2 O.R.; To D.R.S. 1 O.R.; Disch. 7 O.R.; Reng. 1 Off. 96 O.R.	
(H.Q.) CHAUNY A.26.a.2.6.	9/3/18	10.30am	D.D.M.S. III Corps and A.D.M.S. 58 Div. arrived Headquarters & inspected the Premises.	
" "	"	Noon.	Lieut. R.LONG, M.O.R.C., reported on his return to the Unit from Course at Fifth Army School of Instruction.	x Includes 2 Italians
" "	"	"	Daily State: Sick: Recd. 5 Off. 2 O.R.; Adnd. 8 O.R.; Evacd. 8 O.R.; Reng. 5 Off. 20 O.R.	
" "	"	"	" " Wounded: Recd. 3 O.R. 2 Off.; To D.R.S. 2 O.R.; Reng. 1 O.R.	
" "	"	"	" " Scabies: Recd. 1 Off. 96 O.R.; Adnd. 10 O.R.; Evacd. 6 O.R.; Disch. 7 O.R.; Reng. 1 Off. 93 O.R.	
A.D.S. (SINCENY) G.10.c.6.5.	"	3pm.	O.C. A.D.S. forwards report received from 7th Bn. LOND. REGT.: "I am in a temporary structure at H.27.b.9.1. This R.A.P. was not Gun itself to being made 'gas-proof.' I am opening the "No permanent R.A.P." (when it is eventually) soon be made gas-proof."	
(H.Q.) CHAUNY A.26.a.2.6.	10/3/18	9am.	Lieut. R. LONG, M.O.R.C., detailed for duty at FIFTH ARMY ADVANCED OPERATING CENTRE, ABBECOURT.	
" "	"	Noon.	Daily State: Sick: Recd. 5 Off. 2 O.R.; Adnd. 4 O.R.; Evacd. 4 O.R.; Disch. 1 Off.; Reng. 4 Off. 2 O.R.	
" "	"	"	" " Wounded: Recd. 1 O.R.; Reng. 1 O.R.	
" "	"	"	" " Scabies: Recd. 1 Off. 93 O.R.; Adnd. 1 Off. 14 O.R.; Evacd. 3 O.R.; To D.R.S. 1 O.R.; Disch. 6 O.R.; Reng. 2 Off. 97 O.R.	
" "	"	2.30pm.	Maj. Gen. MACPHERSON, D.G.M.S.; Maj. Gen. SKINNER, D.M.S.; & D.D.M.S. III Corps inspected the Premises.	

Army Form C. 2118.

WAR DIARY
or
INTELLIGENCE SUMMARY.
(Erase heading not required.)

Instructions regarding War Diaries and Intelligence Summaries are contained in F. S. Regs., Part II. and the Staff Manual respectively. Title pages will be prepared in manuscript.

Place	Date	Hour	Summary of Events and Information	Remarks and references to Appendices
SHEET 70D (HQ) CHAUNY A.26.a.2.6.	1/3/18	Noon	Daily State: Sick: Remd. 2 O.R.; Admd. 1 Off. 6 O.R.; Evac. 1 Off. 6 O.R.; Remg. 4 Off. 2 O.R.	×Includes 3 Italians
"	"	"	" L " Wounded: Remd. 1 O.R. TO Blk. S. 1 O.R.	
"	"	"	" " Scabies: Remd. 2 Off. 97 O.R.; Admd. 18 O.R.; Evac. 3 O.R.; Disch. 13 O.R.; Remg. 2 Off. 97 O.R.	
A.D.S. SINCENY G.10.c.6.8.	"	3 p.m.	M.O. 1/6 Ed Bn. LOND. REGT. reports through A.D.S.: "Arrangements are being made for the Battalion to build a Regimental Aid Post in the Quarry on the road about Bn. H.Q. In addition the rest in Coy. aid P. will consist of an empty shelter where there are no suitable houses for this purpose. It is arranged that a cellar suitable as an aid post is selected in the "Fragment from Bn. H.Q. around which the [...]"	"UNICORN" 1st Bn. LOND. REGT.
			H.Q. UNICORN (Left sector)	
(HQ) CHAUNY A.26.a.2.6.	12/3/18	—	Extract from Unit Orders for the Day: "1931. HONOURS: The following extract from "The Times" of 9-3-18, is published for the information of all Ranks: LONDON GAZETTE Supplement, March 8th. — WAR OFFICE, March 8th. — The KING has been pleased to approve the following Rewards for Distinguished Service in the Field. Dated Jan. 1st, 1918. — D.S.O. Maj. (A/Lt. Col.) H. FULTON, R.A.M.C."	
"	"	Noon	Daily State: Sick: Remd. 4 Off. 2 O.R.; Admd. 1 Off. 2 O.R.; Evac. 1 Off. 10 O.R.; Disch. 1 Off.; Remg. 3 Off. 2 O.R.	×Includes 5 Italians
"	"	"	" L " Wounded: —	
"	"	"	" " Scabies: Remd. 2 Off. 99 O.R.; Admd. 10 O.R.; Evac. 4 O.R.; Disch. 8 O.R.; Remg. 2 Off. 97 O.R.	
A.D.S. SINCENY G.10.c.6.8.	"	3 p.m.	O.C. A.D.S. reports: — Capt. McKEE has returned from Left Sector of line & reports that the officer is sick at the same place — B.27.b.7.4 — & his likely remain there as the Artillery refuse to vacate the post we looked at with the O.C. 9th LOND. REGT. the other day."	
(H.Q) CHAUNY A.26.a.2.6.	13/3/18	Noon	Daily State: Sick: Remd. 3 Off. 2 O.R.; Admd. 1 O.R.; Evac. 1 Off. 1 O.R.; Remg. 2 Off. 2 O.R.	
"	"	"	" L " Wounded: Admd. 7 O.R.; Remg. 7 O.R.	
"	"	"	" " Scabies: Remd. 2 Off. 9 O.R.; Admd. 20 O.R.; Evac. 2 O.R.; Disch. 7 O.R.; Remg. 2 Off. 108 O.R.	
(HQ) CHAUNY A.26.a.2.6.	14/3/18	8.20 a.m.	Commandant No. 2.6 Med. Army Convalescent and III CORPS DEFENCE SCHEME received.	
"	"	Noon	Daily State: Sick: Remd. 2 Off. 2 O.R.; Admd. 2 O.R.; Evac. 2 O.R.; To D.R.S. 6 O.R.; Remg. 2 O.R.	
"	"	"	" L " Wounded: 7 O.R.; Evac. 1 O.R.; To D.R.S. 6 O.R.; Remg. —	
"	"	"	" " Scabies: " 2 Off. 108 O.R.; Admd. 8 O.R.; Evac. 1 O.R.; Disch. 1 Off. 9 O.R.; Remg. 1 Off. 108 O.R.	

D.D. & L., London, E.C. (A7853) Wt. W6o4/M1672 350,000 1/17 **Sch. 92a.** Forms C/2118/4

WAR DIARY / INTELLIGENCE SUMMARY

Army Form C. 2118.

Place	Date	Hour	Summary of Events and Information	Remarks and references to Appendices
SHEET 70 D (Contd) A.D.S. SINCENY G.10.c.6.8.	14/3/18	3 p.m.	O.C. A.D.S. SINCENY forwards report from M.O. i/c 8th Bn. Lond. Regt.: "My new R.A.P. will probably be completed by tonight or tomorrow."	
(H.Q.) CHAUNY A.26.a.2.6.	"	6 p.m.	12 Reinforcements (O.R. R.A.M.C) joined Unit.	
(H.Q.) CHAUNY A.26.a.2.6.	15/3/18	—	Med. Arr. for "keeps" supplementary to Med. Arr. in connection with III Corps Defence Scheme received.	
		Noon	Daily State: Sick: Remg. 2 O.R.; Disch. 2 O.R.	
			" Wounded: —	
			" Scabies: Remg. 1 Off. 106 O.R.; Admd. 4 O.R.; Evacd. 3 O.R.; To D.R.S. 10 R.; Disch. 9 O.R.; Remg. 1 Off. 97 O.R.	
A.D.S. SINCENY G.10.c.6.8.	"	3 p.m.	Report from M.O. i/c 8th Bn. Lond. Regt. fwded through O.C. A.D.S. SINCENY: "The construction of new R.A.P. has been taken over by the R.E.'s." One N.C.O. killed in line yesterday, no casualties.	
(H.Q.) CHAUNY A.26.a.2.6.	16/3/18	Noon	Daily State: Sick: Admd. 3, Evacd. 3;	
			" Wounded: —	
			" Scabies: Remd. 1 Off. 97 O.R.; Admd. 10 O.R.; To D.R.S. 2 O.R.; Disch. 11 O.R.; Remg. 1 Off. 89 O.R.	
(H.Q.) CHAUNY A.26.a.2.6.	17/3/18	Noon	Daily State: Sick: Admd. 5; Evacd. 5	*Includes 4 Italians
			" Wounded: —	
			" Scabies: Remd. 1 Off. 89 O.R.; Admd. 10 O.R.; Evacd. 4 O.R.; Disch. 9 O.R.; Remg. 1 Off. 86 O.R.	
"	"	3 p.m.	3 O.R. left to attend Course of Instruction at 66 C.C.S. HAM.	
A.D.S. SINCENY G.10.c.6.8.	"	"	Commandant of No.3 S. Med. Arr. in connection with III Corps Defence Scheme received.	
			O.C. A.D.S. reports: "A few shells (H.E.) fell in the vicinity of QUARRY this morning."	
(H.Q.) CHAUNY A.26.a.2.6.	"	3.30 p.m.	LIEUT. GEN. SIR R.H.K. BUTLER, K.C.M.G., C.B. Cmndg. III Army Corps, accompanied by A.D.M.S. 58th Div., visited and inspected III Corps SCABIES Station at H.Q. CHAUNY.	
"	"	"	A few shells fired into the vicinity of Fourbourbo dropped in the vicinity of	
"	"	9.00 p.m.	E/A came over dropping Aerial Bombs. Fourbourbo about 2 kms.	

Army Form C. 2118.

WAR DIARY
or
INTELLIGENCE SUMMARY.

(Erase heading not required.)

Place	Date	Hour	Summary of Events and Information	Remarks and references to Appendices
SHEET 70D. (H.Q.) CHAUNY A.26.a.2.6	18/3/18.	Noon	Daily State: SICK: Admd. 2 O.R.; Evacd 2 O.R.	+Includes 1 Italian.
			" " WOUNDED: —	
			" " SCABIES: Recd. 1 Off. 86 O.R.; Admd. 12 O.R.; Evacd 4 O.R.; Disch. 1 Off. 6 O.R.; Reng. 88 O.R.	
A.D.S. SINCENY. G.10.c.6.8.	"	3 p.m.	O.C. A.D.S. reports: "Slight intermittent shelling from 10.15 a.m. to 11.00 a.m. this morning. No casualties."	
(H.Q.) CHAUNY A.26.a.2.6	19/3/18.	Noon.	Daily State: SICK: Admitted 2 O.R.; Evacd 2 O.R.	
			" " WOUNDED: —	
			" " SCABIES: Recd. 88 O.R.; Admd. 1 Off. 27 O.R.; Evacd. 3 O.R.; To D.R.S. 20 R.; Disch. 10 O.R.; Reng. 1 Off. 100 O.R.	
A.D.S. SINCENY.	"	3 p.m.	O.C. A.D.S. reports: "Sanitation normal."	
"	"	"	M.O. i/c 7th Bn. LOND. Regt. reports: "The sanitation of this area can be much improved if the Trenches were filled with portable buckets with fly-proof covers. The new R.A.P. is in course of construction."	
(H.Q.) CHAUNY A.26.a.2.6	"	10.30 p.m.	Lt.Col. H.FULTON, R.A.M.C.(T.), D.S.O. returned from leave.	
(H.Q.) CHAUNY A.26.a.2.6	20/3/18.	9.0 a.m.	Lt.Col. H.FULTON, R.A.M.C.(-), D.S.O. re-assumed Command of the Unit.	
"	"	Noon	Daily State: SICK: Admitted 10 O.R.; Evacd 9 O.R.; Reng. 1 O.R.	
"	"	"	" " WOUNDED: Recd. 1 Off. 100 O.R.; Admd. 12 O.R.; Evacd 3 O.R.; To D.R.S. 1 O.R.; Disch. 9 O.R.; Reng. 1 Off. 99 O.R.	
"	"	"	" " SCABIES: —	
A.D.S. SINCENY	"	3 p.m.	O.C. A.D.S. reports: "Everything satisfactory."	
"	"	"	M.O. i/c 7th Bn. LOND. Regt. reports: Although A.D.S. "The two Medical Emergency Boxes have been placed in the prescribed positions. The new R.A.P. is in course of construction. I strongly recommend that a new path through the wood to the Cab Post from the new R.A.P. be made for the evacuation of casualties, if not used every day it would be "	

WAR DIARY
INTELLIGENCE SUMMARY

Army Form C. 2118.

Place	Date	Hour	Summary of Events and Information	Remarks and references to Appendices
SHEET 70D. (N.W.) CHALNY. A 26 a 2.6	20/3/18	6.30 p.m	Wire rec'd. "Prepare for attack at once." "Preparations made to evacuate all sick & casualty offensive medical posts in accordance with 58th DIVISIONAL Defence Scheme.	
A.D.S. SINCENY G10.c.6.8.	"	8.00 p.m	M.O. i/c. A.D.S. SINCENY reports. "Everything satisfactory & nothing to report."	
"	"	"	M.O. 7th Bn. LOND. REGT. reports. "The Car available & carrying Cases have been placed in the forward positions. The four R.A.P.s in front of Embuscade & straight through to watch the Car Posts for further "evacuation" All wire road through Canalles. R.A.P. be used for the abnormal of casualties. It for not use any dry stretcher as a useful Kearns Car service has a.	
(ROD. D'HAM) A26.q.2.6.	21/3/18	3. a.m	"Enemy just received from 8th DIV. — A.D.M.S. 58th DIV."	18th DIV Left Sector
"	"	4.30 am	Heavy Barrage heard coming to to our left Sector.	
"	"	5.00 am	Wire rec'd "War Battle positions." Necessary action taken according to pre-arranged plan. All patients evacuated.	
"	"	Noon	DAILY STATE: SICK: Ramft. 1 O.R.; Admd. 2 Off., 2 O.R.; Evac. 2 Off., 2 O.R.; Remg. 1 O.R.	
			WOUNDED:	
			SCABIES: Remd. 1 Off., 99 O.R.; Admd. 14 O.Rs.; Evac. 1 Off., Disch. 9 O.Rs.; Remg. 1 Off., 103 O.Rs.	
A.D.S SINCENY G10.c.6.8.	"	3.00 pm	M.O. i/c A.D.S. SINCENY reports. Heavy shelling all along the line from about 3.40 am. "Rail at ROND D'ORLEANS in the trench & badly cut up. Motor Ambulance Car stuck in shell-hole then and had to be abandoned. Allowed rail along the ROND and through the wood suitable for evacuation found. Cars can go to within 200 yards of ROND and pack up cases there. Heavy gas shelling this area. (Contd. next page)	

Army Form C. 2118.

WAR DIARY
or
INTELLIGENCE SUMMARY.
(Erase heading not required.)

Place	Date	Hour	Summary of Events and Information	Remarks and references to Appendices
Sheet 70.D ADS SINCENY G10.c.6.8	21/3/18	3 p.m.	(cont. from previous page). Position on the above on left was at time of Report. Heavy shelling in rear & around BUTTES DE ROUY. During the day several men were made to go forward to dugouts but R.E. have all not yet gone so much attention to the as before. (Extract from C.O.s report). Weather misty, very sultry, particularly in the morning.	///
(H.Q.) SINCENY G10.c.6.6	22/3/18	8.30 a.m.	O.C. 6/Lond. of N.C.O. details sent to A.D.S. SINCENY. Remainder of personnel & store cart of to QUIERZY. Advanced GAS CENTRE moved to QUIERZY. STABLES STATION closed.	
ADS SINCENY G10.c.6.6	"	—	Capt. A.C. WATKIN reports establishment of GAS CENTRE at New Station.	
"	"	Noon	Casualties to R.A.M.C. personnel reported:– 4 O.R's "Wounded (Gas) Shell" – evacuated 21/3/18 to Advanced GAS CENTRE. One O.R. "G.S.W. (Shell) Neck" – remained at duty.	
"	"	Noon	D. of G. Sect. Sick State. I.O.R. Cond. 29 O.R. Devon. 3 O.R. WOUNDED Cond.–; Admd. 29 O.R; Evacd. 26 O.R; Devon. 3 O.R; Dischd. 1 Off. 100 O.R. SCABIES Remd. 1 Off. 108 O.R's; To DRESS 0 O.Rs; Dischd. 1 Off.	
"	"	2 p.m.	O.C. A.D.S. reports: "Evacuation Route all clear of personnel."	
"	"	"	Weather: No change.	
(A.Q.) SINCENY G10.c.6.8	23/3/18	Noon	4/Lond. Casualty Report. 3 O.R. R.A.M.C. – "Wounded (Gas) Shell" sent to Advanced GAS CENTRE	
"	"	"	D. of G. Sick State (N.C.)	
"	"	3 p.m.	Situation report: M.O. 7 Bn. LOND. RGT. reports:– "There are no casualties awaiting evacuation." O.C. A.D.S. reports: "Becoming impossible to evacuate through AMIGNY on account (cont. next page)	///

Army Form C. 2118.

10

WAR DIARY
INTELLIGENCE SUMMARY.
(Erase heading not required.)

Instructions regarding War Diaries and Intelligence Summaries are contained in F. S. Regs., Part II. and the Staff Manual respectively. Title pages will be prepared in manuscript.

Place	Date	Hour	Summary of Events and Information	Remarks and references to Appendices
SHEET 70D (H.Q.) SINCENY G.10.c.6.8	23/3/18	3 p.m.	REPORT by O.C.A.D.S. (Cont.) "Labelling" Now route with 3 R.P's. being established along edge of March from left. R.A.P. Night side quiet and route clear. No shelling of Rond D'Orleans. Heavy shelling this afternoon of crossroads at east N.E. of SINCENY near "SUGAR FACTORY". Weather fine, with mist	
"	"	7.30 p.m.	Party under Capt. H.S. PALMER about to push various of evacuation.	
"	"	-	E.A. busy in the vicinity during the night, several bombs being dropped	
"	"	9.0 p.m.	Unit details from ADVANCED GAS CENTRE at QUERZY reported at H.Q. Capt. WATKIN assuming	
(H.Q.) SINCENY G.10.c.6.8	24/3/18	10.30 a.m.	Commanding Officer orders "Prepare to Move". Marking of New Route advised.	
"	"	11.15 a.m.	Details at A.D.S. left by Route March taking staves for new A.D.S. Capt G.M. McGILLIVRAY left with 6 O.R's N.C.O.'s & men and wounded R.A.M.C. Personnel at 3 EMERGENCY A.D. POSTS — G.14.a.0.6 (Sheet 70D) L.23.6.7.6 (Sheet 70E) G.28.b.5.2 (Sheet 70D) Joined Unit Details from A.D.S. en route to New Station	
"	"	Noon	Daily Staff: (N.O.)	
"	"	"	Casualties in Unit for previous 24 hrs. 1 O.R. R.A.M.C. "Wounded (Gas) Shell"	
"	"	"	A.D.M.S. met on the Road Consultation with Commanding Officer.	
BICHANCOURT	"	1.30 p.m.	Unit D.R. brings message from Capt. McGILLIVRAY: "The evacuation at present is much the same. No other news. Left. Reporting W.W. by Staff Car to BICHANCOURT & Capt. PALMER & party. Lts. WORD Car broke down & Lts. on way to QUARRY for stretcher	

WAR DIARY
INTELLIGENCE SUMMARY

Army Form C. 2118.

Place	Date	Hour	Summary of Events and Information	Remarks and references to Appendices
BEHANCOURT	24/3/18	1.30 pm	REPORT by O.C A.D.S (Contd.) "Case" FRENCH Armoured Cars taken up defensive position along road in front of "DRESSING STATION." All clear on Rt. of Rd. so far. Still shelling PIERRE AMANDE. "Sent Cage Carts for FORD."	
(Sheet 70.E.) BESME R 14.b.9.4.	"	4.15pm	Unit Details arrived at New Station. (Old Farm Ruins) specially prepared for reception of Wounded. Capt WATKIN joined Unit here.	
" "	"	4.30 pm	Wounded began to arrive. Tent Sub Divisions being kept very busy.	
" "	"	6.0 pm	Capt. McGILLIVRAY reports from PIERRE AMANDE. "Journeyed from SINCENY to PIERRE AMAND this afternoon. BOCHE are in CHAUNY and said to have crossed CANAL East of Letter McCase. Both First Cars out of action. One broke down on way to QUERRY for cases and I moved it in tow of Staff Car sent to QUERZY with Wounded. Weather so stuck at ROND D'ORLEANS hard hard wheel off. 3 cases will cases from left of line before evacuating SINCENY and there were 14 cases at night to clear. So have arranged for cases from right to be brought East if "one was needed stretchers from C.C.P.0.6. I had got to back with 14 and 175 "INFANTRY B.Oe. here. If the First Car that ran on could get the Car "could be repaired a bit there or back well I think so that I could get "the big Stewart Car on to road. Somehow must carry on for the French "but in all require at least two large Case Here. FRENCH old ENGLISH troops "using up 4th or attack between LA.O. & AUTREVILLE. I shall require help here in "so cannot carry on everything with only myself and six cars. Could I have "another M.O.J. Some thing like a Ambulance to the Lire. BOCHE still putting up "fair H.V. shell here."	
" "	"	7 pm	Capt. T. B McKEE and 7 O.Rs. sent to help Capt McGILLVRAY.	
" "	"	-	Arrangements made for evacuation of FRENCH Wounded by Officer Commanding 9th Cavalry Division with D.M.S. FRENCH CAVALRY CORPS.	
" "	"	-	Weather Fine	

Army Form C. 2118.

WAR DIARY
or
INTELLIGENCE SUMMARY.
(Erase heading not required.)

Place	Date	Hour	Summary of Events and Information	Remarks and references to Appendices
BESME R.14.b.94	24/3/18	12 Noon	Two telegrams received from M.O. 9th Bn LOND. RGT :— (1) "Field Post extinct of 12 Noon today by orders of Capt PALMER are orders party at A.D.S. en route for G.28 b." (2) "Send evacuating route to Fermeyer via ULCER RAP."	"ULCER = 9/12 Bn LOND. RGT."
"	"	"	Reply sent "Evacuation route to being re-arranged by M.O. 9/12 A.D.S. PIERRE AMANDE."	
(AND) BESME R142.94	25/3/18	—	Enemy reported to be crossing the OISE. Capt. MASSEY MILES, R.M.O. 6th Bn LOND. RGT. temp. att. for duty at H.Q.	
"	"	11am	Order received to "Stand by". Packing of Wagons commenced.	
"	"	—	Casualties — chiefly FRENCH — still incoming, treated and evacuated.	
"	"	Noon	Daily State: WOUNDED: Officers 5 off, 44 O.R.s; Sick 17 O.R.s. Evact. 17 O.R.s Sick France 1 off; 5 off, 23 O.R.s. Died of wounds 1 O.R.	
"	"	2 p.m.	Transport proceeded to NOUPCEL (Sheet 70.E.W.5). Capt.& Q.M. KNOWLES in charge.	
"	"	—	M.Os. & sufficient R.A.M.C. personnel kept behind at BESME to form an ADVANCED DRESSING STATION. Wounded still received. Casualties evacuated to SOISSONS.	
"	"	—	Ambulances formed of DRESSING STATION every active throughout the afternoon.	
"	"	5.30 p.m.	Request for 2 squads of Stretcher Bearers received from M.O. 3rd Bn LOND RGT.	
"	"	6.00 p.m.	Party detailed for duty in accordance with this request.	
"	"	"	"Stand by" order cancelled	
"	"	"	Transport arrived at NAMPCEL (Sheet 70.E. W.5)	

WAR DIARY
INTELLIGENCE SUMMARY
(Erase heading not required.)

Army Form C. 2118.

Instructions regarding War Diaries and Intelligence Summaries are contained in F. S. Regs., Part II. and the Staff Manual respectively. Title pages will be prepared in manuscript.

Place	Date	Hour	Summary of Events and Information	Remarks and references to Appendices
SHEET 70.E. (A.6) BESME R.14.b.9.4.	25/3/18	6 p.m.	Capt. McGILLIVRAY reports from PIERRE AMANDE. "Heavy shelling with H.V. + H.E. and Gas Shells for an hour the northern & east side of this Village and Rest. a New Rely Post has been established at G.7.l.c.9.6 (Shot 78.D.av.) with 8 Bearers and same came down by weather Track on motor stretcher to this Rely Post to RP called Course Aqent is the Rely Post from AUTREVILLE. Heavy shelling after the ROND D'ORLEANS Rd & the field path to Courcy also for two hours this morning 9 is anticipated tonight. Too risky for Rags + Mulls to get along that way. Cars from P.A. are going through to Q.H.P.A.R. without difficulty. Every vehicle the first casualties Rem. German Barrage on the L.H.R.P. on Blanc Mont & south. as 7.49 P.M. this held MAIGNY ROUX and Regiment Barrer every track & are Rely Post on this line has been frequently uncommunicative from the outer R.A.P. only but on Cap. Aqy) stated his P.A.P.A. has come to a halt, its Ihave tel with his Walkers notified with Bearers carriage from Cose R.A.P. to Rest. via ROND DE LESPIRONS & ROND D'ORLEANS which have already arrived here by that route, satisfactorily, so that routes from all will are closed owing to enemy artillery mostly." Post locations Past. A.D.S. PIERRE AMANDE G.13.b.8.2. Adv R.P. B.26.c.l.l. Quarry Post H.1.c.7.4. Surgery R.D. G.11.c.9.6. Coast R.A.P. H.9.b.37. R.P.A.P. H.27.b.9.1. Car P.6. H.27.a.59	
" "	" "	6 p.m.	Weather fine. Becoming dull in late afternoon.	
" "	" "	8 p.m.	Late Report from Capt. McGILLIVRAY handed by D.R. The A.D.M.S. has just been out & asked me to note to you for two more large Cars to be hired. Col. te is saying "you have none enough to lose just a number of FRENCH Cars with to clear Cars P.A. to TROSLY LOIRE as well + low our to SOISSONS could I have as many Stretcher Bearers as you can the men I have to supply Regiments around here. Things here no test Report"	
" "	" "	10 p.m.	Reports that all our Wounded have been evacuated from Hospitals in SOISSONS to VASSENY – 12 Kilometres south of Soissons.	
			Capt. MASSEY, M.C. E., R.A.M.C. 8th Bn. LOND. Reg. Temp. attached for duty.	

14.

Army Form C. 2118.

WAR DIARY
or
INTELLIGENCE SUMMARY.
(Erase heading not required.)

Instructions regarding War Diaries and Intelligence Summaries are contained in F. S. Regs., Part II. and the Staff Manual respectively. Title pages will be prepared in manuscript.

Place	Date	Hour	Summary of Events and Information	Remarks and references to Appendices
SHEET 70E. P.H.Q. B/S/MG R.M.b.Q.C.	26/3/18	8.00 a.m.	Capt. McGillivray reports from PERREGMANDE. "The 2nd C in C is to SOISSONS with Wounded. Just received word that 6 of 67 from the Drive inform that they are Wounded. Am to expect 70 wounded French and 100 Germans in a VASSENS about 15 kilometers further on, suggest being evacuated at SOISSONS. It is impossible to get in Ch-over ROAD D'OREANS tonight over own carrying Party. Not likely need to evac to SOISSONS. QUARRY W.O.N.1. might even carry in the early of the Division without equipment. New Posts at G.11.A.96 – a cellar with accommodation. I have no accommodation for the Men. Except each find the "Abri" to live in the place is full of FRENCH and Rifle Troops."	
"	"	10 a.m.	Extract from Medical Arrangements by A.D.M.S. 5th Divn. – O.C. 11th Post Amb. with Personnel Casualties at NAMPCEL. These will be evacuated to FRENCH Hospital at COMPEIGNE. 2 Sections 7 Canad. Field Amb. will remain at COMPIEGNE to receive & forward to which ever hosp. is decided on return to him."	
"	"	Noon	Daily State. { Sick: Admit 1 Off. 9 O.Rs.; Evad 1 Off. 9 O.Rs. {Wounded: Admit 1 Off. 43 O.Rs. Evad 1 Off. 41 O.Rs. Disch. to duty 2 O.Rs.	
"	"	"	Capt McGillivray reports that R.M.O's positioned against removal of squads from QUARRY Central "R.A.P. @ 13th R.A.P. & as a result two squads were left at each of these. Our Squads now "allocated as follows: Lt R.P.R. 2 Squads; QUARRY Post, 2 Squads; SINCENY R.P., 1 Squad, Rt. R.A.P., "2 Squads; Can Bat., 3 Squads; Centre R.A.P., 2 Squads.	
"	"	5.25 p.m.	Commanding Officer issues instructions to O.C. A.D.S. PERREGMANDE as follows: Keep "well in touch with 174 and 175 Inf. Bde. "Be prepared to withdraw all your kits and these "immediately in the event of any of the Division falling back in the line of the Chavalu from "NAMPCEL to about M.8.b 57. (Sheet 70.D.) If you have more equipment at front of posts "than personnel can carry get rid of it. You will have to be up and loaded at M.O. "in the Lines and let them withdraw with M.O.s in charge and remain with them. See "that they are standing by fully loaded and equipped from now on. You are "authority here with Yorks Farm Cornel and equipment so long as BDe. H.Q. moves "I warn you that the withdrawal will likely have tonight. Above is confirmed"	

WAR DIARY or INTELLIGENCE SUMMARY

Army Form C. 2118.

Place	Date	Hour	Summary of Events and Information	Remarks and references to Appendices
SHEET 70E 26/3/18 C.H.Q. BESME R.W.D.9a.	26/3/18	5.30pm	Reply from A.D.M.S. 58 DIV. A.D.S. should be established at BESME. Reply from O.C., A.D.S., PIERREAMANDE: "O.K. am near staff. Capt. in 174 and 175 Bdes. and arranged withdrawal of same. The fresh wine takes place tomorrow night and I have arranged to have 1 Sgnd. at each R.A.P. with intercoms in case of casualties. Other medical equipment should get on board from there ready along with spare equipt. I will see Colonel Walters. Personal kit and baggage of R.P.s with the other medical equipment. Personnel light out and should be woven told by not start Carriers to the morning into and hope will then allow me to proceed when they can be withdrawn to BESME. I have practically decided at this port for my A.D.S. and equipment."	
"	"	5.30pm	55 Div. wired: "Withdraw the A.D.S. at PIERREAMANDE to BESME. Withdraw all medical equipment and personnel R.A.M.C. Leave one Squad of bearers with each R.M.O. to BESME. Withdrawal will take place at once. Arrange to be in touch with 174 Bde. Headquarters. The rear and of position from VAUXAINE (inclusive) eastwards to junction of AILETTE River with OISE and AISNE Canal. Thence southwards along Canal to N.8.b.6.7. 173 Bde will be on left. 174 Bde will hold length of Canal to F.28.c.7."	
"	"	7pm	Report received from Capt. McGILLRAY. "Things quiet; meantime nothing fresh to report. All wounded south clear. 9 O.R.s at A.D.S. Civilians are allowed to pass here."	
"	"		Weather during day fine	
SHEET 70E 27/3/18 C.H.Q. BESME R.W.D.9a	27/3/18	Noon	Daily State G: Sick 1 Off. 14 O.R.s Since 1 Off. 14 O.R.s. Admitted. Wounded 1 Off. admitted — decided to duty.	
"	"	12.30 pm	Commanding Officer issued order to O.C. A.D.S. PIERREAMANDE: "Take over as organised line of Headquarters your post at PIERREAMANDE from H.Q. 174 Inf Bde. Whatever job you get your orders and allotment of carry with you. They will be badly wanted."	
"	"		Reply from O.C. A.D.S. PIERREAMANDE: "Have seen to be sure of my men, they are at the moment working to insufficient protection of any sort here and the fact that this place is"	

16

Army Form C. 2118.

WAR DIARY
or
INTELLIGENCE SUMMARY.
(Erase heading not required.)

Instructions regarding War Diaries and Intelligence Summaries are contained in F. S. Regs., Part II, and the Staff Manual respectively. Title pages will be prepared in manuscript.

Place	Date	Hour	Summary of Events and Information	Remarks and references to Appendices
SHEET 70E (A.S.) IBESME R.14.b.9.4.	27/3/18	—	"Enemy 88's bursting beyond and upon church to long to your north, that also just one case of patrol and gun fire. Just near 1 H.E. that missed one of the Officers by about 10 yards. 174th Bde. are practically staying on in PIERREMANDE and am frantically without anything to carry on with and would like instructions."	
"	"	1.10pm	Reply from Commanding Officer :— "Your name is nothing do, nearest. I am sending your best some crackling of you wait of them. Also notify me if you want I will send up to fifty clean up. Move your cars out to place of safety along about Etreppioi and if the village requires it go on up to Bde. to try and find you a piece to occupy in not you must now and I will find you a place to occupy. If anything requires it get up to Bde. to know what you are going. If shelling gets you can come back to village."	
"	"	1.10pm	Commanding Officer communicates with H.Q. 174 INF. BDE :— "As there is practically no shelter for the M.O. and Aid Post in the village of PIERREMANDE I have moved him to our cellar a quarter of a mile down the road. Let me know if you need also his forwarder."	
"	"	3.30pm	General DU CHESNE, Commdg. Staff FRENCH Army visited the nigger in the ambulance.	
"	"	6.00pm	Hostile enemy activity in this time but several C.H.E. shells now fell near the Aid P. Splinters quite strong for about 10 minutes. Two killed and wounded of the 2/10th Bn., "LOND" Regt. reported. Stretcher squads turned out and cases quickly placed.	
"	"	7.00pm	Report from O.C. A.D.S. PIERREMANDE :— "Enemy shelling during night was heavy at intervals this afternoon. Your O.C. is trying to make arrangements to all man this place and that is not a shell-proof cave of any kind. Considering the fact that the BOCHE Balloons are all round having the cold at present and three hours to see the fact that make it safer to stay longer where I am and like the route."	

Weather during day: Fine

Army Form C. 2118.

WAR DIARY
or
INTELLIGENCE SUMMARY.
(Erase heading not required.)

Place	Date	Hour	Summary of Events and Information	Remarks and references to Appendices
SHEET 70 E. (H.Q.) BESSME R.14.b.94.	27/3/18	8.45am	Report from Capt. T.B. McKEE for O.C. A.D.S. PIERREAMANDE. Occurred reporting movement of St John's guide. "Things are quiet here at the moment but Lewisgun Posts are out to [....] get [....] in any information from BRIGADE."	
"	"		Normal conditions resumed at A.D.S. PIERREAMANDE	
SHEET 70 E. (H.Q.) BESSME R.14.b.94	28/3/18		Made a Reconnaissance by A.D.M.S. 18 DIV. No. 16. sent to cars up to face 29/3/18. "Nip" and Chief Secty. — Route of evacuation as follows — to ADVANCED DRESSING STATION PIERREAMANDE Left Sector — Walking Wounded and Stretcher cases to AD- VANCED DRESSING STATION BESSME. Headquarters 3/2 and H.C. FIELD AMBULANCE. From ADVANCED DRESSING STATION PIERREAMANDE and ADVANCED DRESSING STATION BESSME. Sick and Wounded will be evacuated by Motor Ambulance to MAIN DRESSING STATION "HAUTEBRAYE" on the MORSAIN-VIC SUR AISNE Road, the HQ of the 3/HC FIELD AMBULANCE From MAIN DRESSING STATION HAUTEBRAYE, Sick and Wounded will be sent by Motor Ambulance to H.O.E. B/51 at FONTENOY on the COMPIEGNE-SOISSONS road. At H.O.E. B/51 Sick and Wounded will not evacuated to the care of the FRENCH Medical Authorities	
"	"	Noon	Daily State: Sick, Admd. 16 ORs. Evacd. 16 ORs. Wounded: Admd. 19 ORs. Died 1 OR. Evacd. 18 ORs.	
SHEET 70 D. (A.D.S.) PIERREAMANDE G.26.b.52	"	2 p.m.	Capt A.C. WATKIN, relieves Capt N. GILLIVRAY of the charge of A.D.S. PIERREAMANDE. Capt N. GILLIVRAY returning to Headquarters by R.A.M.C. Box Wagon, wiz: Capt MASSEY MILES R.A.M.C. 8th Bn. LOND. REGT., Capt SEAL, returning to his unit.	
(H.Q.) BESSME R.14.b.94	"		Weather: fine.	
"	"		A.A.	
(H.Q.) BESSME R.14.b.94	29/3/18	10.45 a.m.	Enemy aeroplane brought down near Chateau Ribarolles from A/A by FRENCH Aviator. Machine destroyed by fire. pilot taken prisoner upon extricating himself from burning machine. Lieut Col. S.C.A. Watkins, O.C., attempted to render 1st aid assistance & get dressed by FRENCH	
"	"	Noon	Daily State: SICK. Admd. 2 Offs. 8 ORs. Evacd. 2 Offs. 8 ORs. WOUNDED: Admd. 1 N.C.Off. 5 ORs. Died 16 Duty 1 Off. 1 OR. Evacd. 4 ORs.	

WAR DIARY
INTELLIGENCE SUMMARY
(Erase heading not required.)

Army Form C. 2118.

18

Place	Date	Hour	Summary of Events and Information	Remarks and references to Appendices
A.D.S BESME R.14.b.9.4.	29/3/18	Noon	Wire received from M.O. 4/10 12th Bn. LOND. RGT. "It is considered that for the present my Aid Post at LA CAPELLE FARM (R.6.a.6.7) is too far from the line of Outposts. Dressing Aid Posts like VAILLY & BAC d'ABLINCOURT — 11/30 & 8.5 (Sheet 70 E.). In case of a retirement to the OISE and AISNE Canal Line, shall we move back to LA CAPELLE FARM (R.5.a.8.1)? During the 24 hours we have had 4 applications from my Stretcher Bearers. I suggest that 2 on the spot of R.B. + O.S. would be enough for evacuation from 11/30 & 8.5 would be by R.A.M.C. relay from them to R.B.O.S. (Bty.) as is the Our Advance Can Staff re arrange the plans?" Reply from Commanding Officer: "If necessary to retire, not opposed. You will keep the Aid Post with you and I warned A.D.S. PIERREMANDE. Suggest your own when you come down and they will send a Car as my order is to alter the present "Check to stretcher" The R.P. at R.10.X.8.8 and C.C. with your forward Plan. If no guns necessary "CANNOT be opened on the return to A.D.S. BESME. You have 4 cycles so far "R.B.T.O.S. Do you mean M.1.b.0.5? Capt. T.J. GILMORE, R.A.M.C. 7C/c reported for temporary duty	
"	"	2pm	Capt. WATKINS report from A.D.S. PIERREMANDE. "Situation quiet during last 24 hours." Weather Wet.	A
(A.D) BESME R.14.b.9.4.	30/3/18	2 am	Capt. WATKINS report from A.D.S. PIERREMANDE. "No Shelling during last 24 hours. Evacuated enemy Cpl. + other Cpl. Wounded 5; Sick 11. Invalid M.O. 12th Long RGT at BAC D'ABLINCOURT "yesterday and sent him a wheeled stretcher."	
"	"	"	Lieut. J.F. DOOLING and C. DUNAWAY of the M.O.R.C. U.S.A. became attached for temporary duty	
"	"	"	Capt. T.J. GILMORE proceeded to 1/4th SUFFOLK RGT for duty	
"	"	"	Weather. Wet — raining greatly all of day	

WAR DIARY
or
INTELLIGENCE SUMMARY.

(Erase heading not required.)

Army Form C. 2118.

Instructions regarding War Diaries and Intelligence Summaries are contained in F. S. Regs., Part II. and the Staff Manual respectively. Title pages will be prepared in manuscript.

Place	Date	Hour	Summary of Events and Information	Remarks and references to Appendices
H.Q. BESME R.14.d.9.4.	3/3/18	10 a.m.	O.C. No. 1 Coy. rang Officer i/c O.H.A.D.S. PIERREAMANDE: "I am afraid that at Rolf he picked enough for tomorrow morning. I want you to get in any stretchers, blankets & tripods etc. etc. at Rolf & that near the spaces from the post at Battalion H.Q." Retired to come down with the squad.	
		11.00 a.m.	Wire from Capt. WATKIN, Send 17,5 ton rick. "Can you spare me two men & one car in at possible. We RAP a proc. of removed this morning. We have only one car at front and have been had over the river at CHAUNY and the canal. We are about to have just had 2 more stretchers to collect from VINCENT and BIZZIES to ROUX. We had one of 4th AB.J Coll which I am sending with this who had gone down for a car for front. . If things quieten down I can send you the two side cars.	
"	"	2 p.m.	Wire from Capt. WATKIN. Rec'd 2 p.m. Rolf. "The Village wire at Rolf during the night. This Coy. has a most of casualties this morning. Owing to attack by Enemy between CHAUNY and VINCENT. Evacuated thro' 9th Fd. A.R. SICK. 7; BRITISH WOUNDED 25; GERMAN WOUNDED ... R.A.P. Thou. Evacuated from R.A.R. R.14.36.A (Not 70 D); Fus. Boy. 27.0.74 (Sheet 70.E.) 12th LOND. Regt. A.R. G.25.a.1.6 (Sheet 70 D); G. R.A.P. H.1.c.7.6 (Sheet 70 D); Car Post, H.27.a.5.9 (Sheet 70 D); H.Q and ADS, R.14.b.9.a (Sheet 70 E). PIERREGRANDE ADS, G.28. b.52 (Sheet 70 D) WAYLAND HAUTEBRAYE. Weather: Close in the morning, turning fair in the afternoon.	
"	"	6.30 p.m.	E.A. active in the sector; by L.C. driven off by AA.	

Army Form C. 2118.

WAR DIARY
or
INTELLIGENCE SUMMARY.
(Erase heading not required.)

Vol 16

CONFIDENTIAL

MEGICAL

WAR DIARY
of
2/2ND H.C.F.AMB. R.A.M.C.(T)

From: April 1st 1918 to April 30th 1918.

COMMITTEE FOR THE
MEDICAL HISTORY
Date —6 JUN 1918

2/2ND
HOME COUNTIES
FIELD AMBULANCE.
No. MC/145
Date 30/4/18

[signature]
Lt Col. R.A.M.C.(T) O.C.
2/2ND H. C. FLD. AMB.

Army Form C. 2118.

WAR DIARY
or
INTELLIGENCE SUMMARY.
(Erase heading not required.)

Instructions regarding War Diaries and Intelligence Summaries are contained in F. S. Regs., Part II. and the Staff Manual respectively. Title pages will be prepared in manuscript.

Place	Date	Hour	Summary of Events and Information	Remarks and references to Appendices
SHEET 70d (H.Q.) BESME R.II.b.9.4.	1/4/18	10 a.m.	Enemy shells continued to fall in the vicinity. 2 about every half hour + one of the morning. Enemy aeroplanes also came over at intervals. Ground kept wires damaged greatly by A.A.	
"	"	12.15 p.m.	17th Bn. Warwicks Regt. B.M.H./17/4 reports at 3/3/918 present "T/6, 17th Infantry Brigade will be relieved on tonight 1st and 2nd by the 215 Trench Infantry Regt. Formation will remain on the 3 inst. after relief arrange for handing out care as simple [?] out through information."	
"	"	3 p.m.	Cas: Wounds reports from A.D.S. Pearce A.D.S. G.28.b.52 - Sheet 70.D. recent "The Villy" was brought again in enemy by firing of Division. Casualties during last 24 hours as follows:-- "Sick - 6. BRITISH WOUNDED Off. 3. O.R. 9. GERMAN WOUNDED 2." Located. RUS A.R.P., H.27.b.91 (Sheet 75.D.). Rus. 87. R.A.P. L.27.b.74 (70.E.) 1/24 Bn. LOND. R.M.R.A.P. G.25.a.14 (70.D.) L.4 R.A.R.H.C.74 (70.D.) Cas. Rel. H.27.a.59 (7.D.) Waynewman Hauterserre.	
"	"	4 p.m. 5 p.m.	Shelling of Enemy emplacement by Artillery of shells dropping in a quiet. E.A. [?] No casualties. Weather fine but clear during the day.	
"	"		Remainder of day was from of incident - Army Listing through.	
(H.Q.) BESME R.II.b.9.4.	2/4/18	Noon.	A few shells fell on [?] throughout the morning.	
			Operation Order No. 37. d/d 31/3/918 by A.D.M.S. 5.0 Div. issued. Extract: "1. The (H.Q.) of the 1/I and 55 Field Division [?] nights of 1/2 and 2/3 April 1918. (2) The 1/I Field Ambulance (less detachment of 16 O.R. and 2 G.S. Wagons Division of 1st March details) & hereby be arranged since Officer Commanding. Exist Ambulance as above. (3.) The Division or such force may be [?] [?] the SALEUX area (S.W. of AMIENS) by train. (4) Sick O.R. who will normally be evacuated beyond the grouping.	

(A7839) Wt. W6oz/M1671 500,000 4/17 Sch. 52a. Forms/C/2118/14 D.D. & L. London, E.C.

WAR DIARY
INTELLIGENCE SUMMARY.

Place	Date	Hour	Summary of Events and Information	Remarks and references to Appendices
Short T.B (AGS) BFSHE R.14.b.9.6	2/4/18	Noon	Orders received and copies of the same will be received by Officers Commanding Field Ambulances sent from G.O.C. Brigade to march as ordered. 42nd at 6.15 pm - sick Feb 17th Belgian Corps N Nancy. 4a & E.O. at motor lorry to Nancy at 7-30 am.	
"	"	"	"Lord Kitchener spent the day on a road reconnaissance of the route from Epinay to Chaumont." A.D.M.S. of Saieux.	
"	"	3 am	Lt. C. Field Ambulance "No.5" reporting Officers 6th DRAs of Saieux. Ordered to O.O.37 reads "Ref para 5) For Saieux to Isaud 5th instant."	
"	"	"	"Admin Ordnance" Reading 2 Instruction No.2 to accompany 58th Division Order No.101 dd 11/4/18, and "Administrative Arrangements issued in connection with 58th Division Order No.101 dd 11/4/18." received.	
"	"	"	Capt A. Watkins reports from own recent - The Village has been shelled several times ... reports leaving 8.15 pm. The Bearer posts in R.R.A.C. and R.A. Relay Post reports... the troops moved off and at 1 pm to march to HAUTESRAYE. Evacuation during Cat II Sitting - SICK, O.R. 12; BRITISH WOUNDED O.R. 9. FRENCH Injured and Civilians injured - Nil.	
"	"	"	Camp Commandant instruction and placing...	
"	"	7 pm	Several shells fired in field southwest of CHQ, about 150 yards south of CHQ, carrying by E.A.	
"	"	"	Weather Fine and clear	
"	"	11 pm	and north-east Nine Enemy shells this time from enemy CHQ. Personnel moved out and to woodedge on to west in out house at CHQ.	
"	"	Night	Plans formed and lift forward to Wagon lines at HAUTEBRAYE.	
(h.q.) BERRY R.14.b.9 6	3/4/18	6 am	C/O dressing at time of letter bombing at the General and nearly fell in the road by the German Commandant. Orders planning to go north. Front failure or on the ground shewn the intensity - No casualties.	

Seen this made for much.
Feel as be made for much.

WAR DIARY
INTELLIGENCE SUMMARY

(Erase heading not required.)

Army Form C. 2118.

Instructions regarding War Diaries and Intelligence Summaries are contained in F. S. Regs., Part II. and the Staff Manual respectively. Title pages will be prepared in manuscript.

Place	Date	Hour	Summary of Events and Information	Remarks and references to Appendices
Start 10.5 (H·Q) BESME RINE Qu.	3/4/18	12.30am	Remainder of R.A.M.C. personnel & Gen. Baulie in the Staff at A.D.S. PIERREAMANDE and in the Mess party at H.Q. left for HAUTEBRAYE by train a March Cpt PALMER R.S. in charge of Rear party	
"	"	10.30am	Motor Ambulance left for HAUTEBRAYE with H.Q. details	
HAUTEBRAYE	"	11.30am	Sub. Cars arrived. Surgical taken over from 2/3rd N&L Amb. soon after arrival	
"	"	2.30pm	A few wounded from the Line received. Rest. Unit harassed. Marching portion arrived	
"	"	3.30pm	Bearer party has arrived	
"	"	5pm	Capt A.C. WATKIN L. Staff & A.D.S. PIERREAMANDE reported arrival. Some of Rear party also arrived (?)	
"	"		Weather Fine	
"	"	10pm	173 Inf. BDE. Administrative instructions No.9 of 3/4/18 received.	
HAUTEBRAYE	4/4/18	7.30am	173 Inf BDE. Order No.6 received containing amendments to March Table	
"	"	7pm	Unit received O/Ps. marching in rear of 173 BDE.	
"	"	11pm	Unit received & occupied billets for the night	
AMBLENY	5/4/18	12.30am	March to Entraining Station begun as per instruction laid down in 173 BDE Order No.7, of 5/4/18. Destination for Entraining St PIERRE AIGLE.	
ST PIERRE AIGLE	"	2.30pm	Unit halted and then began march to VILLERS COTTERETS Station for entraining in accordance with Programme as laid down in 173 BDE Order No. 8 of 5/4/18	
"	"	7.30pm		
VILLERS COTTERETS	6/4/18	12.30 a.m.	Unit arrived at Entraining Station after very trying march.	
"	"	3.30 a.m.	Entrainment completed.	
"	"	4.00 a.m.	Journey to new Station begun	

WAR DIARY / INTELLIGENCE SUMMARY

Army Form C. 2118.

Instructions regarding War Diaries and Intelligence Summaries are contained in F. S. Regs., Part II. and the Staff Manual respectively. Title pages will be prepared in manuscript.

(Erase heading not required.)

Place	Date	Hour	Summary of Events and Information	Remarks and references to Appendices
CORBIE	6/4/18	11.30am	Unit arrived at Infantry School	
"	"	1.30pm	March to new School commenced	
ECOLE DES JEUNE FILLES FAUBOURG DU HEM, AMIENS	"	3.30pm	Unit arrived at new H.Q.	
"	"		1st Lieut. R.C. EATON, M.C.R.C. U.S.A. reported for duty	
"	"		D.M.S. 4th Army Circ. Memo No. 63 received	
"	7/4/18		Circular CH/B4/63 E.F. of 56th D.N.R. Staff re serving officers held as Units	
"	"	5pm	Detachment from 4th of Fr. Amis (20 O.R.) returned to their Unit	
"	"		E.A. paid programme which during the afternoon	
"	8/4/18	5pm	19 O.R. CRAMC, HT & HMT., loan party returned to Unit having been detached	
"	"		as some type of Rest Camps Barracks and deserted	
"	"	4.30pm	The S.C. & S.B.O. left for evening to visit sites of proposed H.Q. to be erected and struck by bombs in rear of H.Q. building front over B.H.D. in presence of Commanding Officers & Officers Quarters and also H.Q. of the Sister Hosps. Commanding Officers complied with command several ones a hospital firing to proceed. The Officers casualty Regiment	
"	"	4.30pm	Personal evacuated and marched to new H.Q.	
ECOLE DES FILLES FRONTIERES	"	5.30pm	New Headquarters established	
" " " "	"	-	Meml. Am. No. 11 (3 R.N.) D.M.S. French Army Circ. Memo No. 64, Med Arr. French Army Cir. No. 13, Med. Arr. III Corps No. 29, acc. 21-7, 14/18 recd.	

Army Form C. 2118.

WAR DIARY
or
INTELLIGENCE SUMMARY.
(Erase heading not required.)

Instructions regarding War Diaries and Intelligence Summaries are contained in F. S. Regs., Part II. and the Staff Manual respectively. Title pages will be prepared in manuscript.

Place	Date	Hour	Summary of Events and Information	Remarks and references to Appendices
ECOLE DES FILLES, MONTIÈRE	9/4/18	—	Route of Evacuation sent O.O. No. 38, A.D.M.S, 58-Div dy. 8/4/18. read	
" "	"	—	1 O.R. Reinforcement reported.	
" "	10/4/18	—	Nothing to report	
" "	11/4/18	—	Nothing to report	
" "	12/4/18	—	10/Lieut C.R.LONG returned to the Unit and retaken on the strength	
" "	13/4/18	—	Nothing to report	
" "	14/4/18	—	58th Div. Med.Arr. No.18 dy.13/4/18, received.	
" "	"	3 p.m.	7 O.Rs. reported as Reinforcements. 27 O.Rs. 23rd A.T.Coy. attached for duty etc.	
" "	"	—	A few H.E. shells dropped in the vicinity near the Railway line, passing H.Q.	
" "	15/4/18	2 p.m.	Personnel moved & assigned away from Abbeville-Corbie on account of shelling. Unit Evacuated for the night, returning to Headquarters in the morning.	
" "	15/4/18	2.30 p.m.	Motor-ambulance for march to LONGPRÉS. Carrying party to form Dressing Station	
LONGPRÉS	"	8.00 p.m.	Unit arrived at new Station. Camp site being selected near Canal — & within short distance of the Village. One Section marched on to meet Village — ARGŒUVRES — & ten up Château there	
" "	"	11 p.m.	Shells opened fired onto the vicinity of H.Q., one Coy occupied by personnel being ripped to base of Palace. Personnel turned out & marched to ARGŒUVRES to take shelter of Sunken road nearby Château.	
ARGŒUVRES	16/4/18	10 a.m.	Headquarters were opened in wood in rear of CHATEAU.	

WAR DIARY / INTELLIGENCE SUMMARY

Army Form C. 2118.

Place	Date	Hour	Summary of Events and Information	Remarks and references to Appendices
ARGOEUVRES	17/4/18	—	Nothing to Report	
"	18/4/18	7.30 am	2 N.C.O's & 80 Bearers (20 guard) sent for duty with 2/1st N.B.F.Amb. I.C. LONGEAU	
"	"	—	Capt. H.S. PALMER R.A.M.C. & 1st O/C R.C. EATON M.O.R.C. U.S.A. to 1/1st N.B.F.Amb. attached for temporary duty with 2/1st N.B.F.Amb.	
"	"	—	Received Notification of Award of Military Medal for Gallantry in Action to Pte C.A. 42602 Sgt Q.M. "B3ALER" 352587 Pte W. LAWSON 475535 Pte M.A.W. RAINER 475590 Pte. S.T. EDDINGONOUGH. Auth. III C.R.O. No. 206 of 13/4/18 & D.R.O. 1000 of 16/4/18.	
"	19/4/18	2 pm	15 O.R's of 2/1st N.B.F.Amb who were attached, detached to their own Unit.	
"	20/4/18	—	1st Lieut. C.R. LONG M.O.R.C. U.S.A. Recalled in action	
"	21/4/18	—	Pte. G. CHABALLER R.A.M.C. reported sick	
"	22/4/18	—	Nothing to report	
"	23/4/18	—	1 O.R. R.A.M.C. Reinforcement	
"	24/4/18	—	Casualties to Unit — 3 O.R's R.A.M.C. personnel wounded, 1 returning to duty	
"	25/4/18	—	12 O.R's of 2/1st N.B.F.Amb — temporary attached to Unit — returned to their own Unit.	
"	"	—	Capt. H.S. PALMER reported severely wounded. Died later in the day from wounds.	
"	26/4/18	2 pm	Capt. G.M. McGILLIVRAY and Capt. T.B. McKEE and 1 Tent Sub-Division temporary attached to 173 INF. BDE. during change of Station.	
"	27/4/18	Noon	1st Lieut. R.C. EATON M.O.R.C. U.S.A. returned from detached duty with 2/1st N.B.F. Amb.	
"	"	"	Bearers C.B. & C of 1/1st N.B.F. Amb. arrived in relays during the night and early morning	

Army Form C. 2118.

WAR DIARY
INTELLIGENCE SUMMARY

Instructions regarding War Diaries and Intelligence Summaries are contained in F. S. Regs., Part II. and the Staff Manual respectively. Title pages will be prepared in manuscript.

Place	Date	Hour	Summary of Events and Information	Remarks and references to Appendices
AROEUVRES	27/4/18	—	Location of 2/2nd H.C.F.Amb. (from 28th inst) to be VAUCHELLES-les-QUESNOY. (Vide A.D.M.S. 58 Div. O.O. No 41 of 27/4/18).	
(ABBEVILLE) VAUCHELLES les QUESNOY	28/4/18	8.15 a.m.	Unit paraded for March to New Station, moving off about 9 A.M. 30 mile march.	
"	"	6.00 p.m.	Unit arrived at New Station.	
"	29/4/18	Noon	1st/Lieut R.C.EATON, M.O.R.C. U.S.A. departed admitted to Field Ambulance Hospital its previous day as a Battle Casualty, there being pronounced Blistro on legs as a result of a recent gas poisoning.	
"	"	—	Hospital preparations in Village for the reception of patients.	
"	"	5.30 p.m.	Medical Arrangements No.19 58th DIV. for BUIGNY Area received: Extract — from 58 Field Ambulance, M.O.s promptly from Infantry are at 174 INF. BDE. and Artillery "Only case likely to be fit within one week due to SICKNESS "Sick will be evacuated ... from 1st, 2nd & 3rd Amb. to No.12 C.C.S. LONGPRÉ, or No.2 Stationary Hospital Rue ABBEVILLE."	
"	"	8.20 p.m.	Capt. E. McGILVRAY returned unfit that Sub Division — Ord Capt. T.B. McKEE and small Rear Party from NEUILLY L'HOPITAL, after duty with 173 BDE.	
"	30/4/18	—	G.S. I. 524/1 from A.B.E. CATOR, Maj. Gen. Comndg 58th (LOND.) Div. of 28/4/18, published that Oriental work this evening: "the Rear Guard which tried to bring up the Division from the OISE to SOMME, the BUIGNY Area has been in front from the commencing field." "Never, notwithstanding this long period of action and fighting the Division has more than upheld its old fighting reputation Break after break it did day by day all ranks to FRENCH Villa— Comng. wore Rear Regiments told me on the five Big Chief gallantry they had showed in the Division. The G.O.C. French Army let know I envy

WAR DIARY
INTELLIGENCE SUMMARY.
(Erase heading not required.)

Army Form C. 2118.

Instructions regarding War Diaries and Intelligence Summaries are contained in F. S. Regs., Part II, and the Staff Manual respectively. Title pages will be prepared in manuscript.

Place	Date	Hour	Summary of Events and Information	Remarks and references to Appendices
(ABBEVILLE) VAUCHELLES les QUESNOY	30/4/18		"The following of congratulations to all Ranks has been sent by the Army Commander to the G.O.C. of the Division:— "AMIENS. During the two weeks fighting on the Division has been sent of no less than three different GERMAN Divisions in front of them, and the greatest difficulties that your rate and opportunity of relieving are completely relieved. You have had all the fighting and no period of rest in the fighting line. "Advances and changes in the line by tired troops are always difficult, but in spite of this the Divn. for the last ten days has held a wide front. "Nearly every inch of ground taken by the enemy has been retaken by counter attack. "The Division must feel a great satisfaction in the knowledge that they are now being relieved after a very successful and gallant [?]. During the time that the Division has been engaged in the AMIENS battle the Americans are coming in to France but it will soon take to replace our men in the line with men more than we have lost. "During our period of rest I want to have no training in the afternoon, but I wish every man to remember that he must be wont to do it when needed. "Trying to practice a great deal of attention must be paid to the most important points. The importance of fire effect on the Enemy in the defensive until that of manoeuvre & fire can be taught on the edge of a wood. The attack on the front VILLERS BRETONNEUX HANGARD Wood taught us on the 24/25 Ap. as being repeated and I wish you to impress upon all Ranks the necessity of defence, so limited to preach the effect of fire on enemy and instil with the confidence that will he equal to the necessary. Once again I congratulate all ranks of the 18th Division who have done so in the Great battle."	

Army Form C. 2118.

CONFIDENTIAL.

MEDICAL
VOL 16
40/3783.

WAR DIARY
or
INTELLIGENCE SUMMARY.
(Erase heading not required.)

Instructions regarding War Diaries and Intelligence Summaries are contained in F. S. Regs., Part II. and the Staff Manual respectively. Title pages will be prepared in manuscript.

Place	Date	Hour	Summary of Events and Information	Remarks and references to Appendices

WAR DIARY
of
2/2ⁿᵈ H.C.F. AMB. R.A.M.C.(T)
From: 1/5/1918 — To: 31/5/18

2/2ND
HOME COUNTIES
FIELD AMBULANCE.
1/6/18

[signature]
Lt. Col. R.A.M.C.(T) O.O.
2/2ND H. C. FLD. AMB.

COMMITTEE FOR THE
MEDICAL HISTORY OF THE WAR
Date 9 JUL 1918

WAR DIARY
INTELLIGENCE SUMMARY.
(Erase heading not required.)

Army Form C. 2118.

Instructions regarding War Diaries and Intelligence Summaries are contained in F. S. Regs., Part II. and the Staff Manual respectively. Title pages will be prepared in manuscript.

Place	Date	Hour	Summary of Events and Information	Remarks and references to Appendices
VAUCHELLES les QUESNOY (ABBEVILLE)	1/5/18	—	1st/Lieut. R.C. EATON, M.O.R.C., U.S.A., discharges to duty having been evacuated "Gassed" (Clinton) Wounded. 28/4/18.	
"	"	—	Sick of 174 BDE. collected.	
"	2/5/18	—	Posted for duty under Orders: "ROYAL ARMY MEDICAL CORPS – the 14/mentioned to be O/C by Major "whilst in Command Section, Field Ambulance. 4 of January 1918 – Capt A.C. WATKIN. "3/2/H.C.F.AM.G."	
"	"	—	Sick of 174 BDE. collected.	
"	3/5/18.	—	One O.R. posted as a casualty from Mounted Gas Poisoning sustained 29/4/18.	
"	"	—	Sick of 174 BDE. collected.	
"	4/5/18.	11:30am	A.D.M.S. MH.51.24/4/5/18 forwarding 58th Div. G.S. 1538 received was to the effect that as a Radio error some confusion in the near future on the left of the FOURTH ARMY front had been decided that the III Corps should take over the left portion of the AUSTRALIAN CORPS front opposite ALBERT on the 6 of May. The 58th DIVISION to be in reserve. The move forward from the present Area to be completed by May 11th. Transport to move the personnel.	
"	"	—	day ... On the night of 6/7th May over the front, the 92 & H.C.F. AMB. to be in the line.	
"	"	7:35pm	A.D.M.S. issues further instructions issue M.H.51. to the effect that FIELD AMBULANCES will move with BRIGADE Groups.	
"	"	9:15pm	174 INF. BDE. issue for issue of Transport by rail (A.24/379) received. Instructions for Unit to march with BRIGADE Group to staging Area at BOURDON on the 5th inst. received.	
"	"	—	Sick of 174 BDE. collected.	
"	5/5/18.	12.30 a.m.	Orders received from 174 INF. BDE. (S.C.76O) to send advance Party of 1 Off & 2 O.R. to BDE. H.Q. at 8 a.m. to proceed to new Area.	
"	"	7:30am	Advance Party left.	
"	"	8:00am	Lieut. R.C. EATON, M.O.R.C., U.S.A. detailed for temporary duty with 4th Bn. LOND. REGT.	
"	"	9:00am	One N.C.O. left to arrange billets for transport for the night 5-6/6/18.	

Army Form C. 2118.

WAR DIARY
of
INTELLIGENCE SUMMARY.
(Erase heading not required.)

Instructions regarding War Diaries and Intelligence Summaries are contained in F. S. Regs., Part II. and the Staff Manual respectively. Title pages will be prepared in manuscript.

Place	Date	Hour	Summary of Events and Information	Remarks and references to Appendices
VAUCHELLES les QUESNOY (ABBEVILLE)	5/5/18	9.45 a.m.	Transport of Unit moved off for march to staging area at BOURDON	
" "	"	1.45 p.m.	Administrative Instructions to 58th DIV. O.O. No. 11, with Bde Programme received	
" "	"	7.45 p.m	17th INF. BDE. Order No 82 with March T366 & Administrative Instructions received	
" "	6/5/18	8.30 a.m.	Dismounted portion of Unit moved off to Embussing Point on ABBEVILLE - ST. RIQUIER Road, at junction of Road leading to NEUF MOULIN. M.T. Ambulances journeyed over.	
(Sheet 57.D.) T.28.a.6.9	"	8 p.m.	Dismounted portion of Unit reached new Billeting Area. Transport also arriving. Billets instained in MIRVAUX and some delay occasioned. Camp site selected in Wood on top of Hill at T.28.a.6.9 (Sheet 57.D.) Tents pitched.	
" "	"	11 p.m.	III Corps Medical Arrangements No. 31 received	
" "	7/5/18	9 a.m.	Headquarters opened on new Site	
" "	8/5/18	"	Medical Arrangements to 58th DIV. No. 20, of 7/5/18 received.	
" "	"	"	A.D.M.S. 58th DIV. M.4479, of 7/5/18, concerning Medical Arrangements in the entirely of reserve Enemy attack gaining a temporary foregrant in the forward zone	
" "	9/5/18	"	Nothing to report.	
" "	10/5/18	"	Lieut. R.G. EATON M.O.R.C. U.S.A. returned to the Unit.	
" "	11/5/18	"	3 O.R's evacuated to Hospital	
" "	12/5/18	"	Amenda No. 1 to Medical Arrangements, 58 DIV. No. 20, received	
" "	13/5/18	"	One N.C.O sent to 18th Class III Corps Gas School to attend for instruction	

WAR DIARY
INTELLIGENCE SUMMARY

Army Form C. 2118.

Place	Date	Hour	Summary of Events and Information	Remarks and references to Appendices
(Sheet 57 D) (T28.a.6.9)	14/5/18	Noon	A.D.M.S. 58 DIV. M.453S. of 13/5/18, forwarding diagram of R.A.P's of Brigades for the 58th Div on taking over the left sector of the VIII Corps Front.	
" "	15/5/18	6 p.m.	Capt. W.B. TANNAHILL R.A.M.C.(T.C) reported & taken on strength.	
" "	"	"	1 O.R. (Reinforcement) also taken on strength.	
" "	16/5/18	9.00 a.m.	Party of personnel under Major A.C. WATKIN marched off to take over ADVANCED COLLECTING POST, HENENCOURT, and Medical Bn— two Non Headquarters at WARLOY. Remainder of personnel transferred to C.B.D. & other Camps, moving later with rest of transport to Wagon Lines situated in ST. GRATIEN WOOD.	
GRANDE RUE DE SOMMIER WARLOY (C.22.c.3.3)	"	1.00 p.m.	New Headquarters taken over from 6th LOND F.D. AMB. Working party from Field Ambulance 147th DIV (24 O.Rs) obtained for duty with incoming Unit. 23 O.Rs of the 2/3rd L.C.F.AMB who had been working with out-going Unit, also renewed for duty.	
" "	"	7.00 p.m.	Major WATKIN, as O.C. ADVANCED COLLECTING POST reports to H.Q. taking over from 6th LOND. F.D. AMB. during the afternoon and the relieving of squads at Relay Posts. Squads at R.A.P.s to be relieved after dark.	
" "	"	"	Capt. W.B. TANNAHILL appointed to M.D.S. VADENCOURT — D.A.H., following G.O. Proceedings.	
" "	"	"	SCHEME FOR WORKING PARTIES in New Area — Work at 3 New Relay Posts. Distant & forward Unit to be taken over. Work to be carried on day and night. Each Relay Post to be ready with 20 bodies. 30 bodies will be carried into Henencourt to ADVANCED COLLECTING POST HENENCOURT (V27.d.29). Orderlies 15 stretcher bearers. Ch: CHATEAU Yard considered most suitable for a Dressing Station on account of its cartilage and its proximity to the Warloy Road, to be occupied accordingly. This is intended primarily to serve as the Collecting area into	

WAR DIARY
INTELLIGENCE SUMMARY

Army Form C. 2118.

Place	Date	Hour	Summary of Events and Information	Remarks and references to Appendices
Sheet 57.D. U.24.c.3.3	16/5/18	—	Barn giving access to the Road and the other into a new Officers Dug-out. When this is constructed works to be fixed up so that cellar will accommodate 20 or rather more. The new Officers Dug-out is to be made to accommodate 8 Officers & be situated within the walls of the Barn so that there will give maximum protection. The Dug-out is to be fairly constructed of top covering of R.S.J's (6"x6") a layer of corrugated iron, a double layer of sand-bags, R.S.J.'s 2 feet apart then above this top Dug-out to be covered with pees to bring level of top of Dug-out to ground. This is to be supported by Dug-out top & to the extent to be similar to the Railhead Dug-outs.	
" " "	17/5/18	—	Large numbers of sick from units in vicinity attended Dressing Room at H.Q. 63 O.R.b 3rd H.C.F.A.M.S. Working Party for A/C.P. & Line Construction attached for this purpose. Work proceeded with much expedition of R.E's (Capt) Shaft Work & cutting Emergency Entrance to Cellar. General R.R. Wilson in near the advance to be cut through the m.t.g.	
" " "	"	4 p.m	Maj. Watkins reports from A.C.P. Henencourt. "A great deal of shelling near to the Dressing Station today. Evacuations are so far quiet." Wounded — O.R. 3. Sick — Off 1. O.R. 16.	
" " "	18/5/18	Noon	Large Sick Parade. Capt. Q.W.M. Andrew reports taken on strength.	
" " "	"	—	Sandbagging exterior wall of Cellar at H.Q. commenced.	
" " "	"	4 p.m	Maj. Watkins reports from A.C.B. "Not much shelling round here today. Evacuations are from yesterday: Wounded O.R.6. Sick O.R.15. I have arranged for all relief of Work to Tonight to take place at night."	
" " "	"	—	Work at H.Q. A.C.P. & at R.P.'s proceeded with away day. A large Red Cross to be painted in red bricks with background of chalk to be laid within garden in — immediately in rear of H.Q. Work for this commenced.	
" " "	19/5/18	Noon	Usual Sick Parade at H.Q. Dressing Room. 63 O.R. & 2 H.C.F.A.M.S. reported for duty as Working Party & Carrying Party & properly attached for this purpose.	
" " "	"	4/5 p.m	Maj. Watkins report from A.C.P. "Evacuations since 4 pm yesterday — Wounded — O.R. 39, Sick —	

Army Form C. 2118.

WAR DIARY
of
INTELLIGENCE SUMMARY.
(Erase heading not required.)

Instructions regarding War Diaries and Intelligence Summaries are contained in F. S. Regs., Part II. and the Staff Manual respectively. Title pages will be prepared in manuscript.

Place	Date	Hour	Summary of Events and Information	Remarks and references to Appendices
(Sheet 57 D.) U26.c.3.3.	19/5/18	8 p.m.	Evacuation through A.C.P. since 4 p.m. — Sick — O.R. 8.	
" "	"	—	Work at H.Q., A.C.P. & R.Ps. proceeded with throughout the day.	
" "	20/5/18	8 a.m.	Evacuation through A.C.P. since 8 p.m. 19/5/18. Wounded — O.R. 8; Sick, Off. 1, O.R. 8.	
" "	"	—	Large sick parade from units in District attended Dressing Room, H.Q.	
" "	"	—	Work according to scheme continued at A.C.P. & R.Ps. during the day. Old disused well clothed with debris, found in garden of H.Q.: cleaned out & disinfected. Small bomb proof protection for same been under of H.Q. carried out. Many of found new were felling in ...	
" "	"	8 p.m.	Evacuation through A.C.P. for 12 hrs.: Wounded — O.R. 7 (returned to unit); Sick — Off. 1, O.R. 9.	
" "	21/5/18	8 a.m.	Evacuation through A.C.P. for previous 12 hrs. — Wounded — Off. 3, O.R. 11; Sick — O.R. 8.	
" "	"	—	Large sick parade at H.Q.	
" "	"	2 a.m.	23 O.Rs. 2/1 H.C.F.AMB. — the first Working Party relieved & returned to Unit.	
" "	"	—	Work carried on as usual.	
" "	"	8 p.m.	Evacuation through A.C.P. for previous 12 hrs. — Wounded — O.R. 13 (returned to unit); Sick — O.R. 10 (?).	
" "	22/5/18	8 a.m.	Evacuation through A.C.P. HENENCOURT for previous 12 hrs. — Wounded — Off. 1, O.R. 11; Sick — O.R. 1. (I.C.R. 9/2 H.C.F.AMB. — "G.S.W." (Sh.Cd.) Gal. E., — returned to Unit.) Usual sick parade at H.R.	
" "	"	Note.	Capt. F.A. DICK attached for temporary duty from 9/H.C.F.AMB.	
" "	"	—	Working arrangements as usual.	
" "	"	8 p.m.	Evacuation through A.C.P. for previous 12 hrs. Wounded — O.R. 8; Sick — O.R. 7. Report on Situation: "Quiet during the day. Shells for four minutes in vicinity of A.C.P. this evening."	
" "	"	"	Major McGULLIVRAY relieved Major WATKIN of 2/1/5/18 acting Lt. Col. allamm & S.O. for Collecting Post at HENENCOURT. Rec. Bn received at K21.d.4.9 and K26.a.9.2 (57.D).	
" "	"	"	A.D.M.S. M.L623 forwarding Divisional arrangements for backing of gas cases received.	
" "	23/5/18	8 a.m.	Evacuation through A.C.P. for previous 12 hrs.: Wounded — O.R. 12, Sick — O.R. 11.	

WAR DIARY or INTELLIGENCE SUMMARY.

(Erase heading not required.)

Army Form C. 2118.

Instructions regarding War Diaries and Intelligence Summaries are contained in F. S. Regs., Part II. and the Staff Manual respectively. Title pages will be prepared in manuscript.

Place	Date	Hour	Summary of Events and Information	Remarks and references to Appendices
(Sheet 57.D) U.24.c.3.3.	23/5/18	—	Usual sick parade at H.Q.	
" "	"	—	Work on Dug Outs started at H.Q. camp.	
" "	"	8 p.m.	Evacuation through A.C.P. for previous 12 hrs.: Wounded — Off. 1; O.R. 5; Sick — O.R. 7.	
" "	24/5/18	8 a.m.	Evacuations through R.A.C.P. for previous 12 hrs.: Wounded — O.R. 6; Sick — O.R. 6. Situation: "Normal".	17
" "	"	—	Capt. R.S. CLARKE, R.A.M.C. taken on the strength.	
" "	"	—	Work carried on around camp by day. Usual sick parade at H.Q.	
" "	"	8 p.m.	Evacuation for previous 12 hrs. through A.C.P.: Wounded — O.R. 6; Sick — Off. 1; O.R. 15. Situation "Normal". 7 O.R. 2/1 H.C.F.Amb. "Gassed" — returned to H.Q.	17
" "	25/5/18	8 a.m.	Evacuations through A.C.P. for previous 12 hrs.: Wounded — O.R. 10; Sick — Off. 1; O.R. 8. Situation: "Normal".	
" "	"	—	Working parties employed as usual. Usual sick parade at H.Q.	
" "	"	8 p.m.	Evacuation through A.C.P. for previous 12 hrs.: Wounded — O.R. 2; Sick — O.R. 15. Situation "Normal".	17
" "	26/5/18	8 a.m.	Evacuations through A.C.P. for previous 12 hrs.: Wounded — Off. 2; O.R. 9; Sick — O.R. 9.	
" "	"	—	Maj. A.C. WATKIN, F.A.M.C. admitted sick to "Spanja".	
" "	"	7 p.m.	58 O.R. 2/1st H.C.F.AMB. (Working Party) returned to Unit. Work carried on Dug outs nearing completion.	
" "	"	8 p.m.	Usual sick parade at H.Q. from Units in vicinity. Evacuation through A.C.P. for previous 12 hrs.: Wounded — O.R. 2; Sick — O.R. 18. Report on Situation: "Normal".	17
" "	27/5/18	8 a.m.	Evacuations through A.C.P. for previous 12 hrs.: Wounded — O.R. 6; Sick — O.R. 9.	
" "	"	—	11 O.R. 7/1st H.C.F.AMB. (Remainder of Working Party) returned to Unit. New Dug outs completed & ready for use.	
" "	"	—	Usual sick parade at H.Q.	
" "	"	Noon	Capt. N. GRAHAM, R.A.M.C. taken on strength.	
" "	"	—	50 O.R. 2/5 H.C.F.Amb. (Burying Party) reported to Unit.	
" "	"	—	Capt. T.B. McKEE relieved Capt. McGILVRAY at A.C.P.	
" "	"	8 p.m.	Evacuation through A.C.P. for previous 12 hrs.: Wounded — O.R. 4; Sick — O.R. 18. Situation: "Normal".	17

WAR DIARY
or
INTELLIGENCE SUMMARY.
(Erase heading not required.)

Army Form C. 2118.

Place	Date	Hour	Summary of Events and Information	Remarks and references to Appendices
Sheet 57D. U.24.c.3.3	28/5/18	—	Usual sick parade at H.Q. Working Party also employed at H.Q.	
" "	"	8am	Evacuation through A.C.P. for previous 12 hrs. Wounded–O.R.3; Sick–O.R.7; Situation "Normal"	
" "	"	3pm	9 O.R. R.A.M.C. (Reinforcements) arrived.	
" "	"	8pm	Evacuation through A.C.P. for previous 12 hrs. Wounded–O.R.3; Sick–O.R.16; Situation: "Normal."	
" "	29/5/18	8am	Evacuation through A.C.P. for previous 12 hrs. Wounded–O.R.5; Sick–O.R.7; Situation "Normal."	
" "	"	—	Usual sick parade at H.Q. Scout-Boy for certain Cellar at H.Q. completed. Entrances now gas-proof. Work at New Dressing Station at A.C.P. completed.	
" "	"	8pm	Evacuation through A.C.P. for previous 12 hrs. Wounded–O.R.4; Sick–O.R.10; Situation: "Normal."	
" "	30/5/18	8am	Usual sick parade at H.Q. Evacuation through A.C.P. for previous 12 hrs. Wounded–O.R.4; Sick–O.R.8; Situation: "Normal."	
" "	"	8pm	O.O. No.43 received from D.A.D.M.S. 58 Div. concerning relief of Division. The Unit to be relieved on Zunday by 56th F.D. Amb. & to move to Wood F.20.C. (57.D.)	
" "	"	8pm	Evacuation through A.C.P. for previous 12 hrs. Wounded–Off.2; O.R.10; Sick–Off.1; O.R.12. Situation: "Normal." Shell casualties caught in N.O. Dressing Room during the night.	
" "	31/5/18	8am	Evacuation through A.C.P. for previous 12 hrs. Wounded–O.R.13; Sick–O.R.12. Situation: "Normal." Between 1 a.m. & 3 a.m. the Wood in which the 1st Lond. Ret. was quartered was shelled with Gas shells. Most of the casualties were above due to N.D.S. from the front.	
" "	"	—	Usual sick parade at H.Q.	
" "	"	—	Capt. P.S. CLARKE, R.A.M.C. transferred to 9th Bn. Lond. Ret. as R.M.O.	
" "	"	8pm	Evacuation through A.C.P. for previous 12 hrs. Wounded–O.R.5; Sick–O.R.9; Situation: "Normal."	

CONFIDENTIAL.

Army Form C. 2118.

WAR DIARY
or
INTELLIGENCE SUMMARY.
(Erase heading not required.)

Vol 17
Med/3078.

WAR DIARY
OF
2/2 H.C.F. Amb. RAMC (T)

FROM 1/6/18 TO 30/6/18

Lt. Col. RAMC (T)

WAR DIARY
or
INTELLIGENCE SUMMARY.

Army Form C. 2118.

(Erase heading not required.)

Instructions regarding War Diaries and Intelligence Summaries are contained in F. S. Regs., Part II. and the Staff Manual respectively. Title pages will be prepared in manuscript.

Place	Date	Hour	Summary of Events and Information	Remarks and references to Appendices
WARLOY U 24 C 3.3	1/6/18		Unit relieved by 56 Fd. Amb. at WARLOY. Adv. C.P. at HENENCOURT and Medical Posts en Routes of Evacuation of Left Sector of III Corps front and returned to the "wood" T 22 C near MIRVAUX. Move Completed 8 P.M.	
	2/6/18	9 a.m	Capt F.A. DICK detailed for duty with 2nd London Fost (ADMS)	
		Noon	Capt F.A. DICK returned to 2/1 F.C.Amb. (ADMS M 4719 A 7/6/18)	
T 22 C nr MIRVAUX	5/6/18	"	Warning Order received to be ready to move at 2 hours' notice (ADMS M/4/59)	
"	7/6/18	3 P.M.	G.O.C. 58th Div. inspected the Transport and expressed himself as greatly pleased with the condition and appearance of horses, harness, and vehicles.	
"	9/6/18	11 a.m	Provisional Administrative Instructions rec'd. if Division should move by bus (ADMS 4729)	
"	10/6/18	6.30 a.m	Amb. and Brigade Groups and Revised Embussing Programme rec'd. for move to CAVILLON AREA 22nd CORPS (ADMS 4737/1)	
"	"	6.30 a.m	O.C. No 44 rec'd from ADMS re 'move' to DREUIL LES MOLLIENS in CAVILLON AREA	
"	"	7.30 a.m	1/1th Inf. Bde. Order No. 92 rec'd re "MOVE" and "S.C.T." 925 re transport Arrangements for march as a Bde. Group	
"	"	9 a.m	Unit (less transport) marched to PUCHEVILLERS - RUBEMPRÉ Rd (Embussing Point)	
"	"	4 P.M.	Unit (less transport) debussed Nr PICQUIGNY and marched to DREUIL LES MOLLIENS (Move Completed 7.30 PM)	
"	"	11 a.m	Transport left and arrived at DREUIL LES MOLLIENS at 8.30 PM	
DREUIL LES MOLLIENS	11/6/18	6.30 a.m	Programme showing Bde. Groups and Alternative Embussing Points for 'Move' North or S.E rec'd. (ADMS 8 (1884))	
"			Small hospital opened for sick of 175 Bde for cases likely to be fit for duty in 4 days	

Army Form C. 2118.

WAR DIARY
or
INTELLIGENCE SUMMARY.
(Erase heading not required.)

Instructions regarding War Diaries and Intelligence Summaries are contained in F. S. Regs., Part II. and the Staff Manual respectively. Title pages will be prepared in manuscript.

Place	Date	Hour	Summary of Events and Information	Remarks and references to Appendices
DREUILLES				
MOLLIENS	11/5/18	Noon	W3185. Adm 11 CCS 11 R.14.	
"	12/5/18	"	W3185. R.14. Adm 24 CCS 11 R.5	
"	"	5.30 PM	Embussing points recd. (CAVILLON - BRIGNEMESNIL Rd.) in event of a move NORTH (ARMS Fitted)	
"	13/5/18	Noon	W3185. R.5 Adm 24 CCS 20 R.9.	
"	14/5/18	"	W3185 R.9 Adm 25 CCS 20 R.14	
"	15/5/18	"	W3185. R.14 Adm 30 CCS 30 Duty 2 R.12.	
"	"	11.45 PM	O.O. No. 112 recd. (121 pt) "Unit to move with 175 Bde to New Area and relieve the 6th London Fd. Amb. at the Rest + Sick station at MIRVAUX and take over the Sick Collecting Station at BEAUCOURT. Return to be completed at 12 Noon 19th. Ford Cars, Lighted Vehicles, + 80 horses to be at the disposal of 2/3 Squad.	
"	16/5/18	Noon	W3185. R.12 Adm 16 CCS 17 Duty 2. R.9.	
"	"	12.45 PM	Ref. O.O. No.115 (1 Aust. S.) Amendment recd. "Move to be completed by Noon 18th instead of Noon 19th. Embussing point to be on CAVILLON + BRIGUESMESNIL Rd at 3.P.M. 18/5/18.	
"	"	11.P.M	175 Inf. Bde O.O. 115 Copy No.5 recd. "Unit to move with Bde by bus to the strand. S.E. MOLLIENS AU BOIS".	
"	"		10 H.T. and Transport to join Bde. Transport at FLOXICOURT - BRIQUESMESNIL "Cross Roads". Capt. N.F. GRAHAM returned from leave.	
"	17/5/18	Noon	W3185 R.9 Adm 22 CCS 19 Duty 2 R.10.	

Army Form C. 2118.

WAR DIARY
or
INTELLIGENCE SUMMARY.
(Erase heading not required.)

Instructions regarding War Diaries and Intelligence Summaries are contained in F. S. Regs., Part II. and the Staff Manual respectively. Title pages will be prepared in manuscript.

Place	Date	Hour	Summary of Events and Information	Remarks and references to Appendices
DREUIL LES	17/6/18	2 a.m.	Advance Party (2 Officers 6 O.R.) left for new area. (Capt McKee + 3 O.R to BEAUCOURT (Sick Collecting Station)	
POLLIENS (A.E. O 30.a.5)	18/6/18	7.45 p.m.	Transport left to join Bde Transport. (Capt KNOWLES - 3 O.R to MIRVAUX (Sick Station) + MIRVAUX WOOD)	
	"	11.45 P.M	Unit marched to Embussing Point } Move Completed to MIRVAUX WOOD at 7 P.M.	
MIRVAUX WOOD	"	8.30 p.m.	9 O.R. sent to report at Sick Collecting Station (BEAUCOURT)	
S.9 D. T.22.C.	"	9 p.m.	"R.S" opened in MIRVAUX WOOD - Accommodation Offrs 4 O.R 112	
			W.3185 R.10 Ade 16 CCS 25 Duty 1 R Mt	
	19/6/18	Noon	W.3185 R Mt Adm 52 CCS 37 R 15	
"	"	9 a.m.	Medical Inspection Room opened at MIRVAUX Village	
"	20/6/18	Noon	W.3185 R 15 Adm 87 CCS 30 Duty 1 R 71	
"	"	2.30 PM	Lieut R C EATON R.A.M.C. Temp. detached as M.O. to 2/10 London Regt (Adm.)	
"	21/6/18	Noon	W 3185 R 71 Adm 91 CCS 64 R 98	
			Large number of cases of Pyrexia (of a mild influenza type) admitted. To provide more accommodation for these a hospital opened in the village for all other cases. Accommodation Offrs 4. O.R. 48	
	22/6/18	Noon	W 3185 R 98 Adm 129 CCS 104 Duty 2 R 121	
	"	2 P.M.	Capt R.L. BARWICK R.A.M.C. attested for duty (Adm.)	
	23/6/18	Noon	W 3185 R 121 Adm 89 CCS 92 R 118	

Army Form C. 2118.

WAR DIARY
or
INTELLIGENCE SUMMARY.
(Erase heading not required.)

Instructions regarding War Diaries and Intelligence Summaries are contained in F. S. Regs., Part II. and the Staff Manual respectively. Title pages will be prepared in manuscript.

Place	Date	Hour	Summary of Events and Information	Remarks and references to Appendices
T22 C	22/6/18		Bath tents for accommodation for Officers at D.R.S. and at MIRVAUX completed	
"	23/6/18		Separate camp at D.R.S. provided for Convalescent Patients	
"	"	Noon	W 3155. R 48 Adm 3 Officers 97 O.R. CCS 2 Off 77 O.R. Duty 1 R 1 officer 137 O.R.	
"	25/6/18	"	W 3155. R 1 Off 137 O.R. Adm 5 Off 60 O.R. CCS 3 Off 50 O.R. Duty 2 R 3 Off 146 O.R.	
"	26/6/18	"	W 3155. R 3 Off 146 O.R. Adm 2 Off 40 O.R. CCS 1 Off 45 O.R. Duty 10 R 4 Off 131 O.R.	
"	"		Erection of "Bath house" at D.R.S. Completed by R.E.s 66th Div.	
"	"	10.30 A.M	O.O. No 46 (copy No 2 issued for APMs. Unit to move tomorrow (27th June) to St GRATIEN WOOD (B20d) on account of further forward advance through Picardie on Somme. The personnel and transport to be clear of MIRVAUX WOOD by NOON 27th inst. Medical Inspection Room and Hospital at MIRVAUX and Sick Collecting Station at BEAUCOURT to be retained.	
"	27/6/18	Noon	W 3155. R 4 Off. 131 O.R. Adm 51 CCS 30 Duty 3 R 4 Off 149 O.R.	
St GRATIEN WOOD	"	2 P.M.	Move of unit completed to St GRATIEN WOOD. Patients temporarily accommodated at MIRVAUX HoSp. and taken to D.R.S in the evening (transfer complete by 7.30 P.M.)	
B2D. B 20 d	"		"Bath tent" dismantled and materials brought to new D.R.S.	
"	"		Working Parties of 25 O.R. supplied by Booth 2/1 H.Q Amb and 2/3 H.Q Amb for digging and levelling Huts etc at D.R.S.	
	28/6/18		Major S. M. McGILVRAY granted Leave 28/6/18 – 12/7/18 (Appx)	

Army Form C. 2118.

WAR DIARY
or
INTELLIGENCE SUMMARY.
(Erase heading not required.)

Instructions regarding War Diaries and Intelligence Summaries are contained in F. S. Regs., Part II. and the Staff Manual respectively. Title pages will be prepared in manuscript.

Place	Date	Hour	Summary of Events and Information	Remarks and references to Appendices
St GRATIEN	28/5/18	Noon	IN 3185 R 4 Off 149 O.R. Adm 2 Off 66 O.R. CCS 45 Evac^d 33 R 6 Off 137 O.R.	
WOOD	29/5/18	"	W 3185 R 6 Off 137 O.R. Adm 7 t O.R. CCS 57 Evac^d 1 R 6 Off 153 O.R.	
62 D B 20d	"	"	"Bath House" re-erected by R.E.s 66th Div. at R.R.S.	
"	30/5/18	"	W 3185 R 6 Off 153 O.R. Adm 2 Off 72 O.R. CCS 3 Off 41 O.R. Evac^d 8 R 5 Off 136 O.R.	

Army Form C. 2118.

WAR DIARY
or
INTELLIGENCE SUMMARY.
(Erase heading not required.)

MEDICAL

98/18

WAR DIARY

OF

2/2 H.C.F. Amb. R.A.M.C. (T)

FROM 1/7/18 to 31/7/18

[Signature]
Lt. Col. R.A.M.C. (T)
O.C.
2/2ND H.C. FLD. AMB.

COMMITTEE FOR THE
MEDICAL HISTORY OF THE WAR
Date 6 SEP 1918

CONFIDENTIAL.
Instructions regarding War Diaries and Intelligence
Summaries are contained in F. S. Regs., Part II.
and the Staff Manual respectively. Title pages
will be prepared in manuscript.

Place	Date	Hour	Summary of Events and Information	Remarks and references to Appendices

WAR DIARY
or
INTELLIGENCE SUMMARY.

(Erase heading not required.)

Army Form C. 2118.

Place	Date	Hour	Summary of Events and Information	Remarks and references to Appendices
St GRATTEN WOOD 62.D B20.d	1/7/18	9 a.m.	Lieut J. DOOLING. M.O.R.C. 2/3 H.C. 2d. Amb. reported for Temp duty as O i/c Convalescent Camp (ADMS)	
"	"	Noon	W3185. R Off 5 O.R 176 Adm. Off 4 O.R 52 CCd Off 2 O.R 14 R Off 3 O.R 172	
"	2/7/18	"	W3185 R Off 3 O.R 172 Adm. Off 5 O.R 59 CCd Off 4 O.R 34 Duty Off 1 O.R 34 R Off 3 O.R 163	
"	"	6.15 P.M	G.O.C. 58th Divsion visited D.R.S. and Hospital at MIRVAUX	
"	3/7/18	Noon	W3185 R Off 3 O.R 163 Adm Off 5 O.R 58. CCd Off 4 O.R 63 Duty O.R 9 R Off 4 O.R 149	
"	"	"	Officers' Ward Closed at MIRVAUX — all officer patients now accommodated at St GRATIEN WOOD	
"	4/7/18	Noon	W3185 R Off 4 O.R 149 Adm. Off 2 O.R 62 CCd 2 Off 46 O.R Duty O.R 8 R Off 4 O.R 157	
"	5/7/18	"	W3185 R Off 4 O.R 157 Adm Off 2 O.R 59 CCd Off 2 O.R 40 Duty Off 10 R1 R Off 3 O.R 175	
"	6/7/18	9 a.m.	Bath House Completed (with cement floor) – Soap trap and pits constructed	
"	"	10 a.m	Capt. R.L.BARWICK RAMC (T.C) det. for temp duty as R.M.O. to 8th London Regt (ADMS M4892 d 5/4/18)	
"	"	"	Capt J.M. SMEATON " 2/1 HOGants det for Temp duty at BEAUCOURT to take over duties	
"	"	"	Performed by Capt. R.L.BARWICK (ADMS M4894 d 6/7/18)	
"	"	Noon	W3185 R Off 3 O.R 175 Adm Off 2 O.R 44 CCd Off 2 O.R 41 Duty O.R 30 R Off 3 O.R 148	
"	"	"	Necessary arrangements completed for admission of diarrhoea cases in a separate part of the camp	
"	7/7/18	Noon	W3185 R Off 3 O.R 148 Adm. Off 1 O.R 60 CCd Off 1 O.R 46 Duty O.R 3 R Off 3 O.R 159	
"	8/7/18	"	W3185 R Off 3 O.R 159 Adm. O.R 43 CCd O.R 46 Duty O.R 12 R Off 3 O.R 144	

WAR DIARY
or
INTELLIGENCE SUMMARY.

Army Form C. 2118.

(Erase heading not required.)

Place	Date	Hour	Summary of Events and Information	Remarks and references to Appendices
ST GRATIEN WOOD 62.D. B.20.d	8/7/18	11.20am	Mirage d 8/7/18 recd. from A.D.M.S. re "Procedure to be carried out on receipt of message Battle Station Practice"	
	"	8.45 PM	"Battle Station Practice" message recd. (A.D.M.S. W730) 12 O.R. sent to 2/3 H.Coy.amb at Car Post C.20.B.4.2 (1 O.R. represented 1 Squad)	
	9/7/18		Extract from List No. 194 d 30/6/18 of "Appointments, Commissions etc. R.A.M.C. — Capt T.B. McKEE 2/2 H.Coy.amb to be Act. Major whilst Commanding Section of Field Amb. (15/6/18)	
	"	11 a.m	Working party of 56 O.R. returned to Unit from 2/3 H.Coy.amb on Completion of new A.D.S. at D.15.d.9.2	
	"	Noon	W3185 R. Off. 3 O.R.144 Adm. Off. 2 O.R.63 C.C.A. Off. 1 O.R.55 Duty Off. 3 O.R.19. R. Off. 1 O.R. 132	
	"	2 P.M.	1/ Lieut R.C. EATON (M.O.R.C.) ret for duty with unit	
	10/7/18	Noon	W3185 R Off. 1 O.R.132. Adm. Off. 2. O.R.65 C.C.A. Off. 2 O.R.42. Duty O.R.17. R Off. 1 O.R.138	
	"	2.30 PM	Instructions recd. from A.D.M.S. (M.5010 d. 10/7/18) that "O.C. 2/2 H.Coy.amb will be given the whole allotment (Off. 8 O.R.100) at the III Corps Rest Station at the Large Chateau, FLESSELLES, which will open 11/7/18 (D.D.M.S. III Corps, No 7389/18.) and will make all arrangements for transport etc	
	"	5.30 PM	Lieut J.F. DOOLING (M.O.R.C.) Ret to his Unit (2/3 H.Coy.amb) = (A.D.M.S. M 5012 d. 10/7/18)	
	11/7/18	Noon	W3185 R Off. 1 O.R.138 Adm. Off. 1. O.R.34. C.C.A. Off. 1 O.R.21 Duty O.R.16. R Off. 1 O.R.135	
	12/7/18	"	" " R Off. 1 O.R. 135 Adm. Off. 1 O.R. 53 C.C.A. Off. 5 O.R.38 Duty O.R.13 R Off. 1 O.R.137	
	13/7/18	11 a.m	D.R.S. Inspected by D.D.M.S. III Corps	

WAR DIARY
or
INTELLIGENCE SUMMARY.

(Erase heading not required.)

Army Form C. 2118.

Instructions regarding War Diaries and Intelligence Summaries are contained in F. S. Regs., Part II. and the Staff Manual respectively. Title pages will be prepared in manuscript.

Place	Date	Hour	Summary of Events and Information	Remarks and references to Appendices
St GRATIEN WOOD	13/7/18	Noon	W 3185 R Off 1 O.R. 137 Adm. O.R. 53 CCS O.R. 45 Duty O.R. 10 R Off 1 O.R. 135	
(62.D - Bde.)	14/7/18	Noon	W 3185 R Off 1 O.R. 135 Adm. Off 2 O.R. 47 CCS Off 2 O.R. 33 III C.R.S. O.R. 10 Duty O.R. 6 R Off 1 O.R. 133	
"	"	"	1/Lieut. EATON R.C. (M.O.R.C) relieved Capt. N.F. GRAHAM (T.C.) as O/c hospital at MIRVAUX	
"	"	"	Capt N.F. GRAHAM to be O/c Conv. Camp at St GRATIEN WOOD	
"	"	2 P.M.	Major G.M. Mc GILLIVRAY (R.A.M.C.T) returned from leave	
"	15/7/18	10 a.m.	Major G.M. Mc GILLIVRAY relieved Major McKEE as Officer i/c at S.C.S. (BEAUCOURT)	
"	"	"	Major T.B. McKEE returned to St GRATIEN	
"	"	Noon	W3185 R Off 1 O.R. 133. Adm. O.R. 141. CCS O.R. 34. III CRS O.R. 6. Duty O.R. 3. R Off 1. O.R. 141	
"	"	5 P.M.	1/Lieut. R.C. EATON (M.O.R.C) detailed to report at A.D.M.S. Office in order to attend presentation of medals by Corps Commander. (M 4999 d 14/7/18) 5032	
"	"	"	Capt. A.C. WATKIN (T.F.) reported for duty with unit (ADMS)	
"	16/7/18	Noon	W 3185 R Off 1 O.R. 141 Adm. O.R. 38 CCS O.R. 25 III CRS O.R. 10 Duty O.R. 3. R Off 1 O.R. 138	
"	"	1 P.M.	Capt N.F. GRAHAM (T.C.) struck off str. of Unit on taking over medical charge of 6th Lond. Regt (Hons M5047 d 14/7/18)	
"	17/7/18	Noon	W3185 R Off 1 O.R. 138. Adm. Off. 1 O.R. 51 CCS Off 1 O.R. 40. III CRS O.R. 9. Duty Off. 1. R O.R. 140	
"	18/7/18	9 a.m.	Working party detailed to erect C. Type Shelter under supervision of N.C.O. det. by C.R.E. 3rd Corps Troops at Reserve Site for M.D.S opposite St GRATIEN WOOD.	

WAR DIARY
or
INTELLIGENCE SUMMARY.

Army Form C. 2118.

Place	Date	Hour	Summary of Events and Information	Remarks and references to Appendices
St-GRATIEN WOOD 62D - B 20 d.	18/7/18	9.5 a.m	O.O. No. 47. Copy No 2 recd from ADMS - "One Tent Sub. Division (with 2 Officers) to be held in readiness to reinforce the C.W.W.C.P at 2 hours' notice.	
"	"	Noon	W 3185. R. O.R. 140. Adm. Off. 2. O.R. 49. CCS Off. 2. O.R. 23. III CRS. O.R. 7. Duty O.R. 7. R. O.R. 152.	
"	19/7/18	10. A.M.	Hospital at MIRVAUX closed. Patients transferred to either DRS, CRS, or CCS.	
"	"		Lieut. R.C. EATON (M.O.R.C) and 2 O.R. det. for temp. duty with 58th Div. Wing.	
"	"	Noon	W 3185. R. O.R. 152. Adm. Off. 1. O.R. 32. CCS Off. 1. O.R. 32. III CRS. O.R. 7. Duty O.R. 1. R. O.R. 144.	
"	20/7/18	10 a.m	Major T.B. McKEE relieved 1/Lieut R.C. EATON (M.O.R.C) as M.O. i/c 58th Div. Wing & Lt EATON ret to St GRATIEN	
"	"	Noon	W 3185. R. O.R. 144. Adm. Off. 2. O.R. 46. CCS Off. 1. O.R. 24. III CRS. O.R. 6. Duty O.R. 6. R. O.R. 145.	
"	21/7/18	"	W 3185. R. Off. 1. O.R. 145. Adm. Off. 1. O.R. 53. CCS Off. 1. O.R. 22. III CRS. O.R. 7. Duty O.R. 11. R. Off. 1. O.R. 158.	
"	22/7/18	"	W 3185. R. Off. 1. O.R. 158. Adm. Off. 1. O.R. 34. III CCS O.R. 42. III CRS O.R. 4. Duty O.R. 3. R. Off. 1. O.R. 159.	
"	23/7/18	"	W 3185. R. Off. 1. O.R. 159. Adm. Off. 1. O.R. 42. CCS Off. 1. O.R. 19. III CRS O.R. 18. Duty O.R. 4. R. Off. 1. O.R. 160.	
"	"	2 P.M	1/Lieut R.C. EATON (M.O.R.C.) det. for temp. duty as M.O. to 3rd London Regt (ADMS M 5966)	
"	24/7/18	Noon	W 3185. R. Off. 1. O.R. 160. Adm. Off. 1. O.R. 54. CCS Off. 1. O.R. 37. III CRS O.R. 13. Duty O.R. 7. R. Off. 1. O.R. 157.	
"	25/7/18	"	W 3185. R. Off. 1. O.R. 157. Adm. O.R. 41. CCS O.R. 26. III CRS O.R. 18 Duty O.R. 2. R. Off. 1. O.R. 152.	
"	"		DDMS III Corps inspected the S.C.S. at BEAUCOURT	
"	"		Hut built for use as Officers' Mess.	

Army Form C. 2118.

WAR DIARY
or
INTELLIGENCE SUMMARY.
(Erase heading not required.)

Place	Date	Hour	Summary of Events and Information	Remarks and references to Appendices
St GRATIEN WOOD. 62.D. B2c.d	26/7/18	9.45am	O.O. 76.148 rec'd from A.D.M.S.	
"		Noon	W 3185 R. Off 1 O.R. 152 Adm. Off 1 O.R. 47 CCS. Off 1 O.R. 39. III CRS. O.R. 18. Duty O.R. 2 R. Off 1 O.R. 140.	
"	27/7/18	"	W 3185 R. Off 1 O.R. 140 Adm. Off 1 O.R 34 CCS Off 1 O.R 29 III CRS. O.R. 1 Duty O.R. 2 R Off 1 O.R. 142	
"	28/7/18	"	W 3185 R. Off 1 O.R. 142 Adm. Off 4 O.R. 40 CCS Off 4 O.R. 20 III CRS O.R. 9 Duty O.R. 5 R Off 1 O.R. 148	
"	"	4 P.M.	Capt. H.C. MULHOLLAND (T.C.) reported for duty with unit. (A.D.M.S)	
"	"	"	Air Raid during night in near neighbourhood	
"	29/7/18	Noon	W 3185 R. Off 1 O.R. 148 Adm. Off 2 O.R. 44 CCS O.R. 33 III CRS Off 1 O.R. 11 Duty O.R. 3 R Off 2 O.R. 148	
"	"	7 P.M	Capt. R.L. BARWICK (T.C.) T.d. to unit from 8th Lond. Regt and detailed for temp. duty with 53rd Div. leaving	
"	"	"	vice Major T. B. McKEE (T.F.) who ret to Unit for duty (ADMS)	
"	30/7/18	7 a.m.	3 N.C.Os and 24 Pvt sent to 2/3 H.C. Amb as a Working Party (ADMS M 5135 d 29/7/18)	
"	"	Noon	W 3185 . R Off 2 O.R. 148. Adm Off 1 O.R.47. CCS O.R. 26. III CRS Off 1 O.R. 14. Duty O.R. 2 R Off 2 O.R. 153	
"	31/7/18	"	W 3185 R Off 2 O.R. 153 Adm. Off 4 O.R. 44 III CRS. O.R. 7. Duty Nil. R Off 2 O.R. 157	
"	"	"	Air Raid during night in near neighbourhood lasting 5 hours.	

WAR DIARY
or
INTELLIGENCE SUMMARY.

(Erase heading not required.)

Army Form C. 2118.

MEDICAL

Vol 19

140/3200

CONFIDENTIAL

War Diary
of
2/2 H.C.Fd. RAMC (T)

From 1/8/18 To 31/8/18

Lt Col RAMC (T)
O.C:
2/2nd H.C. FLD. AMB

COMMITTEE FOR THE
MEDICAL HISTORY
Date 5 OCT 1936

2/2ND
HOME COUNTIES
FIELD AMBULANCE
No. HC 2522
Date 4/9/18

WAR DIARY
or
INTELLIGENCE SUMMARY.

Army Form C. 2118.

Place	Date	Hour	Summary of Events and Information	Remarks and references to Appendices
S. GRATIEN WOOD G.2.D. B20.d	1/8/18	10.20 a.m.	Administrative Instructions in Connection with move to VIGNACOURT AREA recd. from A.D.M.S.	
"	"	11 a.m.	Lieut R.C. EATON (M.O.R.C.) returned to Unit from temp duty with 3rd London Regt.	
"	"	Noon	W.3185 R Off.2 O.R.157 Adm. Off.3 O.R.48 CCS Off.3 O.R. 34 III CCS Off.1 O.R.+ Duty O.R.1 R Off.1 O.R.166	
"	"	2 P.M.	O.O. No.49 recd. from A.D.M.S. "Fd. Amb." to move with 174 Inf. Bde. to HAVERNAS after relief by 36th Fd Amb on the morning of the 2nd inst.	
"	"	"	Rear Party to be left (1 Off. 60 O.R.) until sick of Division are returned to duty	
"	"	"	Lorry to report at M.R.S. on 5th, 6th & 7th at 10 a.m. to convey patients fit for duty to VIGNACOURT AREA	
"	"	5.30 P.M.	O.O. No. 104 recd. from 174 Inf. Bde. - Unit (Less transport) to be at embussing point - BEHENCOURT - BAZIEUX Rd at 4 P.M. 2/8/18	
"	2/8/18	11 a.m.	Transport left for HAVERNAS - arrived 3.30 P.M.	
"	"	Noon	W.3185 R Off.1 O.R.166 Adm O.R. 39 CCS O.R.36 III CCS O.R.14 Duty O.R.11 R Off.1 O.R. 143	
"	"	2.30 P.M.	Unit left for Embussing Point	
"	"	9.30 P.M.	Move completed to HAVERNAS	
HAVERNAS 57E R.21 C.61	3/8/18	10 a.m.	Arrangements made for collection of sick of 174 Inf. Bde. Hospital opened to accommodate patients likely to be fit for duty within 3 days	

Army Form C. 2118.

WAR DIARY
or
INTELLIGENCE SUMMARY.
(Erase heading not required.)

Instructions regarding War Diaries and Intelligence Summaries are contained in F. S. Regs., Part II. and the Staff Manual respectively. Title pages will be prepared in manuscript.

Place	Date	Hour	Summary of Events and Information	Remarks and references to Appendices
57 E. R.31.C.6.4.	3/8/18	Noon	W.3185. R. Off 1. O.R. 143 Adm. O.R. 14. CCS. O.R. 22 III CRS. O.R. 12 Trans. to 36 Fld. Amb. O.R. 14 Duty O.R. 5 R. Off	I. O.R. 104
"	"	11.30 P.M	Major T. B. McKEE with 3 O.R. proceeded to new area (KEY WOOD 62 D 14 a) to change site for unit	
"	4/8/18	11.45 a.m	O.O. No. 50 recd from ADMS. "O.C. to arrange direct with 114 Inf. Bde. as to time + place for Embussing"	
"	"	Noon	W.3185 R. Off 1. O.R. 104 Adm. O.R. 5 CCA. O.R. 28 R. Off.	I. O.R. 81
"	"	3.30 P.M	O.O. No. 105, Copy No. 8 recd from 114 Inf. Bde. "Unit to move to New Area with Bde - embussing point - CANAPLES - HAVERNAS Rd - to be at embussing point at 8.45 P.M.	
"	"	11.30 P.M	Transport left + arrived at KEY WOOD 11.30 P.M	
KEY WOOD 62 D 14 a	5/8/18	4.30 a.m	Unit arrived at KEY WOOD	
"	"	Noon	W.3185 R. Off 1. O.R. 81 Adm. O.R. 3 CCA O.R. 16 III CRS. O.R. 11 Trans. from 36 Fd Amb. O.R. 6 Duty Off. 1. R. O.R. 73	
"	"	2 P.M	Medical Inspection Room opened at Billet No 13 LAHOUSSOYE. Major McKEE M.O.i/c	
"	6/8/18	9 a.m	Major G. M. McGILLIVRAY left for Temp. duty with 2/1 H.O.Amb	
"	"	"	1/Lieut G. S. SILLIMAN (M.O.R.C) 2/1 H.O.G.A. rep. to Unit for Temp. duty.	
"	"	Noon	W.3185. R. O.R. 73 Adm. O.R. 11 CCS. O.R. 11 III CRS. O.R. 10 Duty 8 R 55	
"	7/8/18	"	All Motor amb. Cars (except one large one) placed at disposal of O.C. 2/1 H.O.Amb. Also 7 pairs of Stretcher wheels, one tarpaulin, 50 Blankets, + 316 stretchers in accordance with A.D.M.S. M.5185 d 4/8/18	
"	"	Noon	W.3185 R. O.R. 55 Adm. Nil. CCA O.R. 15 III CRS. O.R. 20 Duty O.R. 20 R. Nil	

A6945 Wt. W.14422/M.1160 350,000 12/16 D. D. & L. Forms/C./2118/14.

Army Form C. 2118.

WAR DIARY
OR
INTELLIGENCE SUMMARY.
(Erase heading not required.)

Place	Date	Hour	Summary of Events and Information	Remarks and references to Appendices
62.D.16.a	7/8/18		Rear Party from St GRATIEN, WOOD rejoined Unit on completion of Our Sick being discharged to duty or evacuated.	
"	"	3 P.M.	1/Lieut. R.C EATON + 10 O.R left to report at III C.W.W.C.P MONTIGNY	
"	"	"	Capt ANDREW, Capt MULHOLLAND + 1/Lieut SILLIMAN + 33 O.R (New Tent sub division) left to report at M.D.S. (QUERRIEU)	
"	"	5 P.M.	Major McKEE, 3 Sergts, + 20 O.R (Stretcher Bearers) left to report to 2/1 H.C.Amb for duty at I30 C.5.6.	
"	"	5 P.M.	3 Horse Ambs. left to report at Hqrs 5th Fld. Amb (I.4.6.) for Conveyance of to-w from 9/Lt a. to BONNAY	
"	"	7 P.M.	50 O.R "58 Rinr. Battle Surplus" reported for duty as reserve bearer squads. (A.D.M.S. 520.d 7/8/18)	
"	"	8 P.M.	3 Officers 2 Sergts 80 O.R 2/3 H.C.Amb reported for duty as bearer squads.	
8/8/18	"	9 A.M.	3 Off. 1 Sergt 40 O.R 2/3 H.C.Amb left to report to O.C. 2/1 H.C.Amb at A.D.S. (I30.a.)	
"	"	Noon	W 3185 Q.M. 26 O.R CCs. 26 O.R.	
"	"	4 P.M.	1 Sergt. 40 O.R 2/3 H.C.Amb left to report to O.C. 2/1 H.C.Amb at A.D.S. (I30.a.)	
"	"		Medical Inspection Room at 13 Drapery St., LAHOUSSOYE closed.	
"	9/8/18	8 P.M.	50 O.R "Battle Surplus, 38 Divn" left to report to O.C. 2/1 H.C.Amb at A.D.S as bearer squads.	
"	10/8/18	4.45 A.M	1 Sergt 12 O.R left to report to O.C. 2/1 H.C.Amb at "A.D.S as bearer squads.	
"	"	3 P.M.	O.O. No 51 recd. from A.D.M.S." Unit to take over M.D.S. at QUERRIEU from 56th Fld Amb. by 6 P.M. 10/8/18	
"	"	3.30 P.M	Anvance west recd. to O.O. No 51. " M.D.S. to be taken over on the 11th inst	
"	"		Air Raid during the night in near neighbourhood	

Army Form C. 2118.

WAR DIARY
or
INTELLIGENCE SUMMARY.
(Erase heading not required.)

Instructions regarding War Diaries and Intelligence Summaries are contained in F. S. Regs., Part II. and the Staff Manual respectively. Title pages will be prepared in manuscript.

Place	Date	Hour	Summary of Events and Information	Remarks and references to Appendices
QUERRIEU H10 a 8.6	11/8/18	4 P.M.	Move Completed to M.D.S.	
"	"	5 P.M.	Detachment (less 2 O.R.) ret. to Unit from III Corps C.P.	
"	"	11 P.M.	50 O.R. "Battle Surplus" ret. to Unit from 2/1 H.C.Amb.	
"	12/8/18		Capt. G.W.M. ANDREW granted leave from 12 - 26/8/18.	
"	"	Noon	The King passed the M.D.S. on his way to inspect detachments of 4th Army at the CHATEAU at QUERRIEU	
"	"	1.30 P.M.	O.O. No. 53 recd. from ADMS. "Unit to be relieved by 1st London Fld. Amb. at M.D.S. & to return to KEN WOOD	
"	"	5 P.M.	"Battle Surplus" of 175 Inf. Bde. returned to Bde. Hqrs.	
"	13/8/18	11 a.m.	" " " " " " 174 " " " "	
"	"	3 P.M.	Move Completed to KEN WOOD. All detachments rejoined Unit there	
KEN WOOD G2.D I 14 a	"		Major McGILLIVRAY ret. from 2/1 H.Ca. 1/Lieut SILLMAN returned to 2/1 H.Ca.	
"	"	6 P.M.	Capt. H.C. MULHOLLAND (T.C.) struck off strength on being transferred to 2nd Life Guards M.G. Bn. (ADMS M/521 d 13/8/18)	
"	"	"	1/Lieut H.W. MAHON (M.O.R.C.) reported to Unit for duty vice Capt H.C. MULHOLLAND (" " ")	
"	"	"	-Air Raid during night in near neighbourhood.	
"	14/8/18	9 a.m.	Medical Inspection Room reopened at LAHOUSSOYE - sick evac. to 2/3 H.Ca. at St GRATIEN WOOD	
"	17/8/18	Noon	1/Lieut. R.C. EATON. M.O.R.C. struck off strength on proceeding to 3rd Division A.E.F. for duty (DMS No 10153 d 12/8/18)	
"	18/8/18		Adm. O.R. 1. CCA O.R.1.	

W 2115

Army Form C. 2118.

WAR DIARY
or
INTELLIGENCE SUMMARY.
(Erase heading not required.)

Instructions regarding War Diaries and Intelligence Summaries are contained in F. S. Regs., Part II. and the Staff Manual respectively. Title pages will be prepared in manuscript.

Place	Date	Hour	Summary of Events and Information	Remarks and references to Appendices
62 D T14a	19/8/18	1.30 p.m.	Lieut. H.W. MAHON (H.O.R.C.) det. for temp. duty with 21st Bde R.G.A (Ref. M 5284 d. 18/8/18)	
	20/8/18	Noon	W 3185 Adm. O.R.1 C.C.S. O.R.1	
	"	"	Extract from List No. 200 d 11/8/18 of Appointments & Commissions etc (58th Div O/2/3125 d 19/8/18) "RAMC" - Capt. A.C. WATKIN	
	"	"	R.A.M.C.(T) To be Actg Major Whilst Comndg a section of Field Amb from 30/7/18.	
	"	"	Capt T.B. McKEE R.A.M.C (T) relinquished acting rank of Major from 29/7/18 on ceasing to Command section of Fd. Amb.	
	21/8/18	10 a.m.	Administrative Instructions in the Event of an Advance recd. (ADMS M 5304 d 19/8/18)	
	"	"	Notes of "Q" Conference held at QUERRIEU on 14/8/18 (III Corps A.Q.D. 14/18 d 16/8/18) recd. from A.D.M.S (M 5304 d 19/8/18)	
	"	Noon	W 3185 Adm. O.R.1. C.C.S. O.R.1.	
	"	11.15 a.m.	Explosion of a land mine (said to be Australian) in LAHOUSSOYE. FORD AMB. No 15563 Considerably damaged - several holes being made in the hood and damage done to the interior. Engine undamaged. Pvt DOYLE Considerably shaken.	
	22/8/18		"Medical Instructions" No. 25 d 22/8/18 recd. from ADMS. The 2/2 H.C.J.A. will remain closed ready to move at two hours' notice. Daily Collection of sick to be continued.	
	"		Sick to be sent to 2/1 HCJA at MONTIGNY FARM (D.R.S.)	
	23/8/18	Noon	W 3185 Adm. O.R.2 CCS O.R.1 Duty O.R.1.	
	"	7 p.m.	M 5322 d. 23/8/18 recd. from ADMS. 2/2 HCJA will remain responsible for collection of sick	

A6945. Wt. W14422/M1160 350,000 12/16 D. D. & L. Forms/C/2118/14.

WAR DIARY
or
INTELLIGENCE SUMMARY.
(Erase heading not required.)

Army Form C. 2118.

Place	Date	Hour	Summary of Events and Information	Remarks and references to Appendices
KEY WOOD 62.D.I.14.a	23/8/18	7 P.M	from 173 Inf. Bde. until further orders. Bearers may be req'd. for collection of Casualties from any or all Bdes. of this Division and will work under Fd. Amb. of Division running the line.	
"	"		Capt & Q.M. G. KNOWLES granted leave to ROUEN from 23/8/18 to 1/9/18 (A.F.W.S. M/497 & 23/8/18)	
"	"	10 P.M.	Warning Order rec'd from A.D.M.S. (M 3338) "Unit to take over A.D.S. + Posts on Route of Evacuation of the 14th Division & to arrange to reconnoitre first thing on the morning of the 24th inst."	
"	24/8/18		Capt. R.L. BARWICK granted leave to U.K. from 24/8/18 – 7/9/18	
"	"	1.30 a.m	O.O. No 56 rec'd from A.D.M.S. "Unit to take over A.D.S. + Bearer Posts from 6th London Fd. Amb. Rear Officer & 80 O.R. from each of the 2/1 + 2/3 Hogamba at disposal of O.C. 2/2 Fd. Amb. Also all wheeled Stretchers, also 2 large cars of 2/1 Hoza and 3 large cars of 2/3 Hoza and all Ford Cars of both these Fd. Ambs.	
"	"	4 a.m.	The A.D.M.S., O.C. + Major Mc GILLIVRAY left to reconnoitre Posts on Route of Evacuation	
"	"	9 a.m	Capt Major T.B. McKEE, 80 Bearers left to take over Posts of Evacuation. Also small detachment for A.D.S (9 24 b. 6.8)	
"	"	Noon	Remainder of Unit and transport left + arrived at A.D.S. 4 P.M	
CEMETERY COPSE. J 24 b 6.8.	"	6 P.M	Relief at A.D.S. and Bearer Posts Completed.	

WAR DIARY
or
INTELLIGENCE SUMMARY.
(Erase heading not required.)

Army Form C. 2118.

Place	Date	Hour	Summary of Events and Information	Remarks and references to Appendices
62 D.	24/8/18	9 P.M.	Report rec'd from Major McGILLIVRAY from "Car Post" (K16 C.2.2). "Bearers posted as follows on	
J.24 c.6.2.			the Div. Front. 2 Squads of 2/2 HCCA with each battalion of the 173 Inf. Bde. 3 Squads of 2/1 HCCA	
"			with each battalion of the 175 Inf. Bde. 6 Squads of 2/3 HCCA at Relay Post No 2. + 5 Squads	
"			of 2/2 HCCA at Relay Post No 1. — " In front of Relay Post "No 2" to the R.A.P.s very	
"			heavy shelling especially in Happy Valley to the south of it."	
"	25/8/18	8 A.M.	2 Off. 73 O.R. 58th Bn. "Battle Surplus" reported for duty - only to be used if German prisoners are	
			insufficient (ASPac M 53+5)	
"			S/stk for new A.T.S. reconnoitred and taken possession of at K 16 C.9.7	
"			Heavy Amb. + W.W. Lorries "Post" now at L 9 d.0.4 - Ford Ambs. passed from there to Div. C.P. at	
			L.3 d.5.6.	
"			Old route of Evacuation given up owing to length of carry + possibility of using cars forward	
"			along CORBIE - BRAY road	
"	25/8/18	Noon	"J 24 c 6.8" now taken over as M.D.S. by 2/3 Hegambs	
K17 c.7.4	26/8/18	4 P.M.	Work now completed to K17 c.7.4. Instead of K18 C.9.7, owing to shelling at latter place on	
"			arrival there	
			Major A.C. WATKIN evac. sick (gastritis) by 2/3 HCCA to 2/1 HCCA and by 2/1 HCCA to 53 CCA 27/8/18	

Army Form C. 2118.

WAR DIARY
or
INTELLIGENCE SUMMARY.
(Erase heading not required.)

Instructions regarding War Diaries and Intelligence Summaries are contained in F. S. Regs., Part II. and the Staff Manual respectively. Title pages will be prepared in manuscript.

Place	Date	Hour	Summary of Events and Information	Remarks and references to Appendices
K.17.6.9.4.	26/6/18		1/Lieut. H.W. MAHON ret. from 27 Bde. R.G.A. and detailed as M.O. i/c 10th London Regt (A.S.C.S.)	
"	"	3 P.M.	Medical Arrangements No. 27 recd. from A.D.M.S.	
"	"	7-8 P.M.	Shelling near H.qrs. - 2 Crashes of about 12 rounds - some landing about 50 yards away and part of ammunition dump there blown up	
"	27/6/18	6 A.M.	Report recd. from Major McGillivray. "Disposition of squads now as follows. 2/2 London Regt. 4 squads (3/2 H.Qrs. Bearers) 3rd London Regt (3K from 2/3 H.Qrs. + 1 from 2/1 H.O.S.R.), 4th London Regt 4 squads (2/1 H.Qrs. Bearers) and 4 squads at each of the 174 Inf. Bde. R.A.P.s (all 2/1 H.Qrs. Bearers) - relief was completed by 4.30 A.M. - no casualties to report and all R.A.P.'s were clear when visited. There was considerable shelling along the road about 1500 yards ahead of BRONFAY FARM and machine gun was trained on the road at about J.24.c.6.5. where there is a Boche Ambce Car. It was too hot to stay & examine but may get it in during the day	
"	"		Adv. C.P. now at BRONFAY FARM between BRAY & MARICOURT. Large ambs. are collecting lying wounded from here	
"	"		K.W.W. C.P. + Car Post now at L.10.a.5.8. (site of old C.C.S.)	
"	"		Corps C.P. opened at MEAULTE at 12 (NOON)	
"	28/6/18		The following medical arrangements were made for an attack by 58th Divn. at zero hour 11.55 A.M.	

WAR DIARY
or
INTELLIGENCE SUMMARY.

(Erase heading not required.)

Army Form C. 2118.

Place	Date	Hour	Summary of Events and Information	Remarks and references to Appendices
K.17.c.7.4.	28/8/18	6 a.m.	3 Horse Ambs sent to Adv C.P. to convey M.O.W. to W.W.C.P. Cases on horses were also sent for this purpose.	
"	"	"	4 Squads were attached to each of the 4 R.M.O.s to act as 100 bearers "Battle Surplus" went as additional bearers and loading parties.	
"	"	8 a.m.	A Car Post for Ford Ambs established at A.21.C.4.8. - just clear of MARICOURT village.	
L.10.a.5.9.	"	3 P.M.	Unit H.Qrs. moved to site of old C.C.S. - (Transport lines still at K.17.c.7.4.) - All motor ambs now held in reserve here - also horse ambs.	
"	"	11.30 P.M.	The following report rec'd from Major McGILLIVRAY of the day's operations. "An Adv. Car Post was established at A.21.C.4.8. just clear of MARICOURT village and Ford Cars running between BRONFAY FARM and that point since 8 a.m. I visited all R.A.P.s of 173 Inf. Bde. and found everything satisfactory - cases all being cleared quickly - no accumulation of wounded on left Div. front. A demand for stretchers rec'd from 17th Inf. Bde about 10 a.m. and sent up in a Ford Amb & distributed to M.Os of the Bde. Lieut. KENNEDY visited all R.A.P.s of 174 Inf. Bde + reported that all R.A.P.s were clear but some cases were still out in front waiting to be brought in. 6 Squads "Battle Surplus" bearers M/C Capt Ffrench went out to clear the line and on return stated that all cases were collected but that were not many & called when they got there.	

Army Form C. 2118.

WAR DIARY
or
INTELLIGENCE SUMMARY.
(Erase heading not required.)

Instructions regarding War Diaries and Intelligence Summaries are contained in F. S. Regs., Part II. and the Staff Manual respectively. Title pages will be prepared in manuscript.

Place	Date	Hour	Summary of Events and Information	Remarks and references to Appendices
L.10.a.5.b.	28/8/18		The Horse amb. were kept at Adv. C.P. till 3.30 P.M. and W.W. lorries carried about 50 or 60 cases during the morning.	
"			The RAPs of 1/3 Inf. Bde were moved up during the afternoon - 2nd + 3rd London Regts established posts about 50 yards north of our Adv. C.P + 3rd London Regt in MARICOURT village at A.21.8.6.	
"			slightly in front of Car Post.	
"			Evacuation from all posts on the line satisfactory + all cases cleared with ease during the day.	
"	29/8/18	2.45 PM	O.O. No 56 recd. from ADMS - Unit HdQrs to move 30th inst with transport to MARICOURT (A.21.c.2.9.)	
"			Unit to be established there. Move to be completed by noon.	
A.21.c.2.9	30/8/18	Noon	HdQrs Unit established. Aldr Collecting Post opened. Adv. Car Post at B.14.c.3.1.	
"		8 P.M.	Sunbeam Amb. No 45581 had radiator damaged by shell fire at B.14.c.3.1.	
"		"	O.O. No 57 recd. from ADMS. Unit HdQrs + bearers to move to Hut Camp A.30.b.3.9. by noon 31st inst	
"		"	Arrangements made in connection with an attack to be made by 174 Inf. Bde in the morning.	
"		"	Large Motor Amb sent with N.C.O + 4 bearers to bring back any casualties at dressing point	
"		"	Capt JARDINE detailed to proceed to Adv. Car Post at dawn to take charge of medical operations in the forward area, to keep in touch with the R.M.Os + to establish suitable R.P.s + Car Posts.	
"		"	Wheeled stretchers, dressings + stretchers sent in reserve to Adv. Car Post (B.14.c.3.1.)	

Army Form C. 2118.

WAR DIARY
or
INTELLIGENCE SUMMARY.
(Erase heading not required.)

Place	Date	Hour	Summary of Events and Information	Remarks and references to Appendices
A.30.c.2.3.	31/8/18	Noon	Move completed + W.W.C.P. opened. Collecting Post established at B.15.a + Adv Car Post at B.23.d.6.6.	
"	"	9.15 A.M.	Arrangements made in connection with an attack to be made by 173 Inf. Bde in the morning. Lieut KENNEDY detailed to reconnoitre + establish a Car Post somewhere on the road between here and CLERY by 6.30 a.m. on 1/9/18. - An N.C.O. + 2 orderlies to be there with a supply of dressings.	
"	"		A Relay Post with 3 squads + wheeled stretchers to be established along the CLERY - BOUCHAVESNES Rd by 6.30 a.m. or as soon after as practicable.	

Army Form C. 2118.

WAR DIARY
or
INTELLIGENCE SUMMARY.

MEDICAL

CONFIDENTIAL

WAR DIARY
— OF —
2/2 HCFAND. R.A.M.C.(T)

From 1-9-18 to 30-9-18

W.O. 19
14/3259

G. McGillivray Lieut
O.C.
2/2nd H.C. FLD. AMB

2/2ND
HOME COUNTIES
FIELD AMBULANCE.
H.C. 2257

COMMITTEE FOR THE
MEDICAL HISTORY OF THE WAR
9 NOV 1923

WAR DIARY
or
INTELLIGENCE SUMMARY.

Army Form C. 2118.

(Erase heading not required.)

Place	Date	Hour	Summary of Events and Information	Remarks and references to Appendices
M30 B.3.b.	1/9/18	9.05 a.m.	Report received from LIEUT KENNEDY on arrangements made in connection with an attack by the 173. INF BDE. "I have established a Coy Pol at CLERY on the main road behind the village. Also a relay pol with that Signal on the CLERY-BOUCHAVESNES road under the crest of the ridge about two kilometres up the hill. So far only Australian casualties have come through. We are in front of g.h.Q. to forward AID POS along RLY as fast and as much as possible. I have directed them though for our own line of evacuation." Both pols unknown during the day. "Looking after Signal Soyly.	
"	"	12.30 pm	Left in charge	
"	"	4.30 pm	Further report received from CAPT. JARDINE R.C. – "So far as I know objectives taken and wounded all evacuated thru the artillery C20.b. and C19.d.7.c. – 2nd London Regiment Aid Pol at C19.a.9.3. probably moving up to old QUARRY C20 central. 3rd London Regiment Aid Pol at B29.a.9.9. probably moving up to some spot shortly. 4th London Regiment Aid Pol has left B2H.d.9.9 for C20 c.R.c. Very few walking wounded that cannot be conveyed by Coves – Bvts. Cabling	

WAR DIARY
or
INTELLIGENCE SUMMARY.
(Erase heading not required.)

Army Form C. 2118.

Place	Date	Hour	Summary of Events and Information	Remarks and references to Appendices
M30 c.5.9	1/9/18	12.30p	Wounded) moved up to B16.b.5.9	
"		9.30p	Before arrangements by Officer Commanding 2/2 H.C.F.A.916 can be carried out with ADMS Operation Order No 58 of 1/9/18 (1) the 74th Division will relieve the 53rd Division on the line tonight (2) the 74th Division will attack at an hour to be notified later. Objectives will also be notified when known (3) Officer Commanding 2/2 H.C.F.A.916 will be responsible for collection and evacuation of wounded during the operations having at his disposal the cars and provisions of the 231st F.A.D. M16 (4) Two squads of 74th Div. Bearers (R.A.M.C.) will be attached to each M.D.S. of the attacking Brigades i.e. 229th and 230th. These are already with R.A.O.s (5) There will be two routes of evacuation :- (a) the Northern through MAUREPAS, LE FOREST and HOSPITAL FARM (b) the southern through Relay Pol at C.19.d.9,2 and Car Pol at C.26.a.2.8 thence by main CLERY – MARICOURT Road (6) Walking Wounded Collecting Posts will be established at B18.B50 and C.17.a.2.8	[signature]

WAR DIARY or INTELLIGENCE SUMMARY.

Army Form C. 2118.

(Erase heading not required.)

Place	Date	Hour	Summary of Events and Information	Remarks and references to Appendices
H20 c 3.5	1/9/18	9.30 p	(1) Walking Wounded will be conveyed by lorries from C26 a 2.8 to Ill corps Walking Wounded Collecting Post. Walking Wounded will be carried on stretchers in ambulances of 231 Fd Amb. to Cauroy at QUARRY in LE FOREST. B16 b 8.6. thence by C.M.W.C. (Mangicourt) Motor Ambulances to levies will be in position 1/2 hour after zero & during 1st 1/2 of One N.C.O. and four bearers will be stationed at ex A at D18 b 50. A sweeping party will be stationed at QUARRY in C19 d 9.2. They will sweep east and west against Walking Wounded to lay hold of as k.z. These posts and arrangements are liable to subsequent modifications at revision by the Army officers responsible for the evacuation routes. (2) Lying wounded will be evacuated by cars and lorries — D3 x 5.8 on further information to Main Dressing station — by Cars evac from C26 a 2.8 viâ C.T. to M.D.S. The third cars of 1/4 Division will be at disposal of the lorries route — he will act then at the division forward of Hospital Farm — they will bear wounded back at QUARRY in LE FOREST by 30 or by lorries two	

WAR DIARY
or
INTELLIGENCE SUMMARY.
(Erase heading not required.)

Army Form C. 2118.

Place	Date	Hour	Summary of Events and Information	Remarks and references to Appendices
HQ E.18	14/5/9 of		Orders for placing Wombat wire fly in each route. Wombat placed will close to point down in any returning enemy forces that are available. (1) A new Key to (2) Q62Md99 - one officer 58 Division and one 74th Division will be here with three N.C.O.s of 231 Field Coy and 10 appts of Searchg of 74th Division. Wheeled vehicles of 74th Division will also to roll. As soon as established. (10) Rear posts will be manned by R.E. Crews flags. (11) A piece of charge of placking over before, as advanced one posts. (12) officer in charge of Northern Route will be Major McGillivray of 1/2 H.C.F.M.R. He will liaise with Captain Dix and Captain Mason of 231 Fd M/R. Captain Thorburn I.C. armd 1/2 HCFM/R will be in charge of Southern Route - he will have Capt Bissett Major McGillivray will give any necessary orders in rear of Northern and Southern routes considering. He will remain with Rear Division. Length of 1/2 HCFM/R route to inner wall. (13) Remarks of Officers of 1/2 HCFM/R will be told back when relieved at discretion of officer in route. (14) Zero hour about 5 a.m.	[signature]

Army Form C. 2118.

WAR DIARY
or
INTELLIGENCE SUMMARY.
(Erase heading not required.)

Instructions regarding War Diaries and Intelligence Summaries are contained in F. S. Regs., Part II. and the Staff Manual respectively. Title pages will be prepared in manuscript.

Place	Date	Hour	Summary of Events and Information	Remarks and references to Appendices
A2.c.5.8	2/4/18	12 noon	Relief of Unit by 231 FLD AMB at A2.d.8.8 completed at 1200 and move of Hd.Quarters to A2.d.9.7	
A2.d.9.7		4p	Relief completed of Adv. Dressing Stns on route of Bucquoy-Donnay.	
	3.4.18	1.1.4p	231 F.D. MTRS	
			Water Trolly & Capt Andrews and three lorrys remained with 231 FLD AMB 24 hours after that had been relieved to assist in kinds of Evacuation	
			Medical Arrangements received from HQRS "Wick" of 1/3rd and 1/7th	G.W.G.
	3/4/18	7pm	INFANTRY BRIGADES were to collect daily by 2/2 Her Amb from transferred to Burrow at LICK following officers and Red Hudson Capt. To Trees left to act as Liason officer to 102 LONDON Res arr	
	5/4/18	9am	1st LIEUT. H.W. HAMON, C.A.M.C. who proceeded on leave (orders 1127,1342,1348) 58th DIVISION arr	G.W.G.
	6/4/15		Warning Order received from AQMS (13499-0/A/M/18) 58th Division arr	G.W.G.
			Probably relieve 175th DIVISION during night of 6th and 7th inst	
	"	4p	Main Egads of Brasens left to embus with Hd 173rd Inf Bde at A2d 9.7 Inf 606 at B27.a.02 Advce Egads to report to Medical Officer of each Battalion of the	G.W.G.

WAR DIARY or INTELLIGENCE SUMMARY

Army Form C. 2118.

(Erase heading not required.)

Instructions regarding War Diaries and Intelligence Summaries are contained in F. S. Regs., Part II. and the Staff Manual respectively. Title pages will be prepared in manuscript.

Place	Date	Hour	Summary of Events and Information	Remarks and references to Appendices
Acheux	6/9/16	7 pm	Brigade (inc. 6th Yr and 8th London Regt) all ordered to report tomorrow to 2/3 H.C.Fd.Ambs. at A.D.S. Cadre q.l.	
"	7/9/16	9 am	Orders for men No. 55 received from A.D.S. 2/3 H.C.F.A.'s and 2/1 H.C.F.A.'s are to be collected by 2/1 H.C.F.A. and 2/3 H.C.F.A. as follows: 2/1 H.C.F.A. to evacuate by own ambces all sick cases to a pot collecting station from whence they will be evacuated by motor ambces to No. 58 C.C.S.	Gully
"	"	"	There left are to report to 2/3 H.C.F.A.'s at A.D.S. for orders. 2/3 H.C.F.A. are then to keep all serious cases and evacuate lying cases to A.D.S. by motor ambces (21 Corps) standing by.	Gully
"	"	"	All cases of lying personnel (others) left to report for duty at III Corps Hd. Qrs. at D.Z 8. c. 5. 4. Only two of these hospitals (D 20 c) will be under this Corps (D 20 c). Nothing to report to the Corps.	
B.D.S. CASTEL (D19.B.7.33)	8/9/16	10am	2/3 H.C.F.A. received from A.D.S. their order to move to a new base of to D.S.(C.B.C.) moving by route now in advance.	Gully
"	"	"	All to report there tomorrow.	

WAR DIARY
or
INTELLIGENCE SUMMARY.
(Erase heading not required.)

Army Form C. 2118.

Place	Date	Hour	Summary of Events and Information	Remarks and references to Appendices
B15/5/b	8/9/18	Noon	N.3185 Transferred of one N.C.O. and 10 O.R. 7 Am. O.R. 16 C.Cl. O.R. 12 R. O.R.11.-	
"	"	1.30 p	1 C.S.O. reported from 10th MAC for temporary duty	G.McG
"	"		Capt. Andrew and 10 OR proceeded to C.I.B.C.	
"	"		Captain (Aviator) G.A. McGillivray awarded the "Military Cross"	
"	"		(III Corps Routine Orders 4/5.9.18 No 135 para 574. 58 Div R.O. 4.6.9.18)	
C.I.B.C. (Poisennes)	9/9/18	2.30 p	Unit moved to C.I.B.C. - N.K.101 on the way to new area few	G.McG
"	"		Drama Indian Serg¹ 11170S Daries attached to conf. team who had	
"	"		been wounded by an enemy bomb that they were in[tense?]	
"	"		fire and and dispatched on a passing lorry to the nearest	
"	"		[ambulance] unit.	
"	"	Noon	N.315 - R.O.R 11 at O.1 O.R 11 C.Cl. O.R 13 Duty O.R.g R.N11.	G.McG
"	10/9/18	"	N.3185 at O.1 Any C.Cl. O.C.7 R.O.1	G.McG
"	"		Air raid during the night on near neighbourhood	
"	11/9/18	"	N.3185 R.O.1 An O.2 O.R 11 C.Cl. O.R 3 O.R. 11 R. N11	G.McG
"	12/9/18	"	N.3185 F.N.W Rd O.R 19 C.Cl. O.R 17 F O.R 2	G.McG
"	13/9/18	"	N.3185 F O.R 2 An O.R 28 C.Cl. O.R 17 O.R 2	G.McG

Army Form C. 2118.

WAR DIARY
or
INTELLIGENCE SUMMARY.
(Erase heading not required.)

Instructions regarding War Diaries and Intelligence Summaries are contained in F. S. Regs., Part II. and the Staff Manual respectively. Title pages will be prepared in manuscript.

Place	Date	Hour	Summary of Events and Information	Remarks and references to Appendices
CISC	13/9/18	9.0 a.m	Lieut. Lee O.R.S (Bearers) returned to unit from 2/3 H.C.F.A 918 — O.C 2/3 H.C.F.A 918	[sig]
			reports he now has five M.O's	
			W.O cars returned from A.D.S. (EIKHABS)	
	14/9/18	11.0 a.m	1st Lieut C.E Dunaway 11.C. (M.O.R.C U.S.A) reported for duty from the LONDON	[sig]
			area, was sent to duties Officer (A.D.M.S. 75th Div)	
		Noon	W.V.B.S 1 O.R 2 adm 0.3 O.R 26 C.C.S O.N. evac 28 R NYK	[sig]
	15/9/18	"	W.V.B.S 1 O.R 2 adm O.R 26 C.C.S 14 R O.R 12	[sig]
	16/9/18	10.a.m	Ambulances received from A.D.M.S to be prepared to return at short	[sig]
			notice which may be refused to be fit for discharge on 17.10	
			day, on account of 175 Inf B.O.S leaving, and of the evac. they	
		Noon	W.V.B.S 1 O.R 12 Long from S/F.R.O O.R 1, ad O.R 26 C.C.O.R 15 R O.R 11	[sig]
		1.0p	Returned from Clyps H.C.F.A 918 to relive Bearers evac at the M/r most	
	17/9/18	Noon	W.V.B.S 1 O.R 21 O.R O.1 O.R 31 C.C 1 O.R 15, 19 Duty O.R (W) 1 R O.R 32	[sig]
		12.N	Arrived Medical Arrangements No 28 Fwd A.D.S giving news of	
			Field Ambulances and location of posts	
		4.pm	One Sgt. 2 Orderly ascents officials of Bearers left to report to	

Noo15. Wt. W1422/M100 350,000 12/16 D. D. & L. Form/C./2118/14.

WAR DIARY
or
INTELLIGENCE SUMMARY.

(Erase heading not required.)

Army Form C. 2118.

Instructions regarding War Diaries and Intelligence Summaries are contained in F. S. Regs., Part II. and the Staff Manual respectively. Title pages will be prepared in manuscript.

Place	Date	Hour	Summary of Events and Information	Remarks and references to Appendices
C.C.S.	17/9/18	6 p.m.	O/C 2/3 H.C.H.F.A. to A.D.M.S. E.W.A.S. (O.L.62.C.) One Jack and two Lanterns also sent	GMcG
	18/9/18	noon	W. 3185 – R on 32 Ann or 33 Col. or 31 R or 36 405309 Cpl. Fox. R.A.M. 50843 (G. E. Willcocks awarded the Military Medal) (Authority 38th Div. R.O. 191 dt. 17-9-18)	GMcG
		1.30	2nd Echelon from A.D.M.S. 38 Division to send 1st Lieut. Dunaway U.S. Corps	
			30 O.R. to III Corps W.V.S. for temporary duty	
		11.30	16 O.R.s reported back from 2/3 H.C.F.A.	
	19/9/18	9 a.m.	1st Lieut. Dunaway U.S. Corps and 30 O.R.s left for temporary duty with III Corps W.V.S.	GMcG
		noon	W.3185 – A.C.I. 36 of or on 11.7.1855 re Mess O.R.2 Indy C.A.S.R etc.	
			Lieut. Col. H. Fulton D.S.O. granted leave to United Kingdom 20-9-18 – Lieut. Col. H. Fulton D.S.O. III Corps R.S./ 4373/18 – (Source)	
		4. 10 – 18	Ausy III Corps R.S./ 4373/18 – (Source)	
			Major G.N. McGillivray t/c took over tempy command since Lieut. Col. H. Fulton D.S.O.	
	20/9/18	noon	M 3185 A.C.I. 80 Pam O.I.O.R. 16 C.I.D.I.O.N.T - R.O.R. 69 Ram O.I.O.R. 16 C.I.D.I.O.N.T - R.O.R. 69	GMcG

M5045. Wt. W14427/M1160 350,000 12/16. D. D. & L. Forms/C/2118/14.

WAR DIARY
or
INTELLIGENCE SUMMARY.

Army Form C. 2118.

(Erase heading not required.)

Place	Date	Hour	Summary of Events and Information	Remarks and references to Appendices
C I S C	31/7/18	10.30am	Instructions from ADMS to open all cars to MDS (Ellis & S) and to evacuate sick by bearer squads	fully
		noon	W3151 - R O K 69 T from 55 FAR 80 R3 Bx OR 15 CC OR 18 Duty OK I OR 77	
		2.5pm	Wng Order received from ADMS - Divisions will probably be relieved night of 2/3/8.3-1 Ref. to 107 ADMS and to M1150 - 53 DIVISION CGQ 82 - went to same effect	
			Orders and instructions from ADMS - Reference CGQ 82 - relief may not occur till close on the night of 23/24- Ref known	
	2/8/18		W3151 - R O R 71 T from 55 FAR 18 OR 4 CR 0 OR 14 CCl OR 17 & OR 77 W3151 - R O K 77 T from 38 FAR OR 1 S F AR 20 R2 Bx OR 1 OR 6	fully fully
			C R 0 1 CR 25 Duty O R 1 R OR 57	
		4.5pm	Warning Orders N O 2 received from ADMS - Division will be relieved night of 23/24th to 24th by 12th DIVISION - 1/2 H C F AMB to proceed to FRANCOURT O C A 20B - odd of horses - frequent Nos. Only 3 officer only	
			Further Instructions N O 1 in connection with III Corps OO NO 325 of- from ADMS	
			MSS 18 Warning from ADMS	

WAR DIARY
INTELLIGENCE SUMMARY

Army Form C. 2118.

Place	Date	Hour	Summary of Events and Information	Remarks and references to Appendices
C/15C	25/9/18	2.14.	C/o then Order to be issued for H.Q.U.S with embussing pts given.	G.V.R.
"	"	6 p	attached	
"	"	"	Received Operation Order No. 56 from 173 INF. BDE. re embussing.	
"	"	"	2/3 H.C.F. Bde. embuses at 11.30 a.m.	
"	"	11.24	Received instructions from C.R.E. of 173 INF. BDE. Group re a rendezvous with above order - time of embussing changed to 3 p.m. – embussing point MOISLAINS CHURCH	
"	26/9/18	"	Capt. T.S. VICKERS and Capt. T. OTR. G. KNOWLES given on leave to ???? Kingdom 25.9.17 - 9.10.18 (A.D.F.S. 113 nos of 23.9.18).	G.V.R.
"	"	9 am	Rare received that Major CAPT. ANDREW left to exchange to Russian C.	
"	"	"	Real later allinscount and to of ??? ??? to come to station	
"	"	Noon	Cars attached from 2/3 H.C.F.A.M.O	
"	"	Noon	N3/85 – R.E. & 59 mares from 35 F.A.M.B. O.R. 2 Rums O.1 or 10 OC101	
"	"	"	C.R.S. Ray OR.17 – R. on 46	
"	"	6.30	2/3 Bn. arrived at HARCOURT (B15c51 – 42.62 NW)	
"	"	"	Rare Adv. Hd. of Bde. in rit. 2/3 H.C.F. Pris. refs. Be Reck	

WAR DIARY
or
INTELLIGENCE SUMMARY.
(Erase heading not required.)

Army Form C. 2118.

Place	Date	Hour	Summary of Events and Information	Remarks and references to Appendices
CONTOURS A15 c 5.1	24/9/18	7.30p	Warning Order received from NRDLS to move to HEILLY 25th inst	G.M.J.
"			Instructions received from ADMS to detail 1 officer & 1 N.C.O to	
			proceed with 50mm 25th inst in motor ambulance to AUDIGNY	
			(S1 104 - PHASE RD) to meet D.M. C 50 Division at 12.30 p.m. for	
			1 loan of artillery	
"	25/9/18		Met D.A.D.M.S. N.E. (M.C.O.C) and Medical Officer 50 Div. reported from III Corps	G.M.J.
			M.D.S	
			N.355. R.A.P. 16 A.M.C R1 Dap O.R. 2 - R.O.R. 45	
"		1.30 noon	at 1 ambulance at HEILLY	G.M.J
"		1.30	Issued Running instructions authorizing & in accordance with A.S. 25/5 of 9 June 18	
		3.30	Handing party of 1 N.C.O and 50 O.R's reported to Entraining Officers at	G.M.J
HEILLY		4.30pm	MERICOURT Station to load 1 hospital	
"		noon	R.O.C N on 65 CO. C.K. 29 Duty Orch & Nil.	
"		"	1 use of RAVINE-RAILENE STATION	
"		"	1 death 51 Pour JENKINS (Q 35 and 3 W. MS)	
CORBIE N 35 a 3.3	27/9/18		Orders received to entrain for our A.D.M.S - 2/2 M.T FORM to relieve	G.M.J
(see a.g.)				

Army Form C. 2118.

WAR DIARY
or
INTELLIGENCE SUMMARY.
(Erase heading not required.)

Instructions regarding War Diaries and Intelligence Summaries are contained in F. S. Regs., Part II. and the Staff Manual respectively. Title pages will be prepared in manuscript.

Place	Date	Hour	Summary of Events and Information	Remarks and references to Appendices
COUY-SERVINS G.35.d.3.3. (Sht 8)	27/9/18	4pm	No 74th FIELD AMB. at the Main Dressing Station Fosse 10 (R8.c.c.- M46)	G.H.H.
			on the 30th inst relief to be completed by noon	
"	28/9/18	3pm	Motor Ambulance to No 2.9 received from A.D.M.S. in connection with Operation Order No 61	G.H.H.
"	29/9/18	2pm	Capt Andrew and 15 O.R. proceeded to Fosse 10 (R.8.c.c.- M46) to act as Advance Party	G.H.H.
"	30/9/18	10.30am	74th arrived at Main Dressing Station at Fosse 10 (R.8.c.c.- M.8) — relief complete.	G.H.H.
"	30/9/18			

Army Form C. 2118.

Army Form C. 2118.

WAR DIARY
or
INTELLIGENCE SUMMARY

(Erase heading not required.)

MEDICAL

Vol 21

WO 95/4932Y

CONFIDENTIAL

WAR DIARY

OF

2/2 Home Counties Fd. Amb. R.A.M.C.(T)

FROM 1/10/18 TO 31/10/18.

[Stamp: COMMITTEE FOR THE MEDICAL HISTORY OF THE WAR, 4 DEC 1918]

Lt. Col. R.A.M.C. (T)
O.C.
2/2 H.C.Fd. R.A.M.C. (T)

[Stamp: 2/2ND HOME COUNTIES FIELD AMBULANCE]

Army Form C. 2118.

WAR DIARY
or
INTELLIGENCE SUMMARY.
(Erase heading not required.)

Instructions regarding War Diaries and Intelligence Summaries are contained in F. S. Regs., Part II. and the Staff Manual respectively. Title pages will be prepared in manuscript.

Place	Date	Hour	Summary of Events and Information	Remarks and references to Appendices
FOSSE 10 Sheet 44 B R 8 Central	1/10/18	11 A.M	Lieut. P.A. MANSFIELD (T.C.) reported for duty. (A.D.M.S.)	
"	"	18.30	W 3185 Adm. Off. 1 O.R. 16 CCS O.R.6 DRS O.R.6 R Off. 1 O.R. 4 Capt. R.L. BARWICK (T.C.) and 1 O.R. rejoined Unit from 58th Div. Amy	17
"	2/10/18	10.00	Capt. R.L. BARWICK (T.C.) struck off strength on leaving to report to A.D.M.S. 2nd Division for duty. (Assus.6210d 1/10/18)	17
"	3/10/18		W 3185. R Off. 1 O.R. 4 Adm. O.R. 28 CCS Off. 1 O.R. 12 DRS O.R. 12 Corps Skin Dept O.R. 2 R.O.R. 15	17
"	"		W 3185 R O.R. 15 Adm. Off. 2 O.R. 86 CCS Off. 2 O.R. 43 DRS O.R. 12 CSD O.R. 2 R.O.R. 42	17
"	"	7.00	4 Aguada (bearers) sent to 2/1 H.Coamb for duty - to report at A.D.S. (M11 C 8.9)	
"	"	14.30	1 Sergt + 4 " " " " " "	
"	4/10/18		W 3185 R O.R. 42 Adm. Off. 2 O.R. 62 CCS Off. 1 O.R. 34 DRS O.R. 43 Duty Off. 1 R O.R. 27	17
"	"	7.00	1 Sergt + 4 Aguada sent to 2/1 H.Coamb for duty - to report at A.D.S. (M11 C 8-9)	17
"	5/10/18		W 3185 R O.R. 27 Adm. Off. 3 O.R. 94 CCS Off. 3 O.R. 61 DRS O.R. 18 CSD O.R. 3 Duty O.R. 2 R O.R. 37	17
"	6/10/18		W 3185 R O.R. 37 Adm. Off. 2 O.R. 44 CCS Off. 2 O.R. 22 DRS O.R. 19 R O.R. 40	17
"	7/10/18		W 3185 R O.R. 40 Adm. Off. 1 O.R. 37 CCS Off. 1 O.R. 26 DRS O.R. 26 Duty O.R. 1 R O.R. 24	17
"	8/10/18		W 3185 R O.R. 24 Adm. O.R. 34 CCS O.R. 17 DRS O.R. 18 CSD O.R. 1 R O.R. 22	17

Army Form C. 2118.

WAR DIARY
or
INTELLIGENCE SUMMARY.
(Erase heading not required.)

Instructions regarding War Diaries and Intelligence Summaries are contained in F.S. Regs., Part II. and the Staff Manual respectively. Title pages will be prepared in manuscript.

Place	Date	Hour	Summary of Events and Information	Remarks and references to Appendices
FOSSE 10 44B. R 8 Central	9/10/18		W 3185. R.O.R. 22. Adm. Off. 1 O.R. 29 C.C.S. O.R. 17 D.R.S. O.R. 5 Duty O.R. 1 R Off. 1 O.R. 28	17
"	10/10/18		W 3185 R Off. 1 O.R. 28 Adm. Off. 2 O.R. 28. C.C.S. Off. 1 O.R. 16 D.R.S. O.R. 17 Duty Off. 1 O.R. 1 R Off. 1 O.R. 22	17
"		10.15	M.D.S. and Transport Lines inspected by Major General F.W. RAMSAY, C.M.G., D.S.O., Commanding 58th (London) Div	17
"	11/10/18		W 3185 R Off. 1 O.R. 22. Adm. Off. 1 O.R. 38. C.C.S. Off. 1 O.R. 16 D.R.S. O.R. 27 C.S.D. O.R. 1 Died O.R. 2 Duty O.R. 2 R Off. 1 O.R. 12.	
"		12.00	Major T.B. McKEE returned from leave.	17
"	12/10/18		W 3185 R Off. 1 O.R. 12. Adm. Off. 4 O.R. 58. C.C.S Off. 3 O.R. 23 D.R.S. O.R. 25 C.S.D Off. 1 Duty O.R. 5 R Off. 1 O.R. 17	17
"		8.30	O.O. No. 62 recd. from A.D.M.S. "Unit to move to St PIERRE and take over A.D.S. and JUNCTION POST (M12.a.9.f.) - move to be completed by 12.00 hrs 13th inst."	
"		14.30	Capt GESER, Lieut. MANSFIELD and 10 O.R left as Advance Party.	17
St PIERRE 44 A. M11 C.7.9.	13/10/18	11.00	Move Completed to St PIERRE.	
"			W 3185 R Off. 1 O.R. 17 Adm. Off. 4 O.R. 34 C.C.S Off. 4 O.R. 37 D.R.S O.R. 7 Duty Off. 1 O.R. 7 R NIL.	17
"	14/10/18		Capt. A.R. GESER granted leave 14 — 28/10/18	17
"			W 3185 Adm. Off. 5 O.R. 86 C.C.S. Off. 2 O.R. 48 D.R.S. Off. 2 O.R. 36 C.S.D. O.R. 2 Duty Off. 1 R NIL.	17

Army Form C. 2118.

WAR DIARY
or
INTELLIGENCE SUMMARY.
(Erase heading not required.)

Instructions regarding War Diaries and Intelligence Summaries are contained in F. S. Regs., Part II. and the Staff Manual respectively. Title pages will be prepared in manuscript.

Place	Date	Hour	Summary of Events and Information	Remarks and references to Appendices
St PIERRE 44A. M11c79	15/10/18		W3185 Adm. Off 2 O.R. 108 C.C.A. Off 2 O.R. 54. D.R.S. O.R. 148. Duty O.R. 6. R. Nil	
	"	20.30	O.O. No. 63 rec'd from ADMS. "The 2/2 HCOamb. (M.D.S.) will move on the 17th inst. to FOUQUIERES (O.21.a.4.5)	1/7
			- Move to be completed by 12.00 hrs "	
"	16/10/18	08.00	Major T.B. McKEE left as Advance Party for new site.	1/7
			+20 O.R.	
	"		W3185. Adm. Off 6 O.R. 42. C.C.A. Off 3 O.R. 23 D.R.S. Off 2 O.R. 19. R Nil	
"	17/10/18		W3185 Adm. Off 2 O.R. 34. C.C.A. Off 2 O.R. DRS O.R. 9. Died O.R. 1 R Nil.	
	"	07.00	M.D.S opened by Advance Party at FOUQUIERES	1/7
FOUQUIERES 44A. O21a.4.5	"	12.30	Move Completed to FOUQUIERES. A holding party of 1 N.C.O. + 4 men left at St PIERRE.	
"	18/10/18	10.00	Capt. G.W.M. ANDREW left to report to 2/1 HCOamb. for temp duty (ADMS M5746 d 17/10/18)	
	"		W3185. Adm. Off 1 O.R. 30. C.C.A. Off 1 O.R. 16. D.R.S. O.R. 9 R O.R. 7	
	"	11.00	O.O. No. 64 rec'd from ADMS "Unit to move tomorrow to OSTRICOURT (44 A. P6.6.3.3 and establish	1/7
			M.D.S. there. Present M.D.S. to be taken over by 2/3 HCOfA. as D.R.S.	
	"	14.00	Major T.B. McKEE + 19 O.R. left as Advance Party	
OSTRICOURT 44 A. P6.6.3.3	19/10/18	07.00	M.D.S. opened by Advance Party	
	"	13.30	Move Completed to OSTRICOURT	
	"		W3185. R O.R. 7. Adm. Off 1 O.R. 49. C.C.A Off 1 O.R. 25 Died O.R. 2 R O.R. 29.	1/7
	"	18.00	Movement Order rec'd. from ADMS. "Unit to move tomorrow to MONS AREA and establish M.D.S on	
			the site vacated by 2/1 HCOamb.	1/7

WAR DIARY
or
INTELLIGENCE SUMMARY.
(Erase heading not required.)

Army Form C. 2118.

Place	Date	Hour	Summary of Events and Information	Remarks and references to Appendices
OSTRICOURT 44 A. P6.b.3.3	19/10/18	19.00	Major T.B. McKEE and 18 O.R. left as Advance Party	
MONS EN PÉVÈLE 44 A. K24 a.0.4	20/10/18	7.00	M.D.S. opened by Advance Party.	
"	"	11.15	Move Completed to K24 a 0.4.	
"	"	"	W3185 R.O.R. 29 Adm. O.R. 39. C.C.S O.R. 13 B.R.S. O.R. 55. R. Nil	
"	"	15.30	O.O. No. 65. recd. from A.D.M.S "Unit to move tomorrow to VERT BOIS (G.14 a 5.7) and establish M.D.S. there"	
"	"	"	Major T.B. McKEE + 18 O.R. left as Advance Party.	
"	"	"	Treatment of Civilians Commenced.	
VERT BOIS 44 G.14 a.5.7	21/10/18	7.00	M.D.S. opened by Advance Party	
"	"	11.15	Move Completed to G.14 a.5.7.	
"	"	"	W3185. Adm. O.R. 24. C.C.S. O.R. 3. B.R.S. O.R. 6 R. O.R. 15	
"	22/10/18		W3185. R O.R. 15 Adm. Off. 3 O.R. 47 C.C.S Off. 3 O.R. 46 B.R.S O.R. 15 R.O.R. 1	
"	23/10/18		W3185 R O.R.1 Adm. Off. 3 O.R. 64. CCS Off. 10 R. 24. B.R.S. Off. 2 O.R. 29 Died O.R. 3 R.O.R.6	
"	"	9.30	Sick Evacuating Station opened near the "Refilling Point" at NOMAIN. All sick cases (except serious) for CCS and W. Wounded to be sent there from M.D.S. for evacuation to CCS by returning Supply Lorries	

Army Form C. 2118.

WAR DIARY
or
INTELLIGENCE SUMMARY.
(Erase heading not required.)

Instructions regarding War Diaries and Intelligence Summaries are contained in F. S. Regs., Part II. and the Staff Manual respectively. Title pages will be prepared in manuscript.

Place	Date	Hour	Summary of Events and Information	Remarks and references to Appendices
VERT BOIS. S.H. G.14.a.5.7	24/10/18	16.00	W3185 R. O.R.6. Adm. Off. 2 O.R. 101 C.C.S. O.R. 75 D.P.S. Off. 2 O.R. 25 Died O.R. 2 R.O.R. 5 "Sick Evacuating Station" closed. "Refilling Point" moved from NOMAIN. Civilians medically treated 27. Evac. to C.C.S 3	[sig]
"	25/10/18		W3185 R O.R.5. Adm. Off. 3 O.R. 42. C.C.S. Off. 2 O.R. 89 D.P.S Off. 1 O.R. 3 Duty O.R. 4 R.O.R. 1 Civilians medically treated 16. Evac. to C.C.S 7	[sig]
"	26/10/18		W3185 R O.R.1. Adm. Off. 2 O.R. 100. C.C.S. Off. 1 O.R. 47 Died O.R. 3 Duty O.R. 10 R Off. 1 O.R. 4	
"	"	13.00	M 5795 d 26/10/18 rec'd from ARTH'S "Small advance party to be sent to the Brewery, I.7.d.8.3. RUMEGIES to take over site as next M.D.S.	
"	"	15.00	Major T. B. McKEE and 10 O.R. left as "Advance Party"	
"	"	21.30	M 5795/1 rec'd from ARTH'S "Move of unit to new site not to take place at present — Advance Party to remain at Mes I.7.d.8.3. until move forward takes place." Civilians medically treated 17. Evac. to C.C.S 5	[sig]
"	27/10/18	11.00	W3185 R Off. 1 O.R. 41 Adm. Off. 4 O.R. 45 C.C.S Off. 4 O.R. 60 D.P.S. O.R. 21 Duty O.R. 1 R Off. 1 O.R. 4. M 5798 rec'd from ARTH'S "Medical officer to visit daily the S.A.A. Section at NOMAIN. All Civilians (for hospital) to be evacuated to ST EUGÉNIE HOSP. at LILLE. No treated 7.	[sig]

Army Form C. 2118.

WAR DIARY
or
INTELLIGENCE SUMMARY.
(Erase heading not required.)

Instructions regarding War Diaries and Intelligence Summaries are contained in F. S. Regs., Part II. and the Staff Manual respectively. Title pages will be prepared in manuscript.

Place	Date	Hour	Summary of Events and Information	Remarks and references to Appendices
VERT BOIS G14 a 5.7	28/10/18		W3185. R.O.R.4. Adm. Off. 1 O.R.46. C.C.S. O.R.46. D.R.S. Off. 1 O.R.1. Died Off. 1 O.R.9	
	"	16.00	Medical Inspection Room opened at NOMAIN for Civilians - to be visited daily by M.O. Civilians treated. 7.	
"	29/10/18		W3185. R.O.R.9. Adm. Off. 1 O.R.69 C.C.S. O.R.25. D.R.S. Off. 1 O.R.16 Duty O.R.1 R.O.R.36 Civilians treated 33. Sent to hospital 3	
"	30/10/18		W3185. R.O.R.36 Adm. O.R.84. C.C.S. O.R.42. D.R.S. O.R.26 Died O.R.1 Duty O.R.1 R.O.R.50	
	"	15.30	M5814 d 30/10/18 recd. from ARMS " A medical officer to take the daily sick parades of the 509, 510, 511, 512 H.T. Coys - all billeted in the NOMAIN area."	
	"	17.00	Capt A.R. GEYER rejoined unit from leave. Civilians treated 43. Sent to hospital 6.	
"	31/10/18		W3185. R.O.R.50 Adm. Off. 1 O.R.58 C.C.S. O.R.44 D.R.S. O.R.21 R Off. 1 O.R.43. Civilians treated 47. Sent to hospital 8	

Army Form C. 2118.

WAR DIARY
or
INTELLIGENCE SUMMARY.
(Erase heading not required.)

MEDICAL

WAR DIARY

of

2/2 Home Counties Fld. Amb. R.A.M.C.(T)

FROM Nov. 1st 1918 to Nov. 30th 1918.

CONFIDENTIAL.

Lt. Col. R.A.M.C.(T)
O.C.
2/2 H.C.Fd. R.A.M.C.(T)

WO/MM/919

2/2nd
HOME COUNTIES
FIELD AMBULANCE.
HC 261

Army Form C. 2118.

WAR DIARY
or
INTELLIGENCE SUMMARY.

(Erase heading not required.)

Instructions regarding War Diaries and Intelligence Summaries are contained in F. S. Regs., Part II. and the Staff Manual respectively. Title pages will be prepared in manuscript.

Place	Date	Hour	Summary of Events and Information	Remarks and references to Appendices
VERT BOIS N4. G/4 a 5.7.	1/11/18		W3185 R. Off. 1 O.R. 43 Adm. Off. 2 O.R. 53. C.C.S. Off. 1 O.R. 16 D.R.S. Off. 1 O.R. 30 Died O.R. 1 R. Off. 1 O.R. 49. Civilians medically treated 52.	☩
"	2/11/18		W3185 R. Off. 1 O.R. 49 Adm. Off. 2 O.R. 34 C.C.S. Off. 2 O.R. 12 D.R.S. Off. 1 O.R. 44 Duty O.R. 1 R. O.R. 26 Civilians treated 54. Evacuated 4.	☩
"	"	14.00	Major T. B. McKEE returned from "Advance Party" at RUMEGIES to M.D.S. for duty.	☩
"	3/11/18		W3185 R. O.R. 26 Adm. O.R. 36 C.C.S. O.R. 9 D.R.S. O.R. 23. R.O.R. 30 Civilians treated 54. Evacuated 2.	☩
"	4/11/18		W3185 R. O.R. 30 Adm. Off. 1 O.R. 49. C.C.S. O.R. 1 D.R.S. O.R. 51 Duty O.R. 1. R.O.R. 27. Civilians treated 46. Evacuated 2.	☩
"	"	22.30	M.550 (Warning Order) recd. from ADMS. "The 1st Corps has been ordered to be in readiness to attack at 24 hours notice from 12.00 hrs 6/11/18 in conjunction with other attacks to be made North & South. D.C. 2/2 N.Ggds. will forthwith proceed to dispose of sick in M.D.S. by evacuation to D.R.S.	☩
"	5/11/18	07.00	Sick evacuation to D.R.S. Completed.	
"	"		W3185 R. O.R. 27 Adm. Off. 1 O.R. 39 C.C.S. Off. 1 O.R. 20 D.R.S. O.R. 43. R.O.R. 2. Civilians treated 29.	☩
"	6/11/18		W3185. R. O.R. 2 Adm. Off. 5 O.R. 44 C.C.S. O.R. 16 D.R.S. Off. 4 O.R. 20. Died Off. 1 Duty O.R. 1 R.O.R. 9. Civilians treated 44. Evacuated 1.	☩

Army Form C. 2118.

WAR DIARY
or
INTELLIGENCE SUMMARY.
(Erase heading not required.)

Instructions regarding War Diaries and Intelligence Summaries are contained in F. S. Regs., Part II. and the Staff Manual respectively. Title pages will be prepared in manuscript.

Place	Date	Hour	Summary of Events and Information	Remarks and references to Appendices
VERT BOIS H4.G.W.a.5.7	6/4/18	09.30	Capt. A.R. GEYER struck off strength on leaving to report to O.C. 4th Suffolk Regt. for duty. (ADMS M.5857 of 6/4/18)	W
"	7/4/18	01.00	O.O. No. 66 recd. from ADMS. 2/3 H⁰Amb. will move on 7th inst. to AIX and establish D.R.S. there.	
			O.C. 2/2 H⁰Amb. will arrange to accommodate up to 40 patients at the present D.R.S. until accommodation for same has been provided for at AIX. He will loan to 2/3 H⁰Amb. 2 M.A.C. Cars to assist in the evacuation or transport of sick. 2/1 H⁰Amb. will evacuate sick on 7th inst. to M.D.S.	
			W3185 R.O.R.9. Adm. Off. 4 O.R. 52 CCS. Off. 1 O.R. 22 D.R.S. Off. 2 O.R. 24 Duty O.R. 3 R Off. 10 O.R. 12 Civilians treated 37. Evacuated 1	
"		16.30	Information received that a Culvert on the AUCHY to VERT BOIS ROAD had broken down by reason of floods. A working Party detailed and repairs completed by 22.00 hrs enabling traffic up to 30 cwt to pass over it. The C.R.E. and D.A.P.M. notified and traffic diverted during these hours.	W
"	8/4/18		W3185 R Off. 1 O.R. 12 Trans. from D.R.S. O.R. 35 Adm. O.R. 71 CCS Off. 1 O.R. 25 Died O.R. 1 R.O.R. 92 Civilians treated 39. Evacuated 1	W
"	"	11.45	O.O. No. 67 recd. from A.D.M.S. "Unit will move tomorrow to RUMEGIES and establish M.D.S. there. Move to be completed by 14.00 hours."	
"	"	14.30	Major J.B. McKEE left to join Advance Party.	
RUMEGIES Sheet 44 (Bernay)	9/4/18	07.00	M.R.S. opened by Advance Party.	W

WAR DIARY
or
INTELLIGENCE SUMMARY.

Army Form C. 2118.

Place	Date	Hour	Summary of Events and Information	Remarks and references to Appendices
RUMEGIES (Brewery)	9/11/18	13.20	Move Completed.	
"	"	"	W 3/85. R. O.R. 92. Adm. Off. 3 O.R. 124 CCS. Off. 3 O.R. 149 D.P.S. O.R. 60 Duty O.R. 7 R Nil. Civilians treated 6. Evacuated 3.	
"	"	"	Capt. G.W.M. ANDREW rejoined Unit from s/s Hospital	
"	"	15.00	O.O. No. 68 Recd. from A.D.M.S. "Unit to move tomorrow to the Brewery, BLEHARIES. Move to be completed by 12.00 hrs.	
BLEHARIES (Brewery)	10/11/18	09.00	Advance Party under Major T.P. McKEE proceeded by Amb. to open M.D.S. on new site	
"	"	12.30	Move Completed	
"	"	"	W 3/85 Adm. Off. 1 O.R. 22 CCS Off. 1 O.R. 9. D.P.S. O.R.13. Civilians treated 1. Evac. 1	
"	"	15.30	"MXI" recd. from A.D.M.S. – "Unit to move tomorrow to PERUWELZ.	
BASECLES (Convent)	11/11/18	07.00	O.O. No. 69 recd from A.D.M.S. cancelling MXI. "M.D.S. to be opened at the Convent at BASECLES.	
"	"	07.15	Major McKEE with Advance Party left for new M.D.S.	
"	"	15.45	Move Completed	
"	"	"	W 3/85 Adm. Off. 2 O.R. 12 CCS Off. 2 O.R. 12. Civilians treated 1. Evac. 1	
"	12/11/18	"	W 3/85 Adm. O.R. 21 CCS. O.R. 6 D.P.S. O.R. 13 R. O.R. 2. Civilians treated 1	
"	13/11/18	"	W 3/85. Trans. from 1st Cav. Fld. Amb. O.R. } R 2. Adm. O.R. 12. CCS. Off. 1 O.R. 15. D.P.S. O.R. 2. R Nil. 3rd " " Off. 1 O.R. 6} Civilians treated 6. Evac. 4.	

WAR DIARY
or
INTELLIGENCE SUMMARY.
(Erase heading not required)

Army Form C. 2118.

Place	Date	Hour	Summary of Events and Information	Remarks and references to Appendices
BASECLES (General)	14/11/18		W3185. Trans. from 1st Cav. Fd. Amb. O.R.4 Adm. O.R.8 C.C.S. O.R.9 R.O.R.3 Civilians treated 3.	
Sheet 45 A.2 G.4.9.S.	15/11/18		W3185. " " " O.R.5 R.O.R.3 Adm. O.R.3 C.C.S. O.R.11. R Nil " 7	
"	16/11/18		W3185. " " " O.R.13 Adm. O.R.16 C.C.S. O.R.23 B.R.S. O.R.6 R Nil " 4	
"	17/11/18		W3185. " " " O.R.9 Adm. O.R.6 C.C.S. O.R.6 B.R.S. O.R.1 R Nil " 4 Evac. 2.	
"			Wounded P of W. (English) left by the Germans at HAL near BRUSSELS fetched by Motor Amb + evac. to CCS	
"	18/11/18		W3185. Adm. Off. 2 O.R.8 C.C.S. Off 2 O.R.8. Civilians treated 6	
"	19/11/18		W3185. Adm. Off. 1 O.R.6 C.C.S. Off 1 O.R.2 B.R.S. O.R.4. Civilians treated 4	
"	20/11/18		W3185. Adm. O.R.5 B.R.S. O.R.5 " " 4.	
"	21/11/18		W3185. Adm. O.R.12 C.C.S. O.R.4. B.R.S. O.R.8 " " 5. Evac. 2	
"	22/11/18		W3185. Adm. O.R.11 C.C.S. O.R.3. B.R.S. O.R.8 " " 5	
"		12.00	Unit (including H.T. A.S.C. and all available Motor Ambs.) Inspected by A.D.M.S.	

Army Form C. 2118.

WAR DIARY
or
INTELLIGENCE SUMMARY.
(Erase heading not required.)

Instructions regarding War Diaries and Intelligence Summaries are contained in F. S. Regs., Part II. and the Staff Manual respectively. Title pages will be prepared in manuscript.

Place	Date	Hour	Summary of Events and Information	Remarks and references to Appendices
BASECLES (Cornet)	22/11/18	16.00	M.5945 recd. from A.D.M.S. "The 5 SUNBEAM AMBS to be exchanged for 5 NAPIER AMBS from 74th Division"	17
Shut 45. A20 a9.5	"	19.00	W.1451 " " cancelling same.	
"	23/11/18		W.3185 Adm. O.R. 7. CCS O.R. 2. D.R.S. O.R. 5. Civilians treated 4	17
"	24/11/18		W.3185 Adm. O.R. 8 CCS O.R. 4 D.R.S O.R.4 " " 11	17
"	25/11/18		W.3185 Adm. O.R. 3 CCS O.R 3 " " 8	17
"	"	09.30	Major G. M. McGILLIVRAY left to report to O.C. No 8 B.R.C.S. Hospital for transit to the Convalescent Hosp at CAP MARTIN (ADM.S 58 Div.)	
"	26/11/18		W.3185. Adm. O.R. 12. CCS O.R. 2. D.R.S O.R. 10. Civilians treated 18	17
"	"	18.00	"Medical Arrangements" No 31 recd from A.D.M.S. "The 2/1 Hogans. will move to BONSECOURS tomorrow and establish R.A.S. there on 28th inst. 2/3 Hoga. will continue to admit and dispose of all special cases (including dental and ophthalmia). Sick hitherto collected by 2/1 Hoga will from 27th be collected by 2/2 Hogant."	
"	27/11/18		W.3185 Adm. O.R. 6. CCS O.R. 2. D.R.S O.R 3 R.O.R.1. Civilians treated 24	17

WAR DIARY
or
INTELLIGENCE SUMMARY.

Army Form C. 2118.

Place	Date	Hour	Summary of Events and Information	Remarks and references to Appendices
BASECLES. (Convent) No. 5. A 20 a 9.3	28/11/18	11.00	W3185. R.O.R.1. Adm O.R.9. D.P.S. O.R.10. Civilians treated 19.	
			M5916 d 27/11/18 recd from ADMS. "The ADMS was very pleased with the result of his inspection of the Unit on the 24th inst. It was evident that the transport section had worked hard, and the result was shown in the smart appearance of the horses, and the care taken in the adjustment of the harness etc."	
"	29/11/18		W3185. Adm. O.R. 16. D.P.S. O.R. 16. Civilians treated 28.	
		20.00	M/6002 recd. from ADMS. "Le 2/2 HoAmb. (less Transport) will represent the 3 Divisional Fld. Amb. at the Divisional Review (by the Army Commander) on Monday 2/12/18 at the GRAND&LISE Aviation ground at 11.00 hrs. Personnel reqd. to complete establishment will be loaned from 2/3 Fld Amb. There will be a Divisional Practice on 30/11/18. - Fld. Amb. to arrive on parade ground at 10.30 hrs. Dress - Drill Order.	
"	30/11/18	09.00	W3185. Adm. Off. 2 O.R. 21 C.C.S. Off 1 O.R 8 D.P.S. Off 1 O.R. 13. Civilians treated 30.	
			Unit paraded to Review Ground for Divisional Practice.	
"		16.00	M/6021 recd. from ADMS. "The 3 Horsed Amb. will parade at the Army Commanders review on Monday 2/3 Hos Amb. to supply transport for collection of sick on Dec 1st + 2nd.	

Army Form C. 2118.

WAR DIARY
or
INTELLIGENCE SUMMARY.
(Erase heading not required.)

MEDICAL

CONFIDENTIAL

WAR DIARY

OF

2/2 HOME COUNTIES FIELD AMB. R.A.M.C. (T.)

1/12/18 — 31/12/18

Lt. Col. RAMC (T)
O.C.
2/2 H.C.F.A. RAMC (T)

COMMITTEE FOR THE
MEDICAL HISTORY OF THIS WAR
Date 6 MAR 1919

WAR DIARY
or
INTELLIGENCE SUMMARY.

Army Form C. 2118.

(Erase heading not required.)

Instructions regarding War Diaries and Intelligence Summaries are contained in F. S. Regs., Part II. and the Staff Manual respectively. Title pages will be prepared in manuscript.

Place	Date	Hour	Summary of Events and Information	Remarks and references to Appendices
BASECLES Sht H-5 A.20.a.9.5	1/12/18	09.30	Unit practice in connection with Army Commander's review on the 2nd inst.	
"	"	"	Major GAMM, Lieut. KENNEDY, 10 O.R. and 3 horsed amb. reported from 2/3 Highland (in accordance with A.D.M.S. instructions) for duty in connection with this review. W3185 Adm. O.R.6 DP8. O.R.6. Civilians treated 26.	
"	2/12/18	08.15	Unit proceeded to Aviation ground at GRANDGLISE for the Divisional Inspection at 11.00 hrs by General Sir H.S. HORNE, K.C.B., K.C.M.G., Commanding First Army.	
"	"	"	W3185 Adm. O.R.12 C.C.S. O.R.5 DP8 O.R.7 Civilians treated 22.	
"	3/12/18	"	W3185 Adm. O.R.10 C.C.S. O.R.1. DP8 O.R.9 " " " 20.	
"	4/12/18	"	W3185 Adm. Off 2 O.R. 12 DP8 Off 2 O.R. 12 " " " 32.	
"	"	"	Capt. C.E. DUNAWAY (M.O.R.C.) granted leave to U.K. 4 — 18/12/18 (ADMS M5399/5060)	
"	"	19.00	The following letter recd. from A.D.M.S. "I wish to thank all ranks of the 2/2 H.F.A. for their splendid turnout at the Army Commander's Inspection last Monday. I also wish to express my appreciation on the way the men marched past and their general appearance on Parade."	
"	5/12/18	"	W3185 Adm. O.R.9 C.C.S. O.R.2. DP8. O.R.7. Civilians treated 26. Evac. 1	

Army Form C. 2118.

WAR DIARY
or
INTELLIGENCE SUMMARY.
(Erase heading not required.)

Instructions regarding War Diaries and Intelligence Summaries are contained in F. S. Regs., Part II. and the Staff Manual respectively. Title pages will be prepared in manuscript.

Place	Date	Hour	Summary of Events and Information	Remarks and references to Appendices
BASECLES. A.20.a.9.5	5/12/18	12.00	Special Order of the Day received. "General Sir H.S. HORNE, K.C.B., K.C.M.G., Commanding the First Army, at his inspection of the Division yesterday expressed to the Divisional Commander entire satisfaction with the appearance and bearing of all ranks. He considered that the general turn-out and conditions of arms and equipment, as well as the steadiness on parade and the march past, were worthy of the highest praise. The Army Commander desired that his congratulations should be conveyed to every individual on this occasion to maintain the high standard of "Esprit de Corps" traditional to the British Army in France. He further signified the pleasure it gave him to have a chance of seeing almost in its entirety a Unit that during long and heavy fighting has made so great a name for itself as has the 58th (London) Division."	
"	6/12/18		W3185. Adm. O.R.4 R O.R.4 Civilians treated 31.	
"	7/12/18		W3185 R O.R.4 C.C.S O.R.1 R.O.R.3 " 31. Evac.1	
"	8/12/18		W3185 R O.R.3 Adm. O.R.1. R.O.R.4. " 29	
"	9/12/18		W3185 R O.R.4 Adm. O.R.1 Duty O.R.1 R.O.R.4 " 29	
"	10/12/18		W3185 R O.R.4 Adm. O.R.1 Duty O.R.1 R.O.R.4 " 24. Evac.1	

Army Form C. 2118.

WAR DIARY
or
INTELLIGENCE SUMMARY.
(Erase heading not required.)

Instructions regarding War Diaries and Intelligence Summaries are contained in F. S. Regs., Part II. and the Staff Manual respectively. Title pages will be prepared in manuscript.

Place	Date	Hour	Summary of Events and Information	Remarks and references to Appendices
BASECLES A 20 a 9.5	11/12/18		W 3185 R.O.R.4 Duty O.R.2 R.O.R.2. Civilians treated 23	
"	12/12/18		W 3185 R.O.R.2 " 22 Evac. 3	
"	"	09.00	M 6399 d 11/12/18 recd. from ADMS. — Lieut. MANSFIELD to be detailed to report to C.R.E. 58 Div. for temp. duty at 10.30 hrs 15th inst. 6037	
"	13/12/18		W 3185 R.O.R.2 Adm. O.R.2 R.O.R.4 Civilians treated 23	
"	14/12/18		W 3185 R.O.R.4 Adm. O.R.1 Duty O.R.2 R.O.R.3 " " 36	
"	15/12/18		W 3185 R.O.R.3 " " 18	
"	16/12/18		W 3185 R.O.R.3 Duty O.R.1 R.O.R.2 " " 18 Evac. 2	
"	17/12/18		W 3185 R.O.R.2 " " 17	
"	18/12/18		W 3185 R.O.R.2 Duty O.R.2 " " 18	
"	19/12/18		W 3185 R NIL " " 16	
"	20/12/18		W 3185 R NIL " " 19	
"	21/12/18		W 3185 R NIL " " 15	

Army Form C. 2118.

WAR DIARY
or
INTELLIGENCE SUMMARY.
(Erase heading not required.)

Instructions regarding War Diaries and Intelligence Summaries are contained in F. S. Regs., Part II. and the Staff Manual respectively. Title pages will be prepared in manuscript.

Place	Date	Hour	Summary of Events and Information	Remarks and references to Appendices
BASECLES A 20 a 9.5.	22/12/18	W 3185	R NIL Civilians treated 13	
	23/12/18	W 3185	R NIL " " 15	
	24/12/18	W 3185	R NIL " " 12	
	25/12/18	W 3185	R NIL " " 8	
	26/12/18	W 3185	Adm. Off. 1 C.C.S. Off. 1 " " 12	
	27/12/18	W 3185	R NIL " " 14	
	28/12/18	W 3185	R NIL " " 13	
	29/12/18	W 3185	R NIL " " 12	
	"		Major G.M. McGILLIVRAY ret. to Unit from Convl. Hosp. at CAP MARTIN.	
	30/12/18	W 3185	R NIL Civilians treated 11	
	31/12/18	W 3185	R NIL " " 9	

CONFIDENTIAL

Army Form C. 2118.

WAR DIARY
or
INTELLIGENCE SUMMARY.
(Erase heading not required.)

58 DIV
Box 286

MEDICAL

140/3690

War Diary
of the
2/2 Home Counties Field Amb. R.A.M.C. (T)

From 1/1/19 to 31/1/19

COMMITTEE FOR THE
MEDICAL HISTORY OF THE WAR

F. W. Rance (T)
O.C.
2/2 H.C.F.A. R.A.M.C. (T)

2/2ND
HOME COUNTIES
FIELD AMBULANCE
No. 2893
Date 4/2/19

Place	Date	Hour	Summary of Events and Information	Remarks and references to Appendices
	Jan 1919			

Army Form C. 2118.

WAR DIARY
INTELLIGENCE SUMMARY.
(Erase heading not required.)

Instructions regarding War Diaries and Intelligence Summaries are contained in F. S. Regs., Part II. and the Staff Manual respectively. Title pages will be prepared in manuscript.

Place	Date	Hour	Summary of Events and Information	Remarks and references to Appendices
BASE-L.F.S (Couvent) Shed 45 A 20 a.g.s	1/1/19	W 3195 NIL	Civilians treated 10	
	2/1/19	W 3195 NIL	" " 9	
	3/1/19	W 3185 NIL	" " 9	
	4/1/19	W 3195 NIL	" " 10	
	"		Capt. G.W.M. ANDREW granted S.L. to U.K. 4 - 18/1/19 (1st Corps S.L. 391)	
	5/1/19		Lieut P.A. MANSFIELD detailed to proceed to 26 Army Bde. R.F.A. as M.O. i/c. (Armys M6163 & 4/1/19)	
		W 3195 NIL	Civilians treated 15	
	6/1/19	W 3195 NIL	" " 14	
	7/1/19	W 3185 NIL	" " 15	
	8/1/19	W 3185 NIL	" " 13	
	9/1/19	W 3195 NIL	" " 12	
	10/1/19	W 3195 NIL	" " 11	
	11/1/19	W 3195 NIL	" " 16	
			Lieut P.A. MANSFIELD granted leave to U.K. 11 - 25/1/19 (Armys M 5391/6103)	

Army Form C. 2118.

WAR DIARY
or
INTELLIGENCE SUMMARY.
(Erase heading not required.)

Instructions regarding War Diaries and Intelligence Summaries are contained in F. S. Regs., Part II. and the Staff Manual respectively. Title pages will be prepared in manuscript.

Place	Date	Hour	Summary of Events and Information	Remarks and references to Appendices
BASETLES	12/1/19		W 3185 NIL Civilians treated 14	
A ROAGE	13/1/19		W 3185 NIL " " 14	
	14/1/19		W 3185 NIL " " 9	
	15/1/19		W 3185 NIL " " 14	
	16/1/19		W 3185 NIL " " 12	
	17/1/19		W 3185 NIL " " 13	
	18/1/19		W 3185 NIL " " 12	
	19/1/19		W 3185 NIL " " 14	
			58 (London) Division — New Years Honours Gazette 1919. MENTION. Capt. (a/Major) T.B.McKEE 2/2 Highland	
	20/1/19		W 3185 NIL Civilians treated 9	
	21/1/19		W 3185 NIL " " 12	
	22/1/19		W 3185 NIL " " 10	
	23/1/19		W 3185 NIL " " 10	
	24/1/19		W 3185 NIL " " 8	

Army Form C. 2118.

WAR DIARY
or
INTELLIGENCE SUMMARY.
(Erase heading not required.)

Instructions regarding War Diaries and Intelligence Summaries are contained in F. S. Regs., Part II. and the Staff Manual respectively. Title pages will be prepared in manuscript.

Place	Date	Hour	Summary of Events and Information	Remarks and references to Appendices
BASEEUX A20a9.5	25/1/19	W 3185	NIL Civilians treated 8	
	26/1/19	W 3185	NIL " 9	
	27/1/19	W 3185	NIL " 11	
	28/1/19	W 3185	NIL " 12	
	29/1/19	W 3185	NIL " 14	
	30/1/19	W 3185	NIL " 11	
	31/1/19	W 3185	NIL " 15	

Army Form C. 2118.

WAR DIARY
or
INTELLIGENCE SUMMARY

(Erase heading not required.)

145/324
MEDICAL

CONFIDENTIAL

WAR DIARY
- OF -
2/2 H.C.F ANG RNCC(T)
FROM 1-2-19 TO 28-2-19

LT. COL. O.C.
2/2ND H.C. FLD. AMB

Army Form C. 2118.

WAR DIARY
or
INTELLIGENCE SUMMARY.
(Erase heading not required.)

Instructions regarding War Diaries and Intelligence Summaries are contained in F. S. Regs., Part II. and the Staff Manual respectively. Title Pages will be prepared in manuscript.

Place	Date	Hour	Summary of Events and Information	Remarks and references to Appendices
FINSECLES (CONVENT) Sun W.S. Hdq n g.s	2/2/19		W3/85 NIL — Civilians treated 30	
	3/2/19		W3/85 NIL — Civilians treated 19	
	4/2/19		27 Cav H. FULTON DSO OC 2/8 H.C.M.G.S granted leave to Wazir King from 4-2-19 - 18-2-19 — WINTON to pickup account to party	
			W3/85 NIL — Civilians treated 16	
	5/2/19		W3/85 NIL — Civilians treated 18	
	6/2/19		W3/85 NIL — Civilians treated 21	
	6/2/19		W3/85 NIL — Civilians treated 15	
	7/2/19		W3/85 NIL — Civilians treated 18	
	8/2/19		W3/85 NIL — Civilians treated 17	
	9/2/19		W3/85 NIL — Civilians treated 18	
	10/2/19		W3/85 NIL — Civilians treated 17	

WAR DIARY
or
INTELLIGENCE SUMMARY

(Erase heading not required.)

Army Form C. 2118.

Place	Date	Hour	Summary of Events and Information	Remarks and references to Appendices
Bulford (Cowdray)	11/2/19		M3/85. NIL. Civilians healed 16	
Sth Ave Road S.P.	12/2/19		M3/85. NIL. Civilians healed 18	
	13/2/19		M3/85. NIL. Civilians healed 22	
	14/2/19		M3/85. NIL. Civilians healed 18	
	15/2/19		M3/85. NIL. Civilians healed 16	
	16/2/19		M3/85. NIL. Civilians healed 15	
	17/2/19		M3/85. NIL. Civilians healed 17. LIEUT ---- returned to Unit 16.2.19. Granted leave 25.1.19 – 1.2.19. Granted extension of leave 1.2.19 – 8.2.19. Proceeded to 51 Casualty Clearing Station 17.2.19. Struck off str---- 17.2.19.	
	18/2/19		M3/85. NIL. Civilians healed 17	
	19/2/19		M3/85. NIL. Civilians healed 15	

WAR DIARY
or
INTELLIGENCE SUMMARY

(Erase heading not required.)

Army Form C. 2118.

Place	Date	Hour	Summary of Events and Information	Remarks and references to Appendices
Brigade (Command) Post 45 Bailleul	19/2/19	10.05	Routine treated 5	
		11.00	Major D.S.O. go on extension of leave to 18/3/19 (Only M.O. from leave 20/2/19. Returned Command of Unit)	
			Major R.L.R.R.C. Gilliway M.C. granted extension of leave to 18/3/19 (Duty M.O. between himself)	
	20/2/19	Nil	Routine treated 11	
	21/2/19	Nil	Routine treated 10	
	22/2/19	Nil	Routine treated 7	
			Case of influenza amongst personnel. Evacuation to No. 2 Gen. Hospital following being reported 23.2.19 (Only Return of Duty M.O. No. 29303 O.R.Q.M.S. Lees, R.Q. for 1 day of Nil returned 23.2.19)	
	23/2/19	Nil	Routine treated 9	
	24/2/19	Nil	Routine treated 9	

WAR DIARY
or
INTELLIGENCE SUMMARY

Army Form C. 2118.

(Erase heading not required.)

Place	Date	Hour	Summary of Events and Information	Remarks and references to Appendices
BRESCHAET (CORNET) SHEET 45 19 20 A 9.5	26/2/19		M 3/85 NIL – Civilians treated 8	Thns.
	27/2/19		M 3/85 NIL – Civilians treated 8	Thns.
	28/2/19		M 3/85 NIL – Civilians treated 10	Thns.
		12.30	Medicine Instruction No 13 received from ADMS 58 Division. 2/2 H.C.F.Amb and 2/3 H.C.F.Amb to be prepared to move at short notice to another address. Advance parties to proceed forward to take over billets etc. On completion of above in order to relieve duties and personnel in the area of 2/2 H.C.F.Amb and 2/3 H.C.F.Amb will report for instructions of duties	Thns.
		15.00	Lt. Col. also Major proceeded to various addresses to see some billets etc	Thns.

Army Form C. 2118.

WAR DIARY
or
INTELLIGENCE SUMMARY.
(Erase heading not required.)

MEDICAL

Instructions regarding War Diaries and Intelligence Summaries are contained in F. S. Regs., Part II. and the Staff Manual respectively. Title pages will be prepared in manuscript.

Hour, Date, Place	Summary of Events and Information	Remarks and references to Appendices

Jul 26   140/3001,

CONFIDENTIAL.

WAR DIARY

OF

O/C H.C.F. AMB. R.A.M.C.(T)

FROM 1.3.19 TO 31.3.19

17 JUL 1919

[signature]
MAJOR O.C.
212th H.C. FLD. AMB

31.3.19

WAR DIARY
or
INTELLIGENCE SUMMARY

(Erase heading not required.)

Army Form C. 2118.

Place	Date	Hour	Summary of Events and Information	Remarks and references to Appendices
BRUSSELS (CAMP) SUB H.Q. H2O A 9.3	1/3/19		M3185 M16 - Strength Rated - 8. Received instructions from A.D.M.S. 58 Div. to send Capt. & W.O.1 Andrew to 3/1 H.C.F. and for duty, also intimation that 1 Lieut. Judkins, M.O.R.C. will report for duty from 291 B.D.E. R.F.A.	
	2/3/19		M3185 Nil - Strength Rated 18	
		8 pm	Received 58 Div. R.A. T.O. order No.70 postponing move to 8 Moselle M. H21705. Order 2 N.Y Ambulance Convoy to 3/1 H.C.F. Ams. for duty	
	3/3/19		M3185 NIL - Strength Rated 10. Lt. Col. H. Pulton, D.S.O. O.C. 4/1 H.C.F. Ams. proceeded to U.K. for demobilgn. (Ceases) Donated on D.M. 32565 (A.M.D.1) dd.15.2.19. Re-enforced notice is sent it so as on arriving to perform duties of M.O. with 4.3.19. Major T.B. Nixon assumed command of unit.	
	4/3/19		M3185 Nil - Strength Rated 16	
	5/3/19		M3185 Nil - Strength Rated 16. 10 am R.T. 2 W.O.S. (M.O.R.C.) joined unit from 291 Bde R.F.A.	

WAR DIARY
or
INTELLIGENCE SUMMARY

Army Form C. 2118.

(Erase heading not required.)

Instructions regarding War Diaries and Intelligence Summaries are contained in F. S. Regs., Part II. and the Staff Manual respectively. Title Pages will be prepared in manuscript.

Place	Date	Hour	Summary of Events and Information	Remarks and references to Appendices
ROUELLES (CONVAL. CAMP) HAVRE B.S.	5/3/19	15.00	Received Warning Order No 72 from P.O.N.S. 58 Div. to move to CHAPELLE - NATTINES on the 8/3/19 also instruction 8/1 H.C.F. Aus moving to CHAPELLE - N- O/S.	
	6/3/19		N.3 R.S. NR 18 - Orders issued 14	
	6/3/19	15.10	Arrival at CHAPELLE - N- NATTINES	
CHAPELLE N-NATTINES	7/3/19		Capt G.I. EVANS (S.R.) taken on strength of Unit - late M.O. /s 58 Div R.E. now serving at H.Q.R.S. Office 58 Div	
	7/3/19		Capt. C.F. SUMMERVILLE (M.O.R.C) proceeded to American Base Depot for duty (Army Ed. Sch. No. Army/32596 d/-21.2.19)	
	8/3/19		Capt C.F. EVANS (S.R.) F/ceased to serve in U.K. for demobilsation from DONS office in cms. (A.M.Y./32596 M. cms. 147/31 d/-27.3.19	
	8/3/19		1 Sgmn 1 Cpl 10 O.R.s proceeded to 51 C.C.S. TOURMAI for 6 days duty numb - instructions received from P.O.N.S. 58 Div.	

Army Form C. 2118.

WAR DIARY
or
INTELLIGENCE SUMMARY

(Erase heading not required.)

Instructions regarding War Diaries and Intelligence Summaries are contained in F. S. Regs., Part II. and the Staff Manual respectively. Title Pages will be prepared in manuscript.

CONFIDENTIAL

WAR DAIRY

— OF —

2/2 H.C.F. AMB. R.A.M.C.

FROM. 1-5-19. TO. 31-5-19.

Major Ramc.
O.C.
2/2ND H.Q. FLD. AMB

Army Form C. 2118.

WAR DIARY
or
INTELLIGENCE SUMMARY.
(Erase heading not required.)

Instructions regarding War Diaries and Intelligence Summaries are contained in F.S. Regs., Part II. and the Staff Manual respectively. Title pages will be prepared in manuscript.

Hour, Date, Place	Summary of Events and Information	Remarks and references to Appendices
CHAPELLE à WATTINES. 4-5-19.	CAPT. & Q.M. KNOWLES .G. Granted Leave 5- 19/5/19.	Minute
30.5-19.	MOVEMENT ORDER No. O.G. 2424, received from 58rd Div. Group. Unit to move to LEUZE, Move to be completed by 10noon 2-6-19.	From

Army Form C. 2118.

WAR DIARY
or
INTELLIGENCE SUMMARY
(Erase heading not required.)

MEDICAL

WC 27
140/3vrs

CONFIDENTIAL

WAR DIARY

— OF —

2/2 H.C.F.AMB. R.A.M.C.(T)

From 1-4-19 TO 30-4-19

17 JUL 1919

MAJOR O.C.
2/2ND H.C. FLD. AMB

Place	Date	Hour	Summary of Events and Information	Remarks and references to Appendices

Army Form C. 2118.

WAR DIARY
or
INTELLIGENCE SUMMARY
(Erase heading not required.)

Instructions regarding War Diaries and Intelligence Summaries are contained in F. S. Regs., Part II. and the Staff Manual respectively. Title Pages will be prepared in manuscript.

Place	Date	Hour	Summary of Events and Information	Remarks and references to Appendices
CHARLES HOSPITAL BEIRUT	4/9/19	-	1st Lt R J Judkins (M.O.R.C) proceeded to 2/1. H.C Paris for temporary duty	Jan
	13/9/19	-	1st Lt R J Judkins (M.O.R.C) returned from 2/1. M.C.F Paris	Jan
	25/9/19	-	1st Lt R J Judkins (M.O.R.C) proceeded to St Aignon Headquarters	Jan

Transport.

Transport consists of
(a) ~~25 H.P. Morris Utility Truck Ltd.~~
(b) 500.c.c. B.S.A motorcycle.

www.ingramcontent.com/pod-product-compliance
Lightning Source LLC
Chambersburg PA
CBHW080848230426
43662CB00013B/2048